A Practical Guide to INTERPOL and Red Notices

Second Edition

A Practical Guide to INTERPOL and Red Notices

Second Edition

Ben Brandon

Partner, Barrister, Mishcon de Reya LLP

Christopher David

Partner, Clifford Chance LLP

Nicholas Hearn

Barrister, Furnival Chambers

Bloomsbury Professional

LONDON • DUBLIN • EDINBURGH • NEW YORK • NEW DELHI • SYDNEY

BLOOMSBURY PROFESSIONAL

Bloomsbury Publishing Plc
50 Bedford Square, London, WC1B 3DP, UK
1385 Broadway, New York, 10018, USA
29 Earlsfort Terrace, Dublin 2, Ireland

BLOOMSBURY and the Diana logo are trademarks of Bloomsbury Publishing Plc

First published in Great Britain 2024

British Library Cataloguing-in-Publication Data

A catalogue record for this book is available from the British Library.

ISBN:	PB:	978 1 52652 786 8
	Epdf:	978 1 52652 788 2
	Epub:	978 1 52652 787 5

Typeset by Evolution Design & Digital (Kent)
Printed and bound by CPI Group (UK) Ltd, Croydon, CR0 4YY

Foreword

It is a great pleasure to be asked to contribute the Foreword to the Second Edition of this important work. The authors have unrivalled expertise in their subject, and this book should be front and centre on the shelves of all those whose work may bring them into contact with INTERPOL, which celebrated its centenary in 2023, making the publication of this new edition especially timely.

As the authors explain, the origins of INTERPOL can be traced to the First International Criminal Police Congress held in Monaco in 1914 at the invitation of Prince Albert I, when 24 countries and states discussed the possibility of establishing an international criminal records office and harmonising extradition procedures. Plans then went on hold following the outbreak of the First World War. So it was not until 1923 when Dr Johannes Schober, Chief of Police in Vienna, Austria, organised the second International Criminal Police Congress that set up the International Criminal Police Commission (ICPC), with headquarters in Vienna.

The ICPC was INTERPOL's predecessor. The idea lying behind these developments was to find ways to help police in different countries to cooperate on solving crimes, notably through arrest and extradition procedures, identification techniques and the idea of centralised criminal records. Although, then, crime was still mainly local, the growing need for international co-operation was obvious.

A common portrayal of INTERPOL in popular culture is that of its agents travelling the world as a kind of global FBI, tracking down criminals and bringing them to justice. Contrary to that characterisation, there is actually no such thing as an INTERPOL agent, and it is not a police force. Instead, INTERPOL's aim, according to Article 2 of its Constitution, is 'to ensure and promote the widest possible mutual assistance between all criminal police authorities.'

INTERPOL, then, is less a police agency than an instrument of co-operative policing: it streamlines information sharing to enable collaboration in crime-fighting across borders. Today, it has 196 member countries as well as co-operation agreements with numerous international organisations, including the United Nations and the EU. It works alongside its member countries and partner agencies across a wide range of areas, using many different techniques, including border management; criminal intelligence analysis; forensics; fugitive investigation support; and many others.

INTERPOL is probably best known to the general public for its system of colour-coded Notices (including the well-known Red Notice to locate a wanted fugitive – often popularly, but wrongly, referred to an international arrest warrant). INTERPOL's Notices enable countries to share alerts and requests for information worldwide, for example, in relation to missing persons or objects or (most recently) those subject to UN sanctions. It typically issues more than 10,000 Red Notices each year, most of which remain secret and are never published.

Invaluable though its work is in the fight against crime – and in particular transnational crime – as many have observed, for a long time INTERPOL lacked any transparency. Pretty much immune from legal challenge in domestic courts, it went about its work largely unchecked (see eg Savino, Mario, 'Global Administrative Law Meets "Soft" Powers: The Uncomfortable Case of Interpol Red Notices' (5 June 2010); New York University Journal of International Law and Politics, Vol 43, No 2, 2010). The ability of repressive regimes to have INTERPOL issue Red Notices in order to harass political opponents became (and is still) a topic of much comment among international criminal lawyers.

One well known case occurred in January 2019, when NBA player Enes Freedom, then of the New York Knicks, and of Turkish heritage, was served with a Red Notice issued at the request of Turkey because of his criticisms of President Erdoğan's style of rule. Freedom was immune on American soil, but travelling abroad to play risked arrest and extradition to Turkey, and likely imprisonment. Freedom was able to evade extradition, and became a US citizen in 2021. But many saw Turkey as being able to use the Red Notice system as a long range weapon with which to precisely target a prominent critic. Another example is that of the financier Bill Browder, author of *Red Notice* (Penguin, 2016) who, it is widely thought, became the target of a Red Notice after falling foul of President Putin. Many take the view that such cases happen far too frequently, and that there is little that can be done to mount effective challenges when they occur.

For obvious reasons a lot of what INTERPOL does has to remain secret. However in recent times, INTERPOL has introduced systems to allow for a degree of scrutiny of its processes. Nonetheless, in practice it still can be difficult for those subject to a Red Notice (or who think they might be) to challenge it, or even to find out if they have been named. Applications can be made to the Commission for the Control of INTERPOL's Files (CCF), but many have said this can be a slow and frustrating process.

This book provides a clear and detailed guide to those who may need to know about how INTERPOL works and what they (or their clients) can do should they come to INTERPOL's attention. The authors provide clear and detailed analysis of INTERPOL's history; how it functions today; how to challenge a Red Notice; how to use data protection laws in different countries in relation to INTERPOL; the criticisms of Red Notices, and recent reform efforts; and much more besides. It will be of great interest and use to defence lawyers; prosecutors; law enforcement professionals; academics; students; and judges. I congratulate the authors, and warmly commend it to you.

Sir Julian Knowles

Preface

The last 30 years have seen a huge increase in co-operation between international law enforcement agencies in the investigation of cross-border and transnational crime. A significant facilitator of this increased co-operation is the International Criminal Police Organization, more commonly known as Interpol. The day-to-day investigation of criminal offences remains the preserve of local law enforcement agencies. However, Interpol has a significant role in the sharing of intelligence and, more pertinently for this book, the circulation of Red Notices and other alerts such as Diffusions (both of which request the arrest and detention of suspects by local law enforcement agencies). As a consequence of increased law enforcement co-operation across borders, practitioners have seen an increase in clients who are, or may be, the subject of a Red Notice. The purpose of this book is to provide context by way of a brief background and history to Interpol, before exploring, in a practical way, what Red Notices are, how they can be identified and how they can be challenged.

The full history of Interpol is beyond the scope of this work. However, a knowledge of its history (see Chapter 1) provides the practitioner with valuable context. It informs an understanding of how, and why, Interpol acts in the way it does today. An awareness of how its different parts are structured (see Chapter 2) is also crucial when engaging with Interpol in any capacity.

That said, the focus of this book is Interpol's processing of Red Notices and Diffusions. They are undoubtedly its most important and controversial tool. As any criminal lawyer will confirm, a law enforcement agency's power of arrest and detention is the most significant power they hold. Interpol is at the centre of how different police forces communicate their requests for individuals to be detained extraterritorially. In 2021, the most recent year for which we have been able to find figures, over 10,000 Red Notices were issued. Chapter 3 examines the process and requirements with which a requesting police force must comply, as well as how police forces are expected to respond to a Red Notice.

The increased use of Red Notices is not without criticism. In the Preface to the first edition of this book we quoted an excerpt from the then President of Interpol, Meng Hongwei's, closing address to the eighty-sixth Interpol General Assembly. In this address he said:

> 'We must build strength. Security is a basic need for human survival, the common denominator of all countries. A safer world is what we have pursued for a century; a stronger organization is what is needed for fighting crimes and safeguarding peace and justice. This is what all police and the international community expect of us.'[1]

1 See https://www.interpol.int/content/download/5351/file/Speech%20by%20President%20Meng%20Hongwei%2086GA.pdf.

Since that address many would say Interpol has fallen short of those expectations and been mired in controversy. Meng Hongwei was detained by the Chinese government and, after much speculation about his whereabouts, was imprisoned in January 2020 for receiving more than $2m in bribes;[2] one of the candidates for the position of President after Meng Hongwei was Alexander Prokopchuk who was criticised by human rights groups for abusing the Interpol Red Notice system to target critics of Vladimir Putin;[3] and the current President, Ahmed Nasser al-Raisi, has been accused by human rights groups of being complicit in torture.[4]

Non-governmental organisations, such as Fair Trials and Human Rights Watch, have consistently raised concerns about the potential misuse of Interpol Red Notices, by oppressive political regimes who use them to arrest political opponents and activists.

Interpol is certainly aware of these concerns. In November 2023 Interpol's member countries met in Vienna for the ninety-first General Assembly, marking the one-hundred-year anniversary of the organisation. In his directional statement Jürgen Stock, Interpol's Secretary General, said:

> 'This is why, as we contemplate our Vision for 2030, INTERPOL is compelled to serve as an orchestrator … Because INTERPOL is neutral … It is the core principle of our Organization. One we cannot, and will not compromise on … This is a principle we must observe in everything we do – especially in the processing of data. This is why INTERPOL created the Notices and Diffusions Task Force in 2016 – to ensure quality and legal compliance of notices and diffusions with our rules. And why the CCF Statute was reformed – leading the path to its recognition as an effective remedy mechanism for individuals affected by our data processing … As Johannes Schober said in 1923; "The objective that we are pursuing, is devoid of all political aims".'

It is against that backdrop that this book has been written. Chapter 4 examines in more detail these criticisms and looks at the steps Interpol has taken towards reform.

Away from the politics of Red Notices, it is certainly a fact that the number of Red Notices being challenged is increasing. In 1986, Interpol set up an independent body, the Commission for the Control of Flies, to supervise the control of information being received from police forces around the world. In its first year, it received ten requests to review such information. By 2022, that number had increased to over 2,258 requests or applications for the revision of

2 See https://www.bbc.co.uk/news/world-asia-china-51185838.
3 See https://www.bbc.co.uk/news/world-europe-46274261.
4 See https://www.bbc.co.uk/news/world-middle-east-59417409.

decisions.[5] Finding out about, or even preventing the issue of a Red Notice is an increasing part of a criminal defence lawyer's practice.

Any individual can submit, free of charge, a request to the CCF for access to, correction or deletion of data processed in Interpol's Information System. Chapter 5 examines the ways in which it may be possible to establish whether a client is the subject of a Red Notice. Whilst some Red Notices are published by Interpol, the vast majority remain confidential: the first time an individual becomes aware of the existence of such a notice can be when they are arrested pursuant to it. It should be recognised that, like many European institutions, Interpol can be bureaucratically challenging, and it is essential, to avoid wasting valuable time, to follow the published rules (see the appendices to this book). In preparing this book Interpol has requested that we make clear that the CCF does not collect any fee as part of its activities concerning the processing of requests to access or challenge information in Interpol's files.

Other routes can be used to try and identify whether a Red Notice is in existence, for example, through the requesting police force. Chapter 5 also sets out more formal routes for obtaining information by way of data protection legislation. This edition uses the United Kingdom, France, Germany, Hong Kong, Italy, the Netherlands, Spain, and the United States of America as examples, but all EU territories and many other countries around the world will have their own statutes and are worth exploring.

One of the most valuable strategic issues to consider is whether a Preventative Request should be made directly to Interpol. Chapter 5 provides advice on this procedure which many practitioners have found to be effective (especially where there is a suspicion that the Red Notice may be politically motivated).

Having established that a Red Notice is in place, the obvious next stage is to consider whether it can be challenged (see Chapter 6). This can be achieved either by using Interpol's own rules and procedures or, in some circumstances, by considering domestic remedies.

Finally, Chapter 7 gathers together practical advice from the authors and leading practitioners in relation to all aspects of identifying and challenging Red Notices.

In addition to the chapters summarised above, this book also gathers together all the necessary underlying material to assist a lawyer in relation to their interaction with Interpol relating to Red Notices. These documents are set out in the appendices to this book and are available on the Interpol website which

5 See https://www.interpol.int/en/content/download/20967/file/GA-2023-91-REP-22%20E%20AnnualActivityReportCCF_2022%20%2823Y2486%29%20%28REV%29%282%29.pdf.

is regularly updated.[6] (It should be noted that the RCI (Rules on the Control of Information) are no longer in force but remain available for reference and historical purposes as many previous decisions/submissions/annual reports reference their provisions.)

There is no doubt that a client, who is, or may be, the subject of a Red Notice is under significant pressure; their personal and business lives can be impeded and, understandably, most want the Red Notice challenged and removed as quickly as possible. Unfortunately, Interpol moves slowly and, from a strategic point of view, an immediate challenge to a Red Notice is not necessarily the best course of action. Like many areas of criminal litigation, a calm and measured response is often the best way forward.

It is hoped that this book can provide a solid foundation in terms of how Interpol and Red Notices work and the underlying mechanics of identifying and challenging such notices and, in turn, allowing practitioners to quickly advise their clients.

The opinions expressed in the present publication are in no way endorsed by Interpol. The responsibility for said opinions rests solely with the authors.

The law is stated as at 12 January 2024 but later changes have been incorporated where possible.

Ben Brandon, Christopher David and Nicholas Hearn

6 At the following links: https://www.interpol.int/content/download/590/file/01%20E%20Constitution_2024.pdf
https://www.interpol.int/content/download/5694/file/24%20E%20RPD%20UPDATE%207%2011%2019_ok.pdf
https://www.interpol.int/content/download/5695/file/Statute%20of%20the%20CCF-EN.pdf
https://www.interpol.int/content/download/6813/file/Rules%20on%20the%20Control%20of%20Information%20and%20Access%20to%20INTERPOLs%20Files.pdf
https://www.interpol.int/en/content/download/6807/file/23Y0803%20E%20CCF_AmendmentsOperating%20(OR).pdf
https://www.interpol.int/content/download/15565/file/ACCESS%20DELETION%20REQUEST%20FORM-EN-2023.pdf.

Acknowledgements

A book like this one undoubtedly needs help and support from many professional colleagues. The authors would particularly like to thank the following for their invaluable assistance in writing this updated edition of the book: Adam Squibbs (Furnival Chambers); James Watson and Celia Marr (Mischon de Reya); Abigail Maton-Howarth, Victoria James, Gary Chan, Jaime Streete, Miranda Harrison, Mollie MacGinty (Clifford Chance), as well as the many Clifford Chance colleagues from around the world that provided an international perspective,

Ben would like to thank his wife Patricia Kingori, and their three children, Felix, Amelia and Otis; and Jo Walsh and the White-Collar Crime & Investigations team at Mishcon for their support during this project.

Chris would like to thank Jane, Charlie, Ben and Sam for the love and happiness that they bring to him.

Nick would like to thank his wife Xanthe and his daughter Severiana for their love and support.

Contents

Foreword by Sir Julian Knowles		*v*
Preface		*vii*
Acknowledgments		*xi*
Bibliography		*xvii*
Table of statutes		*xxv*
Table of international legislation		*xxvii*
Table of cases		*xxix*
1	**Interpol – Origins and historical development**	**1**
	Introduction	1
	The First International Police Congress	2
	The 1923 International Criminal Police Congress	3
	The war years	5
	Post-war renewal	7
	Conclusion	9
2	**Interpol today**	**11**
	Introduction	11
	The Constitution	12
	The structure	13
	Funding	18
	International partners	19
	Interpol's work	19
3	**Red Notices and Diffusions**	**21**
	Introduction	21
	Interpol Red Notices – general operation	22
	The NCB request – minimum criteria	22
	Specific criteria	25
	The General Secretariat's discretion	26
	NCB request – minimum data	26
	Further obligations on the requesting NCB – Articles 84–85	26
	Legal review by the General Secretariat	27

	Action to be taken by NCBs pursuant to an Interpol Red Notice	27
	Diffusions	29
4	**Criticisms of Red Notices and Wanted Person Diffusions and efforts toward reform**	**35**
	Introduction	35
	Criticisms	37
	Efforts towards reform	39
	Asylum status – a change in approach?	42
	A new approach to asylum status	44
	Current criticisms of Interpol Red Notices and Wanted Person Diffusions	48
	The future of Interpol	55
	Conclusion	56
5	**Finding out whether a Red Notice exists**	**59**
	Introduction	59
	Interpol	60
	Diffusions	63
	Requesting NCB	64
	Other countries	66
	Other NCBs	78
	Other matters to consider	79
6	**Interpol – Challenging Red Notices and Diffusions**	**83**
	Introduction	83
	Procedure for challenging a Red Notice or Diffusion	84
	Specific approach to Red Notices	90
	Challenges based on Article 2 of the Interpol Constitution	91
	Challenges based on Article 3 of the Interpol Constitution	102
	Challenges based on breaches of the RPD	110
	Challenges based on the 2017 Interpol Refugee Resolution	114
	Challenges in domestic law – example jurisdictions	115
	Conclusion	121
7	**Red Notices – practical guidance**	**123**
	Introduction	123
	First steps	123

Identifying the existence of a Red Notice 124
Preventative Requests 126
Challenging a Red Notice 127
Contents of representations 129
Litigation PR and the media 130
Conclusion 130

Appendices
1. Constitution of the ICPO–Interpol 133
2. Interpol's Rules on the processing of data 143
3. Statute of the Commission for the Control of Interpol's Files 195
4. Rules on the Control of Information and Access to Interpol's Files 209
5. Commission for the Control of Interpol's Files: Operating rules 215
6. Commission for the Control of Interpol's Files: Application Form for Access and/or Correction/Deletion 227

Index **233**

Bibliography

Chapter 1:

Anderson, M *Policing the World – Interpol and the Politics of International Police Co-operation* (Oxford: Clarendon Press, 1989)

Bresler, F *Interpol* (1st edn, London: Sinclair-Stevenson Ltd, 1992)

Chapter 2:

'Activity Report of the CCF 2008 and January–February 2009'. Interpol. Available at: https://www.interpol.int/content/download/6889/file/Annual%20Report%20of%20the%20CCF%202008.pdf.

'Biography of the current Secretary General Jürgen Stock'. Interpol website. Available at: www.interpol.int/Who-we-are/General-Secretariat/Secretary-General/Juergen-Stock-biography.

'Empowering the INTERPOL network of global law enforcement cooperation'. Interpol website. Available at: https://www.interpol.int/News-and-Events/News/2023/INTERPOL-conference-Heightened-urgency-as-police-leaders-discuss-global-crime-threats.

'Financial Statements for the Year Ended 31 December 2021'. International Criminal Police Organization. Available at: https://www.interpol.int/content/download/18417/file/ICPO-INTERPOL%20Audited%20Financial%20Statements%202021.pdf.

'Financial Statements for the Year Ended 31 December 2021'. International Criminal Police Organization. Available at: https://www.interpol.int/content/download/18417/file/ICPO-INTERPOL%20Audited%20Financial%20Statements%202021.

'General Secretariat'. Interpol website. Available at: https://www.interpol.int/Who-we-are/General-Secretariat.

'International Organization Partners'. Interpol website. Available at: https://www.interpol.int/Our-partners/International-organization-partners.

'Interpol Member Country Statutory Contributions 2023'. Interpol website. Available at: https://www.interpol.int/content/download/19208/file/INTERPOL%20MEMBER%20COUNTRY%20STATUTORY%20CONTRIBUTIONS%202023.pdf.

'Our Funding'. Interpol website. Available at: www.interpol.int/Who-we-are/Our-funding.

'Strategic Framework 2022–2025'. Interpol website. Available at: https://www.interpol.int/Who-we-are/Strategy/Strategic-Framework-2022-2025.

'Strategy'. Interpol website. Available at: https://www.interpol.int/Who-we-are/Strategy.

Interpol Constitution (Vienna, June 1956)

'National Central Bureaus (NCBs)', Interpol website. Available at: https://www.interpol.int/en/Who-we-are/Member-countries/National-Central-Bureaus-NCBs.

'Statute of the Commission for the Control of INTERPOL's Files'. Interpol. Available at: https://www.interpol.int/content/download/5695/file/Statute%20of%20the%20CCF-EN.pdf.

Chapter 3:

'Strengthening Respect for Human Rights Strengthening Interpol' *Fair Trials International*

Assange v Swedish Prosecution Authority [2012] UKSC 22

Interpol's Rules on the Processing of Data

'Ukraine: INTERPOL General Secretariat statement'. Interpol website. Available at: https://www.interpol.int/en/News-and-Events/News/2022/Ukraine-INTERPOL-General-Secretariat-statement.

US National Central Bureau of Interpol, *Audit Report 09-35*, September 2009.

Chapter 4:

OSLO DECLARATION of the OSCE Parliamentary Assembly and Resolutions Adopted at the Nineteenth Annual Session. OSCE PA. Available at: https://www.oscepa.org/en/documents/annual-sessions/2010-oslo/declaration-5/267-oslo-declaration-english/file.

Istanbul Declaration and Resolutions Adopted by the OSCE Parliamentary Assembly at the Twenty-Second Annual Session. OSCE PA. Available at: https://www.oscepa.org/en/documents/annual-sessions/2013-istanbul/declaration/1801-istanbul-declaration-eng-1/file#:~:text=Calls%20on%20the%20OSCE%20to,47.

Cochetel, V, '"Terrorism as a Global Phenomenon", UNHCR presentation to the Joint Seminar of the Strategic Committee on Immigration, Frontiers and Asylum (SCIFA) and Committee on Article 36 (CATS)' (UNHCR, 17 January 2008) Available at: https://www.refworld.org/policy/statements/unhcr/2008/en/53109.

Lewis, L, 'Interpol's Red Notices Used by Some to Pursue Political Dissenters, Opponents'. (International Consortium of Investigative Journalists, 18 July

2011). Available at: www.publicintegrity.org/2011/07/18/5179/interpols-red-notices-used-some-pursue-political-dissenters-opponents.

'Strengthening respect for human rights, strengthening INTERPOL'. Fair Trials International (November 2013) Available at: https://www.fairtrials.org/app/uploads/2022/01/Strengthening-respect-for-human-rights-strengthening-INTERPOL4.pdf.

Draft rules relating to the processing of police information, to the control of the processing of personal information, and to the access to that information (Rules relating to the processing of police information). Interpol AG-2002-RES-09 (October 2002) Available at: https://www.interpol.int/content/download/6170/file/GA-2002-71-RES-09%20-%20Draft%20rules%20relating%20to%20the%20processing%20of%20police%20information%20%28Rules%20relating%20to%20the%20processing%20of%20police%20information%29.pdf.

Approval of the 2003 Draft Budget. Interpol AG-2002-RES-14 (October 2002). Available at: https://www.interpol.int/content/download/6163/file/GA-2002-71-FR-RES-14%20-%20Approbation%20du%20projet%20de%20budget%202003.pdf?inLanguage=fre-FR.

'INTERPOL's supervisory mechanisms concerning the processing of data in the INTERPOL Information System'. Interpol (November 2014). Available at: https://www.interpol.int/content/download/5951/file/AG-2014-83-RES-19%20-%20INTERPOL%E2%80%99s%20supervisory%20mechanisms%20concerning%20the%20processing%20of%20data%20in%20the%20INTERPOL%20Information%20System.pdf.

'Annual Activity Report of the CCF for 2014'. Commission for the Control of INTERPOL's Files. Available at: https://www.interpol.int/content/download/6901/file/Annual%20Report%20of%20the%20CCF%202014.pdf.

Press release: '"Fair Trials" recommendations inform major INTERPOL reforms' (2 December 2016) [link not available].

Press release: 'Interpol Red Notice for Julian Assange remains in force'. Interpol (16 August 2012). Available at: https://www.interpol.int/en/News-and-Events/News/2012/INTERPOL-Red-Notice-for-Julian-Assange-remains-in-force.

'Statement of the Prosecutor's Office in Relation to Annulling Interpol Red Notice, International Search warrant against Z Adeishvili'. Prosecutor's Office of Georgia (14 April 2015). Available at: https://pog.gov.ge/en/news/prokuraturis-gancxadeba-z-adeishvilis-mimarT-wiTeli-cirkulariT-saerTashoriso-Zebnis-gauqmebasTan-dak.

Press release: 'Interpol announces new asylum policy at Council of Europe meeting' (29 May 2015). Available at: https://web.archive.org/web/20211128182626/https:/www.fairtrials.org/node/779.

Interpol Text on Refugee Policy – Excerpts. Fair Trials. Available at: https://www.fairtrials.org/app/uploads/2022/01/INTERPOL-TEXT-ON-REFUGEE-POLICY.pdf.

INTERPOL policy on refugees. Interpol GA-2017-86-RES-09 (September 2017). Available at: https://www.interpol.int/content/download/5746/file/GA-2017-86-RES-09%20-%20INTERPOL%20policy%20on%20refugees.pdf.

'Abusive use of the Interpol system: the need for more stringent legal safeguards' Parliamentary Assembly Assemblée parlementaire, Committee on Legal Affairs and Human Rights (29 March 2017). Available at: https://pace.coe.int/en/files/23524/html.

'Misuse of Interpol's Red Notices and impact on human rights – recent developments'. European Parliament (January 2019). Available at: https://www.europarl.europa.eu/RegData/etudes/STUD/2019/603472/EXPO_STU(2019)603472_EN.pdf.

'Compliance and review'. Interpol. Available at: https://www.interpol.int/en/How-we-work/Notices/Compliance-and-review.

'Abusive recourse to the Interpol system: the need for more stringent legal safeguards'. Parliamentary Assembly Resolution 2161 (2017). Available at: https://pace.coe.int/en/files/23714/html.

'Interpol reform and extradition proceedings: building trust by fighting abuse' Parliamentary Assembly Assemblée parlementaire, Committee on Legal Affairs and Human Rights (15 October 2019). Available at: https://pace.coe.int/en/files/28090/html.

'Interpol reform and extradition proceedings: building trust by fighting abuse' Parliamentary Assembly Resolution 2315 (2019) (29 November 2019) Available at: https://pace.coe.int/en/files/28303/html.

Annual Report 2015. Interpol. Available at: https://www.interpol.int/en/content/download/4995/file/Annual%20Report%202015-EN.pdf.

'About Notices'. Interpol. Available at: https://www.interpol.int/en/How-we-work/Notices/About-Notices.

'Improving the quality of supervision measures for data processing'. Interpol GA-2023-91-RES-09 (December 2023). Available at: https://www.interpol.int/content/download/20578/file/GA-2023-91-RES-09%20-%20Improving%20the%20quality%20of%20supervision%20measures%20for%20data%20processing.pdf.

'Red Notices and Wanted Person Diffusions and their use for provisional arrest pending extradition'. Interpol GA-2023-91-RES-10 (December 2023). Available at: https://www.interpol.int/content/download/20579/file/GA-2023-91-RES-10%20-%20Red%20Notices%20and%20Wanted%20

Person%20Diffusions%20and%20their%20use%20for%20provisional%20 arrest%20pending%20extradition.pdf.

'Report of the Working Group to Review Legal Provisions Relating to INTERPOL's Governance Bodies – Process for the expulsion or suspension of a Member of INTERPOL and Draft Resolutions regarding Article 2, 3 and 4 of INTERPOL's Constitution'. Interpol GA-2023-91-RES-06 (December 2023). Available at: https://www.interpol.int/content/download/20574/ file/GA-2023-91-RES-06%20-%20Report%20of%20the%20Working%20 Group%20to%20Review%20Legal%20Provisions%20Relating%20to%20 INTERPOL%E2%80%99s%20Governance%20Bodies%20%E2%80%93%20 Process%20for%20the%20expulsion%20or%20suspension%20of%20a%20 Member%20of%20INTERPOL%20and%20Draft%20Resolutions%20re.pdf.

'Programme of Activities and Draft Budget 2024, and Indications for 2025 and 2026'. Interpol GA-2023-91-RES-14 (December 2023). Available at: https://www.interpol.int/content/download/20585/file/GA-2023-91-RES-14%20E%20Programme%20of%20Activities%20and%20Draft%20 Budget%202024.pdf.

Congressional Record Vol 146 No 91 (14 July 2000).

Chapter 5:

Act on Judicial and Criminal Data (*Wet Justitiële en Strafvorderlijke Gegevens* (WJSG)).

Autoriteit Persoonsgegevens. Available at: https://www.autoriteitpersoonsgegevens.nl/en.

Cinepoly Records Co Ltd v Hong Kong Broadband Network Ltd [2006] 1 HKC 433

'Code on Access to Information: Guidelines on Interpretation and Application'. Available at: https://www.access.gov.hk/filemanager/content/ codeonacctoinfo/guidelines.pdf.

'Commission for the Control of Interpol's files: Operating Rules'. Interpol (28 March 2017). Available at: https://www.interpol.int/en/content/ download/6807/file/23Y0803%20E%20CCF_AmendmentsOperating%20 %28OR%29.pdf.

Data Protection Act 2018

Directive (EU) 2016/680

Directive in the Act on Police Data (*Wet Politiegegevens* (WPG))

Freedom of Information Act (FOIA)

German Federal Criminal Police Act (*Bundeskriminalamtgesetz*, 'BKAG')

German Federal Data Protection Act (*Bundesdatenschutzgesetz*, 'BDSG')

Guidelines for dealings with foreign countries in criminal matters (*Richtlinien für den Verkehr mit dem Ausland in strafrechtlichen Angelegenheiten, RiVASt*)

Loi Informatique et Libertés

Personal Data (Privacy) Law in Hong Kong: A Practical Guide on Compliance (2nd edn)

Personal Data (Privacy) Ordinance (Cap 486, Laws of Hong Kong) (PDPO)

'Statute of the Commission for the Control of INTERPOL's Files'. Interpol. Available at: https://www.interpol.int/content/download/5695/file/Statute%20of%20the%20CCF-EN.pdf.

UK GDPR

'What other exemptions are there?' Information Commissioner's Office. Available at: https://ico.org.uk/for-organisations/uk-gdpr-guidance-and-resources/individual-rights/right-of-access/what-other-exemptions-are-there.

Chapter 6:

CCF Decision Excerpt Number 2 of 2017

CCF Decision Excerpt Number 9 of 2017

CCF Decision Excerpt Number 12 of 2017

CCF Decision Excerpt Number 13 of 2017

CCF Decision Excerpt Number 2 of 2018

CCF Decision Excerpt Number 3 of 2018

CCF Decision Excerpt Number 5 of 2018

CCF Decision Excerpt Number 6 of 2018

CCF Decision Excerpt Number 8 of 2018

CCF Decision Excerpt Number 14 of 2018

CCF Decision Excerpt Number 15 of 2018

CCF Decision Excerpt Number 17 of 2018

CCF Decision Excerpt Number 18 of 2018

CCF Decision Excerpt Number 1 of 2019

CCF Decision Excerpt Number 5 of 2019

CCF Decision Excerpt Number 6 of 2019

CCF Decision Excerpt Number 9 of 2019

Convention Against Torture (CAT)

El Omari v Interpol, 35 F 4th 83 (2nd Cir 2022)

EU Charter of Fundamental Rights

European Convention of Human Rights (ECHR)

German Code of Criminal Procedure (*Strafprozessordnung*, 'StPO')

Gonzalez-Castillo v Garland, 47 F 4th 971 (9th Cir 2022)

Google Spain SL and Google Inc v Agencia Española de Protección de Datos (AEPD) and Mario Costeja González [2014] C-131/12

International Covenant on Civil and Political Rights (ICCPR)

International Organizations Immunities Act (IOIA)

Interpol 2023, Interpol website, accessed 2 October 2023, https://www.interpol.int/en/Who-we-are/Commission-for-the-Control-of-INTERPOL-s-Files-CCF/How-to-submit-a-request.

Interpol Repository of Practice: Application of Article 3.

N v United Kingdom [2008] ECHR 45

National Defense Authorization Act (NDAA)

New Zealand v France (*Rainbow Warrior*). Available at: https://www.google.com/url?sa=t&rct=j&q=&esrc=s&source=web&cd=&cad=rja&uact=8&ved=2ah UKEwi8nvrasMKFAxWzRUEAHRJyAYYQFnoECCIQAQ&url=https%3A%2F%2Fiilj.org%2Fwp-content%2Fuploads%2F2016%2F08%2FArechaga-etal-Rainbow-Warrior-1990.pdf&usg=AOvVaw09Q5Hn1Spw8XBvuS_U1Z1Q&opi=89978449.

Paposhvili v Belgium [2016] ECHR 1113

Privacy Act of 1974

Rules on the Processing of Data (RPD). Available at: https://www.google.com/url?sa=t&rct=j&q=&esrc=s&source=web&cd=&ved=2ahUKEwj5yuzMqsKFAxXAQUEAHUk6CUgQFnoECBoQAQ&url=https%3A%2F%2Fwww.interpol.int%2Fcontent%2Fdownload%2F5694%2Ffile%2F24%2520E%2520RPD%2520UPDATE%25207%252011%252019_ok.pdf&usg=AOvVaw0-iWULJlbiElIQWw09rpR-&opi=89978449.

Schengen Convention (*Schengener Durchführungsübereinkommen*, SDÜ)

Second generation Schengen Information System (SIS II)

Treaty on the Functioning of the European Union (TFEU)

Universal Declaration of Human Rights (UNDHR)

Villalobos Sura v Garland, 8 F 4th 1161 (9th Cir 2021)

Chapter 7:

Soering v United Kingdom [1989] ECHR 14

Table of Statutes

*[All references are to paragraph number. References in **bold** type indicate where the section is set out in part or in full]*

UNITED KINGDOM
Data Protection Act 2018 .... 5.24, 5.25
Equality Act 2010 .... 5.24

FRANCE
Loi Informatique et Libertés (Loi n° 78-17, 6 January 1978) 5.31, 5.38
Art 4, 5 .... 6.98
Title III (arts 87–114) 5.31
104, 105 .... 5.31, 5.33
106 .... 5.31
107 .... 5.31
(I) 5.38, 5.39
(II) (III) 5.39
108 .... 5.31
109 .... 5.31, 5.37
110, 111 .... 5.31

GERMANY
Code of Criminal Procedure (*Strafprozessordnung* (stPO)) ... 6.103
§ 98(2) 6.106
130 .... 6.106
153a(1) 6.103
Federal Criminal Police Act (*Bundeskriminalamgesetz* (BKAG)) 5.49
§ 33 .... 5.42
84(1) 5.49
Federal Data Protection Act (*Bundesdatenschutzgestz* (BDSG)) 5.49
§ 56 .... 5.48
(2), (4) 5.48
57 .... 5.42
(4) 5.48
60 .... 6.100
(1) 6.102
61(1) 6.101

HONG KONG
Interpretation and General Clauses Ordinance (Cap 1) 5.52
Personal Data (Privacy) Ordinance (Cap 486) 5.54
s 2(1) 5.53

Personal Data (Privacy) Ordinance (Cap 486) – *contd*
s 17A 5.53
18(1) **5.52**
19(1) 5.53
28 .... 5.54
Pt 8 (ss 51–63D) 5.56
s 57 .... 5.56
(1) 5.56
58(1) 5.56
(a), (b) 5.56

NETHERLANDS
Act on Judicial and Criminal Data (*Wet Justitiële en Strafvorderlijke Gegevens* (WJSG)) 5.65, 5.67, 5.71; 6.110
Art 18 .... 5.69
20 .... 5.70
21(2) 5.73
25 .... 5.70
26a 6.110
(5) 6.110
31a 6.110
39i 5.69
(1)(c) 5.67
Act on Police Data (*Wet Politiegegevens* (WPG)) 5.65, 5.66, 5.71, 5.73; 6.110
Art 18(c) 5.67
24a(3) 5.68
25(1) 5.68
(c) 5.66
26(3) 5.68
27(1) 5.72
29, 31a 6.110
General Administrative Law Act (*Algemene Wet Bestuursreecht* (AWB)) 6.110

UNITED STATES
Freedom of information Act (5 USC § 552) 5.75, 5.79, 5.80
s 552(c) 5.80

Freedom of Information Act Regulations (28 CFR) 5.77, 5.78
s 16.3 .... 5.75
International Organizations Immunities Act 1945 .... 6.119
National Defense Authorization Act . 6.121
New York State Constitution............ 6.119
Privacy Act 1974.............................. 6.119
United States Constitution 6.122

Table of International Legislation

[All references are to paragraph number. References in ***bold*** *type indicate where the Article is set out in part or in full]*

TREATIES AND CONVENTIONS

United Nations Convention Against Torture and other Cruel, Inhuman or Degrading Treatment or Punishment (New York, 4 February 1985) 6.119

European Convention on Human Rights (Rome, 4 November 1950) 6.35
- Art 2 .... 6.113
- 3 .... 6.53, 6.112, 6.113
- 6 .... 6.53
- Protocol 7
  - Art 4(1) 6.35, 6.47

International Covenant on Civil and Political Rights (New York, 16 December 1966) 6.35
- Art 14(7) 6.35, 6.47

Interpol Constitution (Vienna, 13 June 1956) 2.2, 2.3, 2.4, 2.5, 2.7, 2.8, 2.9, 2.10, 2.12; 4.54; 7.16, 7.19, 7.26
- Art 2 .... 2.4; 3.8, 3.18, 3.24, 3.27; 4.41, 4.47, 4.54; 5.92; 6.32, 6.34, 6.35, 6.36, 6.38, 6.39, 6.42, 6.46, 6.47, 6.48, 6.49, 6.50, 6.51, 6.53
  - (1) 3.24, 3.25; 4.21; 6.33, 6.93
- 3 .... 1.27, 1.28; 2.5; 3.8, 3.18, 3.24, 3.25; 4.21, 4.41, 4.44, 4.54; 6.53, 6.54, 6.55, 6.56, 6.58, 6.59, 6.60, 6.61, 6.62, 6.64, 6.65, 6.66, 6.76, 6.79, 6.93; 7.17, 7.25
- 5 .... 2.8
- 6–8, 13 .... 2.9
- 14 .... 2.10
- 15–17 .... 2.12

Interpol Constitution (Vienna, 13 June 1956) – *contd*
- Art 22 .... 2.11
- 26 .... 2.14
- 28, 29 .... 2.15
- 32 .... 2.16
- 36 .... 2.19
- 38, 39 .... 2.5
- 41 .... 2.6
- 42 .... 2.7

Interpol Rules on the Processing of Data 6.19, 6.25, 6.91, 6.92, 6.93, 6.95; 7.16, 7.17, 7.22, 7.26
- Art 1 .... 6.20
- 2 .... 6.27
- 5(3) 6.40
- 8(3) 6.90
- 10 .... 6.25
  - (1) 6.24
- 12 .... 6.82, 6.91, 6.94
  - (1) 6.84, 6.89
- 34(1) 6.32
  - (3) **6.64**, 6.79
- 35 .... 6.40
  - (1) 6.40
- 51 .... 6.20, 6.21, 6.25
  - (1) 6.22, 6.23
  - (2) 6.22, 6.24
- 73 .... 6.90
- 81(3) **6.29**
  - (c) 6.30
- 82 .... 3.4, 3.17; 6.82
- 83 .... **3.6**, 3.8, 3.9, 3.15; 6.30, 6.85, 6.87, 6.91, 6.94
  - (1) 6.86
    - (b) 3.13, 3.14
    - (c) 3.14
  - (2) 3.28
    - (b) 6.89
- 84 .... 3.16, 3.17

Interpol Rules on the Processing of Data – *contd*,
Art 85 .... 3.16
86 .... 3.18
87 .... **3.20**, 3.21
97(1) 3.22
99 .... 6.82, 6.91
(2) **3.24**, 3.33; 6.93
100 .... 6.31
Convention relating to the Status of Refugees (Geneva, 28 July 1951) 4.4, 4.22, 4.29
Operating Rules of the Commission for the Control of Interpol's Files (adopted 28 March 2017; latest amendments 28 April 2023) 6.15
r 30(1) 6.14
(b) 6.14
(2) 6.15
(4) 6.16
Convention implementing the Schengen Agreement of 14 June 1985 between the Governments of the States of the Benelux Economic Union, the Federal Republic of Germany and the French Republic on the gradual abolition of checks at their common borders (Schengen, 19 June 1990)
Art 54 .... 6.105
Statute of the Commission for the Control of INTERPOL'S Files (11 March 2017) 2.20; 4.37; 4.9; 5.16; 6.12
Ch 4 Sub-Ch 1 (arts 29–32) 5.9
Art 29 .... 5.11, 5.12, 5.41, 5.61, 5.74; 6.4
30(3) 6.4
32(1) 6.5, 6.11
34 .... 6.6
36 .... 6.7
37 .... 6.9
38 .... 6.17
39 .... 6.8
40 .... 6.17
(2) 6.11
41 .... 6.10
130, 131 .... 4.39
Treaty on the Functioning of the European Union (Rome, 25 March 1957)
Art 21 .... 6.104
(1) 6.105
Charter of the United Nations and Statute of the International Court of Justice (San Fransisco, 26 June 1945) 1.23
Art 1 .... 1.24
Ch VII (arts 39–51) 6.77
Universal Declaration of Human Rights (Paris, 10 December 1948) 2.4; 6.34, 6.35, 6.51; 7.23
Art 3 .... 6.37, 6.53
5 .... 6.41, 6.53
10 .... 6.43, 6.53; 7.24
13 .... 6.49
25 .... 6.45, 6.53
29 .... 6.49
(2) 6.46, 6.53

DIRECTIVES

Directive (EU) 2016/680 of the European Parliament and of the Council of 27 April 2016 on the protection of natural persons with regard to the processing of personal data by competent authorities for the purposes of the prevention, investigation, detection or prosecution of criminal offences or the execution of criminal penalties, and on the for movement of such data, and repealing Council Framework Decision 2008/977/JHA 5.64, 5.65
Recital 25 .... 5.64

REGULATIONS

Regulation (EU) 2016/679 of the European Parliament and of the Council of 27 April 2016 on the protection of natural persons with regard to the processing of personal data and on the free movement of such data, and repealing Directive 95/46/EC (General Data Protection Regulation) 5.65; 6.100, 6.110

Table of Cases

A

Assange v Swedish Prosecution Authority; Assange v Sweden [2012] UKSC 22, [2012] 2 AC 471, [2012] 2 WLR 1275 .... 3.16

C

Cinepoly Records Co Ltd v Hong Kong Broadband Network Ltd [2006] 1 HKC 433.. 5.56

E

Eastweek Publisher Ltd v Privacy Comr for Personal Data [2000] 1 HKC 692 .... 5.52
El Omari v Interpol 35 F 4th 83 (2nd Cir, 2022) 6.119

G

Gonzalez-Castillo v Garland 47 F 4th 1971 (9th Cir, 2022) 6.120

N

N v United Kingdom [2008] 5 WLUK 632, (2008) 47 EHRR 39, 25 BHRC 258......... 6.53

P

Paposhivili v Belgium (Application 41738/10) (judgment 13 December 2016)........... 6.53

S

Soering v United Kingdom (A/161) [1989] 7 WLUK 64, (1989) 11 EHRR 439, [1989] ECHR 14 .... 7.23

V

Villalobos Sura v Garland 8 F 4th 1161 (9th Cir, 2021) 6.119

1 Interpol – Origins and historical development

1. Introduction
2. The First International Police Congress
3. The 1923 International Criminal Police Congress
4. The war years
5. Post-war renewal
6. Conclusion

Introduction

1.1

A detailed history of the development of Interpol is beyond the scope of this work. This chapter will, however, consider the organisation's development in order to understand the extent of its work (which is more limited than is popularly understood) and the political and practical restraints under which it operates.

1.2

This chapter will consider two significant challenges that faced those who, in the early part of the twentieth century, were concerned with developing an organisation capable of harmonising co-operation between the police forces of nation states: scepticism and political instability. Both these factors have shaped the development of Interpol and continue to present formidable challenges to the organisation.

1.3

This chapter looks at the development of Interpol and will focus on the periods of the organisation's development which have had the greatest impact on how it operates today.

The First International Police Congress

1.4

The development of Interpol can be traced to the meeting of the 'First International Police Congress' in Monaco in April 1914. The meeting was organised by Prince Albert I of Monaco and he distributed his invitations widely. The list of attendees was genuinely international with 188 official representatives from 24 nation states.[1] However, not all major police forces of the era were represented. The United States and Great Britain both sent representatives to the conference, but neither country sent representatives from their police forces. This is an early example of the scepticism which influenced the approach of both countries to the international movement for greater police co-operation.[2]

1.5

After the assembly in Monaco a 'Summary of the Wishes of the Congress'[3] was published. This document expressed the following aspirations in respect of general police matters:

> 'I. The First International Criminal Police Congress expresses the wish to see direct, official contacts between police forces of the different countries generalized and improved, so as to allow all investigations likely to facilitate the action of criminal justice.
>
> II. The Congress expresses the wish for Governments to agree to allow judicial and police authorities to use international post, telegram and telephone services free of charge in order to facilitate the arrest of criminals.
>
> III. The Congress, recognizing the need for an international language for contacts between police officials belonging to different countries, expresses the wish that, until Esperanto, or any other similar language, is sufficiently widespread to be used for such purposes, the French language be used.
>
> IV. The Congress expresses the wish for training in forensic science to be given to students in all Law Faculties.

---

1 Austria, Belgium, Brazil Bulgaria, Cuba, Denmark, Egypt, El Salvador France, Germany, Guatemala, Hungary, Iran, Italy, Mexico, Monaco, Portugal, Romania, Serbia, Spain, Switzerland, Turkey, Tsarist Russia and the United States of America.

2 As Interpol historian Fenton Bresler has observed, Great Britain was represented by a magistrate from Hove, a barrister and two solicitors who were 'so undistinguished that not one of them merited an entry in the 1914 volume of *Who's Who*'. The United States of America was represented by 'a solitary judge from Dayton, Ohio'. Fenton Bresler, *Interpol* (1st edn, London: Sinclair-Stevenson Ltd, 1992) p 13.

3 First International Criminal Police Congress, Monaco (April 1914) 'Summary of the Wishes of Congress held on 15, 16 and 18 April 2014'.

V. In order to propagate new search techniques among police officers and agents, the Congress expresses the wish for governments to increase the number of practical schools to give this training.

VI. The Congress, recognizing the need to know the biological features of professional criminals in order to combat them effectively, expresses the wish for this matter to be put on the agenda of a future Congress.'

1.6

In addition to these general matters, the Congress urged national governments to implement greater co-operation in three areas of immediate concern: (1) the creation of a system of identifying 'international' offenders; (2) the creation of centralised international records; and (3) the creation of a functioning extradition system.

1.7

The Congress can be considered successful in at least two regards. Firstly, it confirmed a great deal of enthusiasm amongst law enforcement agencies for greater co-operation to combat the growing problem of international crime. Secondly, it identified practical measures where greater international co-operation would yield significant results. It is notable that the areas identified by the Congress would become the focus of co-operation between national law enforcement agencies in the years that followed. The outbreak of World War I later that year, however, meant that many years would pass before the measures suggested by the Congress were implemented.

The 1923 International Criminal Police Congress

1.8

The huge scale of the dislocation of individuals during World War I provided added impetus to implement the measures identified in Monaco in 1914. The Austrian police authorities became the driving force behind a renewed effort to advance international police co-operation. It has been suggested by some commentators that their enthusiasm stemmed more from a desire to monitor those they suspected of fermenting communist revolution rather than the need to combat international crime.[4]

4 Malcolm Anderson, *Policing the World – Interpol and the Politics of International Police Co-operation* (Oxford: Clarendon Press, 1989) pp 39–40.

1.9

In 1923, Johann Schober, the Austrian police chief, invited police chiefs and the leaders of major cities from across the world to attend the 'Second International Police Congress' in Vienna. The Congress took place on 3 September 1923. In attendance were 138 delegates representing 17 different nation states.[5] It is notable that the Congress was dominated by the states of Western Continental Europe. The (then) Soviet Union was conspicuous by its absence. It has been observed by some that this further demonstrated that the objectives of many nation states were far from apolitical.

1.10

Whatever the underlying motives of some participants may have been, the Congress was undoubtedly significant. It is regarded as the birth of the organisation that would later become known as Interpol. At the conclusion of the Congress the formation of an international police organisation was declared. The new organisation was to be called the International Criminal Police Commission (ICPC) and was to be based in Vienna, Austria.

1.11

As has been noted, the formation of the ICPC was driven by the Austrian authorities and the organisation's early years were shaped by this formative influence. Based in Vienna, it was funded by the Austrian government and staffed entirely by Austrians.

1.12

The organisation moved quickly to implement the longstanding aim of a database of international records. The new 'International Criminal Records Office' was, in reality, little more than the records of the Viennese police. Whilst those records were regarded as the most extensive in the world at the time, there was little evidence of any significant progress in international police co-operation. The French lawyer Claude Valleix described the ICPC as 'an office of the federal directorate of the Viennese police handling international crime cases'.[6]

1.13

In 1923, the ICPC's claim to be a genuine international police organisation may have been questionable. However, the organisation developed rapidly. As it grew in size, the ICPC quickly realised that, to implement its aims, it would be necessary for each member country to create a body to interact directly

5 The following nations were represented: Austria, Belgium, China, Egypt, Fiume, France, Germany, Greece, Hungary, Italy, the Netherlands, Poland, Romania, Sweden, Switzerland, the United States and Yugoslavia (two notable absentees include Great Britain and Monaco).

6 Ibid, Bresler, *Interpol*, p 18.

with it. The solution adopted was the creation of a National Central Bureau (NCB) in each member country, through which ICPC communications could be channelled. The first NCB was formed in 1925 by Belgium; other nations quickly followed. This basic structure – national NCBs liaising with a centralised secretariat – remains in place today.

1.14

The year 1925 contained a further significant milestone for the ICPC with the publication of the first 'International Wanted Notices' published in its fortnightly magazine edited by the ICPC's Secretary General, Oskar Dressler. The magazine was published in German, French, English and Italian and was distributed widely. Those early wanted notices can be considered the forerunner of the now infamous 'Interpol Red Notice' which forms the subject of later chapters in this book.

1.15

On the occasion of its tenth anniversary in 1933, the ICPC had members from over 20 nations. Its International Criminal Records Office contained the names of 3,240 international criminals. The ambitious project had been an unquestionable success. However, the organisation was about to enter its most troubled period. The subsequent years would have a profound impact on the course of international police co-operation.

The war years

1.16

The ICPC General Assembly[7] of 1934 was convened in Vienna against a backdrop of huge political uncertainty. The rise of the National Socialist Party in Germany had placed huge pressure on Austrian sovereignty. By the time the conference convened there had already been a Nazi-inspired coup attempt against the Austrian Government. There was concern amongst many delegates that Germany was seeking control of the organisation. In order to check German influence, a resolution was passed that, for a trial period of five years, the head of the Vienna police would automatically become the ICPC president. However, the location of the ICPC in Vienna, which was soon to be enveloped by the Third Reich, meant that there was no internal governance measure that could prevent the organisation from being overtaken by world events.

1.17

On 12 March 1938 'Der Anschluss' took place and Vienna fell under the control of the Third Reich. On the same day, the incumbent President of the ICPC,

7 See Chapter 2 for General Assembly definition.

Dr Michael Skubl, was placed under house arrest. Heinrich Himmler personally demanded Dr Skubl's resignation, which was forthcoming. The Nazis resisted the temptation to immediately install a senior German Nazi as the president of the ICPC. Instead a stopgap was found in the form of Austrian, Otto Steinhausl. A former high-ranking police officer, he was an avowed Nazi who had recently been released from prison where he had been held for crimes against the Austrian State.

1.18

At the ICPC General Assembly in Bucharest in 1938, delegates were welcomed by their new president. In an atmosphere of high tension, a proposal was made by the French delegation that the ICPC headquarters be moved to Geneva, the home of the League of Nations and a neutral territory. The proposal was voted down. At the conclusion of the assembly it was agreed that the ICPC would meet again in Berlin in September 1939. However, the outbreak of World War II meant that it was never convened.

1.19

There has been much academic discussion of whether the ICPC ceased to function as an organisation of international police co-operation during World War II. Although there were no assemblies during the war, the ICPC was not formally disbanded by the Nazis, who moved its headquarters to Berlin and continued to publish its magazine. What is beyond dispute is that the organisation's apparatus fell under the total control of the Nazi regime. It was eventually headed by Reinhard Heydrich, a senior Nazi official, until his assassination in May 1942. What is more uncertain is the extent to which the apparatus of the ICPC was utilised as a tool of genocide. The detailed records held by the ICPC at this time would have been extremely useful to a regime seeking to exterminate individuals based on race, religion or political affiliation. No documentary evidence exists, however, to confirm the records were used by the Nazis in this way.[8]

1.20

The events of World War II and the ability of a totalitarian regime to take complete control of the ICPC apparatus not only delayed the advance of international police co-operation but also had a profound impact on how the ICPC would structure itself in the future. Perhaps most critically, it demonstrated that its viability depended on its ability to demonstrate an apolitical character. This was to be a considerable challenge as the organisation renewed and developed in the post-war era.

8 Bresler, *Interpol* pp 59–63.

Post-war renewal

1.21

The huge dislocation of people caused by a major global conflagration provided a strong incentive to restore international police co-operation as quickly as possible. It is perhaps unsurprising that those nations in continental Europe who had experienced a massive influx of dislocated persons were at the vanguard of a movement to quickly re-establish the ICPC.

1.22

A senior Belgian police official, Flourent Lowage, persuaded the Belgian authorities to host the Fifteenth International Criminal Police Congress which convened on 3 June 1946 in Brussels. The majority of delegates in attendance were representatives of the victorious nations of World War II, although the United States and the (then) Soviet Union were notably absent.[9] There was a broad agreement amongst the delegates about the urgent need for a renewed ICPC in the post-war era. Resolutions were passed establishing the organisation's headquarters in Paris,[10] a statute was adopted requiring the president of the ICPC to be a citizen of the state in which the headquarters were located and English and French were adopted as the official languages (a resolution to include Russian as an official language was defeated). The assembly also approved a statute governing the scope of the ICPC's operations. This document, however, soon required significant amendment.

1.23

In September 1948, at the Seventeenth General Assembly in Prague, the Secretary General of the ICPC, Louis Ducloux, proposed an amendment to formalise the ICPC's apolitical status. He introduced the amendment in the following way:

> 'The strict limitation of our action within the realm of common law has enabled us to extend the influence of the ICPC without opposition, and we consider that its future hangs largely on the strict observance of this neutrality. Now a reading of the Statute [of 1946] brings to light a grave omission in this respect, which I am sure all the adhering states will agree must be rectified as quickly as possible.'[11]

---

9 The following nations were represented: Belgium, Chile, Czechoslovakia, Denmark, Egypt, France, Great Britain, Iran, Luxembourg, The Netherlands, Norway, Poland, Portugal, Sweden, Switzerland, Turkey and Yugoslavia.

10 Most commentators agree that the French did not specifically lobby for these changes. However, their willingness to devote resources was helpful in allowing the organisation to re-establish itself quickly. An inevitable consequence of these changes was that the organisation was influenced by French practices and culture.

11 Bresler, *Interpol*, pp 106–107.

1.24

Mr Ducloux then proposed an amendment to Article 1 of the statute which would forbid the ICPC from intervening in cases of a political character. This self-imposed restriction on the scope of the ICPC remains a principal feature of Interpol's present constitution.[12]

1.25

In the following decade the organisation saw a rapid growth in membership. By 1955 the membership had grown to 55 countries. In 1956, the ICPC adopted a new constitution and the organisation was renamed 'Interpol'.

1.26

Interpol's membership continued to grow and in 1971 was recognised by the United Nations as an intergovernmental organisation. Interpol continued to adopt an intentionally low profile and a resolutely apolitical stance. However, the organisation gradually began to realise that the strict application of its constitution was hampering its efforts to assist in combating the emerging threat of international terrorism.

1.27

In 1984, the General Assembly passed a resolution clarifying how Article 3 of the Interpol Constitution was to be interpreted. The new resolution plainly increased the potential scope of its operations. The changes allowed Interpol to concern itself with a broad range of cases that may previously have been considered to be outside the scope of its permitted operations by virtue of Article 3.

1.28

The new resolution acknowledged that the organisation is strictly forbidden 'to undertake any intervention or activities of a political, military, religious or racial character'. However, it emphasised that this only brought criminal behaviour outside the organisation's scope if the conduct was of 'predominantly political, racial or religious character'. Furthermore, each case must be 'examined separately with due consideration for the specific context'. Crucially, the resolution excluded a broad range of conduct from the operation of Article 3 by stating as follows:

> 'When offences are committed by persons with definite political motives but when the offences committed have no direct connection with the political life of the offenders' country or the cause for which they are fighting, the crime may no longer be deemed to come within

---

12 Article 3 of the Interpol Constitution (Vienna, June 1956).

the scope of Article 3. This is particularly true when offences are committed in countries which are not directly involved (i.e. outside the "conflict area") and when the offences constitute a serious threat to personal freedom, life or property.'

1.29

Further significant changes to Interpol's structure and procedure were again prompted by the spectre of international terrorism. In the aftermath of the attacks on the United States on 11 September 2001, Interpol has invested significantly in its technological capabilities in response to threats of international terrorism and trans-national crime. Interpol has developed 'I-24/7' a secure global communication network. The system was created in January 2003 and allows information about suspected individuals and groups to be exchanged between Interpol's member countries and its General Secretariat.

1.30

Interpol's membership has continued to increase in size, by 2022 reaching 195 member countries. In September 2023, Interpol, celebrated its centenary. The UN General Assembly designated an International Day of Police Cooperation in recognition of the vital need for co-operation within the international law enforcement community.

Conclusion

1.31

It is clear that the obstacles faced by those who wished to form a co-operative international police body at the beginning of the twentieth century – identified at the outset of this chapter – remain significant challenges for Interpol in the modern era. Firstly, effective international police co-operation requires sufficient political stability to provide the environment for such co-operation to take place. Secondly, those co-operating must believe that the conduit of that co-operation is an honest broker. Finally, the agencies seeking to co-operate must believe that co-operation will bear fruit. Chapter 2 explores the modern-day operation of Interpol and how it seeks to meet those challenges.

2 Interpol today

1. Introduction

2. The Constitution

3. The structure

4. Funding

5. International partners

6. Interpol's work

Introduction

2.1

Having considered Interpol's history we now turn to its structure, culture and role today. Headquartered in Lyon, Interpol consists of 196 member countries. There are currently only two UN member countries who are not also members of Interpol.[1] Membership is obtained either as a result of having been involved in the 1956 constitutive process or by application. Applications must be made to the Secretary General of Interpol by the appropriate governmental authority[2] of the prospective member country.

2.2

All applicants must consent to the binding nature of the Interpol Constitution (the Constitution) as an international legal instrument. Membership is then subject to approval by two-thirds majority of the General Assembly.

2.3

This chapter will consider Interpol's Constitution and how each of its component parts, including the General Assembly, operates; as well as setting

1 Democratic People's Republic of Korea and Tuvalu.

2 President of the Republic, Head of State, Prime Minister or government departments, Ministers of Foreign Affairs, Interior and Justice (or Attorney General), or Secretary General of the President of the Republic's office.

out its structure, vision and mission of the organisation, how it is funded and its stated priorities.

The Constitution

2.4

The Constitution was formerly adopted by the General Assembly at its twenty-fifth session in Vienna on 13 June 1956 and has two stated aims:

- to ensure and promote the widest possible mutual assistance between all criminal police authorities within the limits of the laws existing in the different countries and in the spirit of the Universal Declaration of Human Rights; and
- to establish and develop all institutions likely to contribute effectively to prevention and suppression of ordinary law crimes.[3]

2.5

The Constitution forbids Interpol from undertaking any activities of a political, military, religious or racial character.[4] The Constitution also mandates that Interpol's resources are to be provided by financial contributions from members as well as gifts, bequests, subsidies, grants, or other resources after approval by the Executive Committee (see below for more details).[5] The General Assembly establishes the basis of member subscriptions and maximum expenditure according to an estimate provided by the Secretary General.[6]

2.6

Interpol is constitutionally allowed to establish relations and collaborate (after General Assembly approval) with intergovernmental or non-governmental organisations (NGOs) which share its aims and objectives.[7]

2.7

Any amendment to the Constitution may occur on the proposal of a member or the Executive Committee. Any such proposals must be communicated by the Secretary General to members at least three months before submission to the General Assembly for consideration. All amendments must be approved by a two-thirds majority.[8]

---

3 Article 2 of the Constitution.
4 Article 3 of the Constitution.
5 Article 38 of the Constitution.
6 Article 39 of the Constitution.
7 Article 41 of the Constitution.
8 Article 42 of the Constitution.

The structure

2.8

Per its constitution Interpol consists of:

- The General Assembly;
- The Executive Committee;
- The General Secretariat;
- The National Central Bureaus;
- The Advisers;
- The Commission for the Control of Files.[9]

The General Assembly

2.9

The General Assembly is Interpol's supreme governing body and is composed of delegates appointed by each of the member countries.[10] Each member country appoints a delegate (or delegates) but there can only be one delegation head and only one delegate from each country has the right to vote in the General Assembly.[11] The delegation head must be appointed by the competent governmental authority of the member country. The General Assembly meets annually and its functions are contained in Article 8 of the Constitution which are to:

- carry out the duties laid down in the Constitution;
- determine principles and lay down the general measures suitable for attaining the objectives of the organisation;
- examine and approve the general programme of activities prepared by the Secretary General for the coming year;
- determine any other regulations deemed necessary;
- elect persons to perform the functions mentioned in the Constitution;
- adopt resolutions and make recommendations to members on matters with which the organisation is competent to deal;
- determine the financial policy of the organisation; and
- examine and approve any agreements to be made with other organisations.

9 Article 5 of the Constitution.
10 Article 6 of the Constitution.
11 Articles 7 and 13 of the Constitution.

2.10

The General Assembly can also meet in extraordinary session at the request of the Executive Committee or the majority of members. Any decisions made by the General Assembly require a simple majority except where a two-thirds majority is required by the Constitution.[12]

The Executive Committee

2.11

The Executive Committee supervises the execution of decisions made by the General Assembly. It is elected by the General Assembly and meets at least once a year. The Executive Committee's formal role is to:

- supervise the execution of decisions made by the General Assembly;
- prepare the Agenda for sessions of General Assembly;
- submit individual programmes of work or projects to General Assembly;
- supervise the administration and work of the Secretary General; and
- exercise all powers delegated to it by the General Assembly.[13]

2.12

The Executive Committee is headed by the Interpol president who, along with three vice presidents, is elected by the General Assembly. The president is elected for a four-year term and the vice presidents for three years each. Nine additional delegates, who are also elected for a three-year term, complete the Committee. The Constitution requires that the members of the Executive Committee belong to different countries and that a proportional geographical distribution of members is maintained. The president and vice president must be from different continents.[14]

The General Secretariat

2.13

The General Secretariat, along with individual National Central Bureaus (NCBs), is responsible for the implementation of strategic decisions made by the General Assembly and the Executive Committee. It is headquartered in Lyon, France and is served by a further seven regional offices in South America,

12 Article 14 of the Constitution.
13 Article 22 of the Constitution.
14 Articles 15, 16 and 17 of the Constitution.

Central America, Africa and Asia. In addition, there are liaison offices located at the African Union in Addis Ababa, the United Nations in New York and the European Union in Brussels.[15]

2.14

The General Secretariat's role within the organisation is set out in Article 26 of the Constitution. The duties of the General Secretariat are as follows:

- put into application the decisions of the General Assembly and the Executive Committee;
- serve as an international centre in the fight against ordinary crime;
- serve as a technical and information centre;
- ensure the efficient administration of the organisation;
- maintain contact with national and international authorities, whereas questions relative to the search for criminals shall be dealt with through the NCBs;
- produce any publications which may be considered useful;
- organise and perform secretariat work at the sessions of the General Assembly, the Executive Committee and any other body of the organisation;
- draw up a draft programme of work for the coming year for the consideration and approval of the General Assembly and the Executive Committee; and
- maintain, as far as is possible, direct and constant contact with the president of the organisation.

2.15

The Secretary General is appointed for a five-year term. They may be reappointed but must give up their right to hold office upon reaching the age of 65, unless permitted by the Executive Committee to complete the current term.[16] The incumbent Secretary General is Jürgen Stock, a former vice president of the German Federal Criminal Police, who was elected at the Eighty-third General Assembly in November 2014 in Monaco.[17] The Secretary General's role involves budget administration and the management and organisation of staff and departments within the Secretariat. He/she also has the right to engage

15 '*General Secretariat*'. Interpol website. Available at: https://www.interpol.int/Who-we-are/General-Secretariat.

16 Article 28 of the Constitution.

17 '*Biography of the current Secretary General Jürgen Stock*'. Interpol website. Available at: www.interpol.int/Who-we-are/General-Secretariat/Secretary-General/Juergen-Stock-biography.

in discussions held by Interpol's governing bodies, to which he/she may also submit any propositions or projects concerning the work of the organisation.[18]

National Central Bureaus

2.16

Each member country of the organisation is required to connect its national law enforcement officer's force with the wider Interpol network through a National Central Bureau (NCB).[19] In this way, the organisation seeks to maintain a central criminal database to improve communication and operational support in cross-border investigations. It is the job of the NCBs to communicate with all in-country law enforcement departments so that more complete information can be transmitted both to other NCBs and to the General Secretariat.

2.17

Cross-border support and co-operation is central to Interpol's role. The organisation therefore encourages increased use of the NCBs on a regional basis.[20] In an attempt to increase the prominence and efficacy of the NCBs, since 2005, Interpol has organised an annual conference, which is attended by the head of each bureau. In 2023, this brought together around 270 delegates from 133 countries. The conference focused heavily on organised crime, terrorism and cybercrime.[21]

Advisers

2.18

In order to improve the oversight of the organisation, Interpol may consult independent advisers on scientific matters. They act in a purely advisory capacity and have no decision-making powers.[22] Advisers are appointed for a term of three years by the Executive Committee, although their appointment is only certain once notification has been given by the General Assembly, which also has the power to remove them. Advisers are selected based on their reputation within fields that are of some interest to Interpol.[23]

---

18 Article 29 of the Constitution.
19 Article 32 of the Constitution.
20 *'National Central Bureaus (NCBs)'*, Interpol website. Available at: https://www.interpol.int/en/Who-we-are/Member-countries/National-Central-Bureaus-NCBs.
21 'Empowering the INTERPOL network of global law enforcement cooperation'. Interpol website. Available at: https://www.interpol.int/News-and-Events/News/2023/INTERPOL-conference-Heightened-urgency-as-police-leaders-discuss-global-crime-threats.
22 Article 34 of the Constitution.
23 Article 35 of the Constitution.

The Commission for the Control of Files

2.19

An independent Commission for the Control of Files (CCF) ensures personal information is processed in compliance with relevant regulations (Article 36). Given the nature of its work, a large volume of personal data, such as names and fingerprints, flows through Interpol's system on a daily basis. The organisation employs the CCF as an independent body to ensure this personal information is stored and processed in a manner compliant with regulations designed by the organisation.[24] To guarantee the CCF's independence, Interpol has incorporated the former into its internal legal structure, a decision taken at the 2008 General Assembly.[25]

2.20

In 2016, Interpol further formalised the role of the CCF by adopting the Statute of the CCF[26] and abrogating the rules on the Control of Information and Access to Interpol's files. According to the statute, the CCF's function is to:

- ensure the processing of personal data by Interpol is in compliance with Interpol's rules;
- provide Interpol with advice about any project, operation, set of rules or other matter involving the processing of personal data in Interpol's information system; and
- examine and decide on requests for access or deletion of data, processed in Interpol's information system.

The culture

2.21

Interpol maintains clearly defined strategies and priorities that drive its day-to-day functions and the culture of the organisation. The overriding theme of these objectives is the proliferation and facilitation of global mutual assistance in the fight against international crime. Within this overarching objective, there is a strong focus on the provision of support to the NCBs. The organisation's strategies and priorities complement its 'vision and mission'. Its vision is 'connecting police for a safer world'; its mission is 'preventing and fighting

24 Article 36 of the Constitution.
25 '*Activity Report of the CCF 2008 and January–February 2009*' Interpol. Available at: https://www.interpol.int/content/download/6889/file/Annual%20Report%20of%20the%20CCF%202008.pdf.
26 See https://www.interpol.int/content/download/5695/file/Statute%20of%20the%20CCF-EN.pdf.

crime through enhanced co-operation and innovation on police and security matters'.[27]

2.22

Interpol has identified four strategic goals:[28]

- *Trusted information for action:* to serve as the trusted global law enforcement hub for the exchange of actionable information and analysis.
- *Enrich policing through partnerships:* to maximise resources, knowledge and operations through cooperation and strategic partnerships.
- *Advance and innovate policing:* advance the global law enforcement community through research and innovative solutions.
- *Enhance organisational performance and delivery:* be an organisation of excellence that is accountable, transparent and agile.

Funding

2.23

Interpol's consolidated budget comprises three separate sources:

- The Regular Budget;
- Trust Fund;
- Special accounts.[29]

2.24

The organisation produces annual financial statements which are currently audited by the Supreme Audit Office of Poland. The 2021 total revenue was €137.3 million.[30]

2.25

The Regular Budget is made up of the annual statutory contribution that is provided by each member country. Contributions are based on a proportional scale and voted upon annually by the General Assembly. In 2023, the USA was the largest single contributor with €15,931,297 and 31 countries each paid the

27 '*Strategy*'. Interpol website. Available at: https://www.interpol.int/Who-we-are/Strategy.

28 '*Strategic Framework 2022–2025*'. Interpol website. Available at: https://www.interpol.int/Who-we-are/Strategy/Strategic-Framework-2022-2025.

29 '*Our Funding*'. Interpol website. Available at: www.interpol.int/Who-we-are/Our-funding.

30 '*Financial Statements for the Year Ended 31 December 2021*'. International Criminal Police Organization. Available at: https://www.interpol.int/content/download/18417/file/ICPO-INTERPOL%20Audited%20Financial%20Statements%202021.pdf.

lowest contribution of €25,402.[31] These payments fund the general running costs of the General Secretariat and core policing, training and support activities according to strategic priorities.[32]

2.26

Contributions from external donors such as government agencies, NGOs and foundations are in a 'special account'.[33] The organisation's strategic priorities (above) are each linked to a sub-account of the trust fund, while a special account is created for each public entity donation which may have specific reporting requirements. The largest external contribution in 2022, of €12,805,000, was given by the European Commission to support a variety of Interpol's programmes.

International partners

2.27

Interpol co-operates closely with a wide variety of public, private, and strategic partners as well as maintaining its liaison offices at the African Union, UN and the EU.[34] The organisation's other key partners include the European Commission, Federal Ministry for Foreign Affairs (Germany) and the US Department of State and Global Affairs Canada.[35] Interpol's private sector partners include profit-making and not-for-profit organisations. These organisations often possess particular expertise required by Interpol such as ballistics, biometric identification and cyber security.

Interpol's work

2.28

In practical terms, Interpol performs a number of functions in relation to the investigation of global crime (eg training and capacity building; data exchange; databases; notices; command and co-ordination; response teams; forensics; criminal intelligence analysis; and border management).

---

31 '*Interpol Member Country Statutory Contributions 2023*'. Available at: https://www.interpol.int/content/download/19208/file/INTERPOL%20MEMBER%20COUNTRY%20STATUTORY%20CONTRIBUTIONS%202023.pdf.

32 '*Our Funding*'. Interpol website. Available at: www.interpol.int/Who-we-are/Our-funding.

33 '*Financial Statements for the Year Ended 31 December 2021*'. International Criminal Police Organization. Available at: https://www.interpol.int/content/download/18417/file/ICPO-INTERPOL%20Audited%20Financial%20Statements%202021.

34 '*International Organization Partners*'. Interpol website. Available at: https://www.interpol.int/Our-partners/International-organization-partners.

35 '*Our funding*'. Interpol website. Available at: www.https://www.interpol.int/Who-we-are/Our-funding.

2.29

A snapshot of the areas in which Interpol conducted field operations in 2022 and 2023 provides some insight as to its priorities:

- Human trafficking including child trafficking and migrant smuggling.
- Fugitives – helping countries locate wanted individuals.
- Child sexual abuse including seizing and analysing online abuse material as well as identifying victims and perpetrators.
- Cybercrime including online blackmail and internet fraud.
- Drug trafficking focusing on identifying smuggling methods.
- Environmental crime focusing on forestry crime, endangered species and pollution crime.
- Illicit trade, focusing on intellectual property crime.
- Pharmaceutical crime including fake or illicit medicines on sale in shops.

3 Red Notices and Diffusions

1. Introduction

2. Interpol Red Notices – general operation

3. NCB request – minimum criteria

4. Specific criteria

5. The General Secretariat's discretion

6. NCB request – minimum data

7. Further obligations on the requesting NCB – Articles 84–85

8. Legal review by the General Secretariat

9. Action to be taken by NCBs pursuant to an Interpol Red Notice

10. Diffusions

Introduction

3.1

Interpol is arguably most famous for its role in apprehending individuals sought by law enforcement agencies for criminal proceedings. Contrary to frequent media misrepresentation Interpol does not play a direct role in investigating the whereabouts of wanted individuals nor does it play a direct role in effecting their arrest. Nevertheless, it unquestionably plays a critical role in allowing law enforcement agencies to arrest individuals who are sought for prosecution or to enforce an outstanding sentence of imprisonment.

3.2

Interpol adopts two principal roles in the apprehension of wanted individuals. Firstly, it maintains a database of individuals sought by member countries.

Secondly, it acts as conduit between National Central Bureaus (NCBs) where an immediate arrest may be sought. In conducting both roles Interpol's actions have the potential to infringe significantly on the liberty of an individual. A decision to communicate a message between two NCBs may lead to an immediate arrest. A decision to include an individual on Interpol's database may also lead to an immediate arrest or, at the very least, restrict that person's ability both to travel and conduct business.

3.3

This chapter explores how Interpol seeks to carry out these functions and will consider the strength of its internal procedures to ensure that in carrying out its role it does not infringe the fundamental rights of the individuals sought.

Interpol Red Notices – general operation

3.4

Red Notices are 'alerts' issued by Interpol's General Secretariat at the request of NCBs of an Interpol member country. The purpose of a Red Notice is to 'seek the location of a wanted person and his/her detention, arrest or restriction of movement for the purpose of extradition, surrender or similar lawful action'.[1]

3.5

The General Secretariat will only issue a Red Notice when satisfied that: (1) the request from the NCB fulfils certain specified criteria and (2) the NCB has provided necessary information in support of the request.

NCB request – minimum criteria

3.6

The minimum criteria and required information are defined in Article 83 of Interpol's Rules on the Processing of Data (RPD). It provides as follows:

> 'Article 83: Specific conditions for publication of red notices
>
> (1) Minimum criteria
>
> (a) Red notices may be published only if the following cumulative criteria are met:
>
> (i) The offence concerned is a serious ordinary-law crime.

1 Article 82 of Interpol's Rules on the Processing of Data (hereafter RPD).

Red notices may not be published for the following categories of offences:

– offences that in various countries raise controversial issues relating to behavioural or cultural norms;

– offences relating to family/private matters;

– offences originating from a violation of laws or regulations of an administrative nature or deriving from private disputes, unless the criminal activity is aimed at facilitating a serious crime or is suspected of being connected to organized crime.

The General Secretariat shall keep, update and share with National Central Bureaus and international entities a non-exhaustive list of specific offences that fall within the above categories.

(ii) Penalty threshold:

– if the person is sought for prosecution, the conduct constituting an offence is punishable by a maximum deprivation of liberty of at least two years or a more serious penalty;

– if the person is sought to serve a sentence, he/she is sentenced to at least six months of imprisonment and/or there is at least six months of the sentence remaining to be served.

(iii) The request is of interest for the purposes of international police co-operation.

(b) The General Secretariat may decide to publish a red notice where the criteria in (i) and/or (ii) above are not met if, following consultation with the requesting National Central Bureau or international entity, it considers that publication of the requested red notice would be of particular importance to international police cooperation.

(c) Several offences: if the request includes several offences, the red notice may be published for all offences that meet Interpol's Rules provided that at least one offence meets the above criteria.

(2) Minimum data

(a) Identity particulars:

Red notices may be published only when sufficient identifiers have been provided. Sufficient identifiers will be considered to include at least one of the following two combinations of identifiers:

(i) family name, forename, sex, date of birth (at least the year) and one of the following identifiers:

- physical description; or
- DNA profile; or
- fingerprints; or
- data contained in identity documents (e.g. passport, national identity card).

(ii) photograph of good quality with some additional data (e.g. alias, name of the parent(s), further physical description, DNA profile, fingerprints, etc.).

(b) Judicial data:

Red notices may be published only when sufficient judicial data has been provided. Sufficient judicial data will be considered to include at least:

(i) summary of facts of the case, which shall provide a succinct and clear description of the criminal activities of the wanted person, including the time and location of the alleged criminal activity; and

(ii) charge(s); and

(iii) law(s) covering the offence (whenever possible, and subject to national law or the rules governing the operation of the international entity, the requesting National Central Bureau or international entity shall provide the wording of the relevant penal provision(s)); and

(iv) maximum penalty possible, sentence imposed, or sentence remaining to be served; and

(v) reference to a valid arrest warrant or judicial decision having the same effect (whenever possible, and subject to national law or the rules governing the operation of the international entity, the requesting National Central Bureau or international entity shall provide a copy of the arrest warrant or judicial decision).'

3.7

Interpol, when determining whether a request from an NCB for publication of a Red Notice should be acceded to, adopts a two-stage test. The first stage involves a consideration of whether certain positive criteria are met by the request. The second stage involves a consideration of whether the case falls into a category where a failure to meet the positive criteria should not prevent publication of the notice. The result of this approach is to afford the General Secretariat an extremely broad discretion as to whether or not a Red Notice should be published.

Specific criteria

3.8

The first positive criterion is that the request concerns a 'serious ordinary law crime'. This concept is not expressly defined in Article 83. However, since 1946, Interpol has defined its action as being limited to preventing and combating ordinary law crimes. This reflects its stated wish to guarantee its neutrality while respecting the sovereignty of states and is enshrined in Articles 2 and 3 of the Constitution.

3.9

Article 83 provides a list of categories of offence that do not qualify as 'serious ordinary law crime(s)'. Some categories are loosely defined (eg 'offences that in various countries raise controversial issues relating to behavioural or cultural norms'). The Article also provides that:

> 'the General Secretariat shall keep, update and share with National Central Bureaus and international entities a non-exhaustive list of specific offences that fall within the above categories'.

3.10

In this way the General Secretariat can provide guidance to NCBs in relation to categories of offence that will not be deemed suitable for publication of a Red Notice.[2] However, it must be observed that the provision of a 'non-exhaustive list of specific offences' in no way fetters Interpol's discretion in relation to any individual request.

3.11

The second positive criterion is that the request concerns criminal conduct which attracts a maximum sentence in excess of two years in relation to a person accused of a crime or, alternatively, where an individual has already been convicted, a sentence in excess of six months remains to be served.

---

2 The list has not been published, posing further difficulties for those seeking to understand how Interpol applies its own criteria.

3.12

The third positive criterion is expressed in broad terms and simply requires that the request be 'of interest for the purposes of international police cooperation'.

The General Secretariat's discretion

3.13

Where a request from an NCB fails to meet these criteria, the Interpol General Secretariat retains a broad discretion as to whether to publish the Red Notice. This is provided for by the operation of Article 83(1)(b), which permits Interpol to issue a Red Notice in these circumstances if it 'would be of particular importance to international police cooperation'.

3.14

In addition, Article 83(1)(b) permits the Interpol General Secretariat to issue a Red Notice for an unlimited number of multiple offences if any single offence included in the request satisfies the criteria (see Article 83(1)(c)).

NCB request – minimum data

3.15

Article 83 imposes minimum requirements for the information that must be included by an NCB when requesting the publication of a Red Notice. This includes the practical information necessary to identify the intended subject of the Red Notice (name, date of birth, fingerprints etc). Article 83 also requires information necessary for it to determine whether the request meets the criteria described above. Accordingly, a request must include a detailed summary of the facts of the case, the charges faced by the subject, the relevant provisions of the criminal statues in the requesting state, details of the maximum penalty (or penalty imposed) and reference to a 'valid arrest warrant or judicial decision having the same effect'.

Further obligations on the requesting NCB – Articles 84–85

3.16

Article 84 places an obligation on the requesting NCB to provide certain assurances. Firstly, that the authority which issued the arrest warrant (or handed down the judicial decision) which provides the jurisdictional basis for the request has the necessary power to do so. Secondly, that the Red Notice request has been co-ordinated with the relevant authorities responsible for extradition in the requesting state and that extradition will be sought upon arrest of the person. Thirdly, if the arrest warrant has not been issued by a judicial authority (eg by a state minister or some emanation of the police[3]), the laws of the requesting country or the rules governing the operation of the international entity provide for a mechanism of appeal before a judicial authority.

3.17

The need for such assurances is obvious: to ensure the issuing NCB has satisfied itself that the Red Notice is being sought for a proper purpose within the ambit of Article 82 (ie for 'the purpose of extradition, surrender or similar lawful action'). However, although the title of Article 84 refers to 'assurances', it is unclear whether it requires an NCB to give express assurances to Interpol before a Red Notice is published or whether the Article simply creates on obligation for the NCB to self-regulate and ensure that the request is within the ambit of Article 82.

Legal review by the General Secretariat

3.18

The General Secretariat is required to conduct a legal review of all Red Notices prior to their publication to ensure compliance with Interpol's Constitution and Rules. Article 86 emphasises the importance of the requirement that the publication of any Red Notice complies 'in particular' with Articles 2 and 3 of Interpol's Constitution. However, no further information is given as to how this review operates in practice.

3.19

It is clear that the criteria by which the General Secretariat judges a request for the publication of a Red Notice are extremely flexible and afford the General Secretariat a broad discretion in their application. As will be discussed in the following chapters, this poses significant challenges for an individual who seeks to cancel a Red Notice on the basis that it has been improperly issued.

Action to be taken by NCBs pursuant to an Interpol Red Notice

3.20

Article 87 of the RPD sets out the steps that must be taken where an NCB becomes aware of the location of an individual who is the subject of a Red Notice.

3 The phrase 'judicial authority' is given a broad autonomous meaning in many jurisdictions and can even encompass public prosecutors (see *Assange v Swedish Prosecution Authority* [2012] UKSC 22).

'Article 87: Steps to be taken following the location of the person *If a person who is the subject of a Red Notice is located, the following steps shall be taken:*

(a) The country where the person has been located shall:

(i) immediately inform the requesting National Central Bureau or international entity and the General Secretariat of the fact that the person has been located, subject to limitations deriving from national law and applicable international treaties;

(ii) take all other measures permitted under national law and applicable international treaties, such as provisionally arresting the wanted person or monitoring or restricting his/her movement.

(b) The requesting National Central Bureau or international entity shall act immediately once it has been informed that the person has been located in another country and, in particular, shall ensure the swift transmission – within the time limits defined for the case in question – of data and supporting documents requested by the country where the person was located or by the General Secretariat.

(c) The General Secretariat shall provide assistance to the relevant National Central Bureaus or international entities by, inter alia, facilitating the transfer of documents related to the provisional arrest or the extradition procedures in accordance with the relevant national laws and international treaties.'

3.21

It is apparent from the wording of Article 87 that the action that any individual NCB will take pursuant to a Red Notice is determined by the application of domestic law. In some jurisdictions, the existence of a Red Notice may lead to an individual's arrest if encountered by the authorities,[4] while in others it is not, of itself, a sufficient basis for a provisional arrest. An individual may, however, be detained under immigration powers while it is ascertained whether a formal extradition request is to be made.[5]

4 It has been estimated by the United States NCB that as many as one-third of Interpol members will arrest on the basis of a Red Notice (see US National Central Bureau of Interpol, *Audit Report 09-35*, September 2009 at p 11).

5 'Strengthening Respect for Human Rights Strengthening Interpol' *Fair Trials International* at pp 14–15.

Diffusions

3.22

'Diffusion' is the Interpol term for any request for international co-operation or any international alert from an NCB, sent directly to one or several NCBs, which is simultaneously recorded by Interpol. It can be used for a number of different purposes:[6]

- to arrest, detain or restrict the movements of a convicted or accused person;
- to locate and trace;
- to obtain additional information;
- for identification purposes;
- to warn about a person's criminal activities; and
- for information purposes.

3.23

Diffusions accordingly correspond to the Notices colour-coded system, so there are red, yellow, blue, black, green, purple and orange diffusions, and they must comply with Interpol's Constitution and the Rules on the Processing of Data. When seeking a wanted individual an Interpol member country can, as an alternative to adopting the formal procedure for the publication of a Red Notice, seek the arrest of an individual with a view to extradition by issuing a Wanted Person Diffusion.

3.24

A Diffusion is not published by the Interpol General Secretariat, but is simply a message from one NCB which asks another NCB (or multiple NCBs) for assistance. The RPD impose an obligation on the NCB to ensure that arrest and detention is for a lawful purpose and does not contravene Articles 2 and 3 of the Interpol Constitution. Article 99(2) of the RPD provides as follows:

> '(2) Before circulating a diffusion, the National Central Bureau or international entity shall ensure:
>
> (a) the quality and lawfulness of the data it provides in support of its diffusion;
>
> (b) that its diffusion complies with the general conditions for recording data;

6 RPD, Article 97(1).

(c) that the data are of interest for the purposes of international police cooperation;

(d) that its request complies with Interpol's rules, specifically with Articles 2(1) and 3 of the Constitution, as well as with the obligations imposed on the requesting entity under international law.'

The Notices and Diffusions Task Force

3.25

A significant reform of the process for transmitting Diffusions was introduced in 2016 with the creation of the Notices and Diffusions Task Force (NDTF) which is said to conduct a robust quality and legal compliance review of incoming Diffusions prior to their authorisation by the General Secretariat. The NDFT specifically examines whether the request is compliant with Articles 2(1) and 3 of Interpol's Constitution and includes a review of all relevant information, including external sources. It assesses the status of the individual concerned and the general context of the case. If a doubt on compliance arises during the initial screening, the NDTF will engage in further review which may include seeking additional information from the requesting National Central Bureau (NCB) (such as additional judicial data) or information from other NCBs.

3.26

The NDTF was originally tasked with examining new requests, which was no small task given the sheer number of requests for Red Notices and Diffusions each year.[7] Since 2018 its role has expanded to conduct a review of those issued prior to 2016.

3.27

Interpol has published data on the number of refusals or cancellation decisions made by the NDTF for the years 2018 to 2022.[8] Although these figures aggregate the number of refusals or cancellations of Red Notices and Diffusions and include both decisions made during that calendar year and the outcome of the NDTF review of cases from previous years, they do provide an overall indication of the level of activity from the NDTF. The figures provided by Interpol for 2022 state that during that year the work of the NDTF comprised of the following decisions:

7 In 2016, the year the NDTF was created, the Interpol Annual Report states that 12,878 Red Notices were issued.

8 See https://www.interpol.int/en/How-we-work/Notices/Compliance-and-review.

- the NDTF decided in 105 cases to refuse or cancel a request for a Red Notice or Wanted Person Diffusion on the grounds of non-compliance with Article 2 of Interpol's Constitution;
- the NDTF decided in 199 cases to refuse or cancel a request for a Red Notice or Wanted Person Diffusion on the grounds of non-compliance with Article 2 of Interpol's Constitution; and
- the NDTF decided in 1,161 cases to refuse or cancel a request for a Red Notice or Wanted Person Diffusion on other non-specified grounds.

3.28

Whilst the majority of the refusals or cancellations are in the category 'other' so could relate to data inadequacy (eg failure to provide identifying particulars as required by Article 83(2) RPD) rather than an identified abuse of the Red Notice and Wanted Person Diffusion system, the introduction of the NDTF is clearly having an impact and appears to be identifying and filtering out at least some cases where an abuse of the system has taken place.

3.29

Whilst Red Notice and Diffusion requests are not visible to member countries through the Interpol Information System (ie not searchable in the databases) until they have been reviewed and authorised by the NDTF, Diffusions (unlike Red Notices) are immediately received by recipient NCBs in Member States in an email format before the conclusion of the NDTF's review. Therefore, there remains a risk that the local law enforcement agency might act on a Diffusion which has not been vetted by the NDTF and, if the NDTF does refuse the Diffusion the email version of the request may remain on the NCB's own system over which Interpol has no control. The only safeguard against this is that the email warns that these Diffusions are subject to legal review and have not been authorised by the General Secretariat which may not adequately address the risk.

3.30

An important issue for practitioners to consider is the practical consequences of their client being sought under a Diffusion as opposed to a Red Notice.

3.31

As noted above, Diffusions are not 'published' in the same way as Red Notices, but are sent to NCBs and are therefore available to be viewed by domestic law enforcement and immigration officials on local data systems of Member States, whether at ports or elsewhere. Diffusions are targeted to individual Member State NCBs in circumstances where the requesting NCB is aware of the presence of the person sought in the territory of the requested Member State, whether by reason of a positive response to an antecedent Blue Notice or police-to-police request to search and locate the wanted person. In certain circumstances, a Diffusion may be transmitted to more than one NCB, where for example, it is known that the person sought has business interests in a different jurisdiction to their regular domicile, has dual or multiple citizenships, or travels regularly to particular countries. It is not inconceivable that in certain circumstances, Diffusions could be transmitted to multiple NCBs in a particular region that the person sought was suspected to be located, although it is difficult to discern whether this has occurred in practice.

3.32

Given the limited transmission of Diffusions, it might appear attractive to a client to travel or relocate to jurisdictions where they have little or no ties. Quite apart from the obvious risk that the person sought will be regarded as a fugitive from justice in the underlying domestic proceedings with the consequences that flow from such a designation, there is also a risk that a Diffusion, operating as a direct NCB to NCB communication, could be transmitted immediately by email to the 'new' destination prior to its review by the NDTF and authorisation by the General Secretariat. Even if the person sought is travelling to a jurisdiction where there is no extant Diffusion request sitting with the Member State NCB, that position can change rapidly and without warning. It is therefore prudent from a practitioners' perspective to treat Red Notices and Diffusions in the same way.

3.33

As set out in Chapters 6 and 7 and above, given the scope of Article 99(2) RPD, Red Notices and Diffusions are capable of being challenged on similar grounds. In other words, all of the arguments that are potentially available to an applicant who is the subject of a Red Notice which is published in breach of Interpol's Constitution and/or incompatibly with the RPD can be deployed to seek deletion of a Diffusion. Additionally, given the contrasting levels of review and oversight of Diffusions and Red Notices, it is not unreasonable to conclude that the prospects of a successful challenge to a Diffusion as opposed to a Red Notice may be higher, notwithstanding recent reforms.

Russian Diffusions

3.34

As foreshadowed earlier in this chapter and elsewhere in this work, there are concerns that certain Interpol Member States transmit Diffusion requests more readily than request Red Notices. One reason advanced for this practice is the lesser scrutiny afforded by the NDTF as opposed to the General Secretariat and the fact that Diffusions can be transmitted NCB to NCB by email before any effective oversight has taken place.

3.35

Although this rationale was not mentioned in his statement, on 10 March 2022, the then Secretary General of Interpol announced that in response to 'the conflict in Ukraine':

> 'Effective immediately, diffusions can no longer be sent directly by NCB Moscow to member countries. NCB Moscow must now send all diffusions to the General Secretariat to be checked for compliance with Interpol's rules. Only if a diffusion is found compliant will the General Secretariat then disseminate it to member countries.'[9]

The Secretary General indicated in his statement that he and Interpol's Executive Committee had resisted calls to suspend or exclude Russia from the Interpol network but emphasised that compliance with Russian requests for international police cooperation remained a matter for the competent national authorities in member countries.

3.36

The attention paid to Diffusions by the Secretary General, the General Assembly and the General Secretariat in recent years is instructive. It indicates that the use, or arguably misuse of Diffusions is a concern to the organisation, and concrete steps have been taken to address the legitimate concerns expressed about their wrongful use by certain member countries. It remains the case that the impact of a Diffusion on the reputation and liberty of a person sought are, for practical purposes, indistinguishable from the impact that arises from the publication of a Red Notice.

---

9 See https://www.interpol.int/en/News-and-Events/News/2022/Ukraine-INTERPOL-General-Secretariat-statement.

4 Criticisms of Red Notices and Wanted Person Diffusions and efforts toward reform

1. **Introduction**
2. **Criticisms**
3. **Efforts towards reform**
4. **Asylum status – a change in approach?**
5. **A new approach to asylum status**
6. **Current criticisms of Interpol Red Notices and Wanted Person Diffusions**
7. **The future of Interpol**
8. **Conclusion**

Introduction

4.1

This chapter will provide an overview of some of the criticisms made of the Interpol Red Notice and Wanted Person Diffusion systems, identify some of the key reforms introduced by Interpol in response to these criticisms, and assess the extent to which those reforms have been regarded as a success.

4.2

Interpol's Red Notice and Wanted Person Diffusion system has long been subject to the criticism that it is subject to abuse for political purposes. In 2000 the then United States Senator for Delaware Joe Biden warned against the manipulation of Interpol's processes for political purposes[1] when he raised before Congress

1 Congressional Record Vol 146 No 91 (14 July 2000).

the arrest of former Kazakh prime minister Akezhan Kazhegeldin on what he referred to as an Interpol warrant.

4.3

Claims that the Interpol Red Notice and Wanted Person Diffusion system has been deliberately abused by certain states is not confined to isolated case-specific instances. Allegations of systemic abuse has also been raised by several international organisations and INGOs. In 2010, the Parliamentary Assembly of the Organization for Security and Co-operation in Europe (OSCE) called upon participating States to avoid undermining the credibility of Interpol by 'placing politically motivated or otherwise inappropriate notices in the Interpol system',[2] and in 2013 expressed concern that this risk had crystalised as:

> 'some OSCE participating States, including Belarus, the Russian Federation and Ukraine, continue to abuse the Interpol system by seeking the arrest of opponents on politically motivated charges, including but not limited to the cases of Mr Petr Silaev, Mr William Browder, Mr Ilya Katsnelson, Mr Ales Michalevic and Mr Bohdan Danylyshyn'.[3]

4.4

Alongside the claims of politically driven abuse of Red Notices and Wanted Person Diffusions there has been historical criticism that Interpol's systems are at odds with the international legal protections afforded to refugees. In 2008 the then United Nations High Commissioner for Refugees expressed concern that he:

> 'is also confronted by situations whereby refugees recognized under the 1951 Refugee Convention, when traveling outside their country of asylum holding Travel Documents issued under the terms of the Refugee Convention, are apprehended or detained, due to politically-motivated requests made by their countries of origin which are abusing of Interpol's "red notice system".'[4]

4.5

This phenomenon and the existential threat it poses to Interpol has long been recognised by the organisation itself. In a 2011 interview, Mr Joel Sollier (a former Director of Legal Affairs at Interpol) acknowledged the existence of politically motivated requests for Red Notices. He insisted that the agency

2 See https://www.oscepa.org/en/documents/annual-sessions/2010-oslo/declaration-5/267-oslo-declaration-english/file.

3 See https://www.oscepa.org/en/documents/annual-sessions/2013-istanbul/declaration/1801-istanbul-declaration-eng-1/file#:~:text=Calls%20on%20the%20OSCE%20to,47.

4 See https://www.refworld.org/pdfid/4794c7ff2.pdf.

works hard to ferret out cases chiefly motivated by politics, rather than crime. 'If we don't,' he said, 'we are dead.'[5]

4.6

There has also been sustained criticism of the procedures for challenging Red Notices and Wanted Person Diffusions. In November 2013, the NGO Fair Trials International published a report entitled 'Strengthening Respect for Human Rights, Strengthening Interpol'.[6] In the preparation of that report Fair Trials consulted with Interpol and a broad base of stakeholders. As well as highlighting that Interpol's protections against the abuse of Red Notice and Wanted Person Diffusions are ineffective as it assumes that they are requested in good faith, the report also highlighted that those affected by Red Notices lack an opportunity to challenge the dissemination of their information through Interpol's databases in a fair, transparent process.

4.7

The potential for Interpol's processes to be abused and the ability of individuals to challenge Interpol Red Notices and Wanted Person Diffusions are closely linked issues, not least because the latter has the potential to act as a significant counterweight to the former. In this chapter we will consider those historical criticisms, the extent to which Interpol has sought to introduce reforms to address them, and more recent assessments of Interpol's Red Notice and Wanted Person Diffusion system to consider whether those reforms have addressed the concerns.

Criticisms

4.8

The historical criticism of Interpol come from a variety of governmental and non-governmental organisations sources and can also be found in academic literature. The following section of this chapter will focus on the criticisms and recommendations made by Fair Trials International in its November 2013 report: however, this document should be viewed in context as forming part of a much wider debate involving many stakeholders that has taken place over a number of years.

5 Libby Lewis 'Interpol's Red Notices Used by Some to Pursue Political Dissenters, Opponents'. Article published on the website of the International Consortium of Investigative Journalists, 18 July 2011. Available at: www.publicintegrity.org/2011/07/18/5179/interpols-red-notices-used-some-pursue-political-dissenters-opponents.

6 See https://www.fairtrials.org/app/uploads/2022/01/Strengthening-respect-for-human-rights-strengthening-INTERPOL4.pdf.

Insufficient procedural protections against abuse

4.9

The November 2013 Fair Trials International report suggested that Interpol's protections against abuse are ineffective and that its internal procedures are not sufficiently robust to prevent abuse by member countries pursuing political objectives.[7]

4.10

The report made the following recommendations to Interpol to address this criticism:

'(a) **Combat persecution**: Interpol should refuse or delete Red Notices where it has substantial grounds to believe the person is being prosecuted for political reasons. National asylum and extradition decisions should, in appropriate cases, be considered decisive.

(b) **Thorough reviews**: Interpol should require national authorities to provide an arrest warrant before they can obtain a Red Notice, and should conduct a thorough review of Red Notice requests and Diffusions against human rights reports and public information.

(c) **Draft Red Notices only in urgency**: Interpol should ensure that Red Notice requests are not visible to other NCBs while under review except in urgent cases; the NCB should justify its use of the urgency exception and Interpol should monitor exception usage closely.

(d) **Continual review**: Interpol should systematically follow up with countries which have reported arrests based on Red Notices, six or 12 months after it is informed of an arrest, and enquire as to the outcome of the proceedings following the arrest.'[8]

Inadequate opportunity to challenge

4.11

The November 2013 Fair Trials International report concluded that Interpol's internal procedures do not provide those affected by Red Notice and Wanted Person Diffusions with an adequate procedure for redress. It concluded that the

7 Ibid p 5.
8 Ibid p 5.

CCF is a 'data protection body' unsuited to the task of providing remedies to those affected by Red Notices and Wanted Person Diffusions.

4.12

The November 2013 Fair Trials International report made the following recommendations:

'(a) **Reform the CCF**: Interpol should develop the competence, expertise and procedures of the CCF to ensure it is able to provide adequate redress for those directly affected by Interpol's activities. It should explore the idea of creating a separate chamber of the CCF dedicated to handling complaints, leaving the existing CCF to advise horizontally on data protection issues.

(b) **Ensure basic standards of due process**: I Interpol should ensure that reforms of the procedures of the CCF provide for the following essential safeguards: (i) adversarial proceedings with a disclosure process; (ii) oral hearings in appropriate cases; (iii) binding, reasoned decisions, which should be published; and (iv) a right to challenge adverse decisions.'[9]

These criticisms are far from unique to Fair Trials International and throughout this chapter these themes will resurface.

Efforts towards reform

4.13

Interpol has been working on reforming the Red Notice system for over 20 years. In 2002 Interpol's General Assembly passed a resolution to set up a working group to discuss and finalise the rules relating to the processing of police information.[10] Over the years the working group's remit has been widened. At the 78th General Assembly in 2009 held in Singapore, the Working Group on the Processing of Information was tasked with examining the operating standards of the NCBs, the procedures for assessing the NCBs, the establishment of monitoring tools and, finally, the procedure to be followed by the General Secretariat in the event of a serious incident at a NCB.[11]

4.14

The significant reforms were introduced between 2015 to 2017 and fall into the following two categories:

9 Ibid p 6.
10 AG-2002-RES-09.
11 AG-2009-RES-14.

- the reforms arising out of the Working Group on the Processing of Information; and
- changes in Interpol's approach to refugee status.

Working Group on the Processing of Information

4.15

In 2014, Interpol mandated the Working Group on the Processing of Information to:

> 'carry out a comprehensive review of Interpol's supervisory mechanisms in the area of data processing, at all levels, at all phases of data processing, and with regard to all entities involved – including the National Central Bureaus, notational and international entities, the General Secretariat and the Commission for the Control of Interpol's Files.'[12]

4.16

The Working Group met for the first time in July 2015. It was clear that it was to have a broad base amongst Interpol's membership: the meeting was attended by more than 60 participants from 30 countries representing all regions of Interpol's membership. The working group was addressed by Interpol's Office of Legal Affairs, Secretary General Jürgen Stock who said:

> 'The obligation to abide by international human rights standards is enshrined in Interpol's constitution, and we have always strived to respect these rights and the rule of law [...] As the processing and review of data shared via Interpol continue to face growing challenges, this full and comprehensive review of the system is timely.'[13]

4.17

In its contemporaneous press releases, Interpol stressed the involvement of Non-Governmental Organisations (NGOs) in the process:

> 'Underlining Interpol's ongoing commitment to encourage dialogue with civil society, a special session was held during the meeting for external representatives including from NGOs specializing in international human rights law and international legal practitioners to provide their input.'[14]

---

12 AG-2014-RES-19.

13 See https://web.archive.org/web/20170706031746/https://www.interpol.int/News-and-media/News/2015/N2015-095.

14 Ibid.

4.18

This sentiment was echoed in the Annual Activity Report of the CCF for 2014 which noted the benefits that could be gained from ensuring the participation of external experts, and specifically referring to earlier reports prepared by Fair Trials International (as above).[15]

4.19

In November 2015, the working group, chaired by Johanna Hervonen, Head of the Interpol's National Central Bureau in Helsinki, presented a number of draft conclusions in relation to the review process of its notices and data processing to the 84th General Assembly in Rwanda. The General Assembly endorsed these draft conclusions and tasked the Working Group to continue its work and present its final report at the 85th General Assembly in Bali.

4.20

The 85th General Assembly adopted resolutions altering both the rules of the CCF and the RPD. It is notable that no significant amendments were made to the RPD in respect of the operation of the Red Notices and Wanted Person Diffusions. However, reforms have been adopted in the CCF to the procedures for challenging them. These reforms have been welcomed by NGOs. Bruno Min, Legal Policy Officer, at Fair Trials International highlighted the following reforms as representing significant improvements:

- Greater independence and influence of the CCF: The CCF's ability to make binding decisions has now been codified into Interpol's rules. In addition, the recent reforms enable the CCF to have a say in budgetary decisions and no longer reliant on the General Secretariat for funding, and the CCF has also been given the powers to enact its own operating rules.
- Improvements to the CCF's capacity and expertise: The CCF has been split into two chambers that concentrate expertise in its two main roles: its role of supervising and advising on Interpol's data-processing activities, and its role of handling individual requests for access to data and complaints. The number of members of the CCF has increased significantly, and the changes to the composition of the CCF means that it has much better expertise to handle complicated requests involving human rights arguments. The new provisions also seem to enable the CCF to consult external experts and international bodies to further enhance its capacity to make informed decisions.
- Better transparency and respect for the equality of arms: The rules on the disclosure of information have changed, which we

15 Annual Activity Report of the CCF for 2014, para 63.

hope will make it easier for individuals to access their data and to challenge it. This is a significant departure from the CCF's previous practice of withholding information from individuals in the absence of explicit permission from NCBs.

- Specified timeframes: Time limits have been introduced to the CCF's procedures, requiring the CCF to make decisions in individual cases within months after it has declared applications to be admissible. Furthermore, the CCF is required to provide information to individuals on relevant timeframes, and reasons for any failures to comply with its own deadlines.
- Reasoned decisions, available to the public: The CCF's recent practice of providing reasoned decisions has been formalised in the Statute, and its commitment to make decisions public could provide some much-needed insight into how Interpol's rules are interpreted, and help individuals whose data has been deleted to protect their reputation and to minimise the risk of arrest.'[16]

4.21

Another important reform was implemented by Interpol in 2016 with the introduction of the Notices and Diffusions Task Force (NDTF). The NDTF, as has been set out in the previous chapter to this book, is tasked to conduct a robust quality and legal compliance review of incoming Red Notices and Diffusions, in particular, whether the request is compliant with Articles 2(1) and 3 of Interpol's Constitution.

Asylum status – a change in approach?

4.22

For many years, Interpol has faced allegations that some member countries utilise its procedures to target political opponents. In 2006 the United Nations High Commissioner for Refugees highlighted individual cases where refugees recognised under the 1951 Refugee Convention had been arrested and detained on the basis of Red Notices requested by their countries of origin. Arrest and detention gives rise to a risk of refoulement or an inability of the person whose arrest and detention is sought to return to their country of asylum.

4.23

Such cases highlight the tension between Interpol's reluctance to be drawn into the political sphere and its stated desire to uphold fundamental rights. On one

16 Press release: '"Fair Trials" recommendations inform major INTERPOL reforms' 2 December 2016. Document no longer available online.

analysis, acknowledging an individual's asylum status (and refusing to process a request for a Red Notice) could itself, in some circumstances, be construed as a political act. However, to take no account of asylum status risks undermining the asylum system and its ability to protect an individual's fundamental rights.

4.24

Historically, the granting of asylum status would not lead to the automatic deletion of a Red Notice or Diffusion. In 2012, WikiLeaks founder, Julian Assange, was resisting extradition to Sweden to face trial in relation to allegations of rape. Mr Assange's final appeal against the decision of the Chief Magistrate of England and Wales to order his extradition to Sweden was dismissed by the UK Supreme Court on 30 May 2012. Mr Assange applied to re-open his appeal. This further application was refused by the Court. Shortly thereafter, Mr Assange entered the Ecuadorian Embassy in London and claimed asylum. In August 2012, Ecuador granted Mr Assange political asylum. However, within a matter of days, Interpol issued a press release confirming that the Red Notice remained in force. The press release stated as follows regarding the status of the Red Notice:

> 'A Red Notice status is a request for any country to identify or locate an individual with a view to their provisional arrest and extradition in accordance with the country's national laws.
>
> Many of Interpol's member countries consider a Red Notice a valid request for provisional arrest, especially if they are linked to the requesting country via a bilateral extradition treaty. In cases where arrests are made based on a Red Notice, these are made by national police officials in Interpol member countries.
>
> Interpol cannot compel any of its 190 member countries to arrest the subject of a Red Notice. Any individual wanted for arrest should be considered innocent until proven guilty.'[17]

4.25

The wording of the press release makes plain that Interpol considered Mr Assange's asylum status to be a matter for the Interpol member countries concerned (in this case, the UK, Sweden and Ecuador). Any decision to act pursuant to the Red Notice would be taken not by Interpol, but by the authorities of the member countries concerned.

17 Press release: 'Interpol Red Notice for Julian Assange remains in force' 16 August 2012. Available at: https://www.interpol.int/en/News-and-Events/News/2012/INTERPOL-Red-Notice-for-Julian-Assange-remains-in-force.

A new approach to asylum status

4.26

In the June 2014 session the Executive Committee of Interpol approved a Refugee Policy. No full text of this policy is available and it remains unclear precisely what this policy is.

4.27

In April 2015, a statement of the Office of the Chief Prosecutor of Georgia led some observers to detect a possible shift in Interpol's approach to individuals with asylum status.[18] The statement related to its decision to delete a Red Notice issued in relation to an individual sought by the Georgian Authorities.

4.28

The individual was Mr Zurab Adeishvili, a high-profile political figure in Georgia, and a member of the UNM political party which occupied senior positions in the former UNM-led government of Georgia. In 2012, the UNM Government was defeated by the Georgian Dream Coalition in parliamentary elections. Many former members of the UNM leadership, including Mr Adeishvili, were charged with corruption offences relating to their time in office and became the subject of extradition requests and requests to Interpol for the issuance of Red Notices. Mr Adeishvili successfully applied for the Red Notice issued in his name to be deleted. The Chief Prosecutor's Office of Georgia issued the following statement:

> 'On April 9, 2015 Office of the Chief Prosecutor of Georgia received a letter from the General Secretariat of Interpol informing the Georgian Party that the General Secretariat of Interpol has annulled the Red Notice Application issued against Zurab Adeishvili. The General Secretariat of Interpol referred to the fact of granting the refugee status [sic] to Z. Adeishvili by one of the states, which is unknown to the Georgian party, as the main ground for annulling the international search of Z. Adeishvili.
>
> It is worth mentioning that the General Secretariat of Interpol has made a decision regarding annulling international search against Z. Adeishvili without requesting additional argumentation or submission of relevant documentation from the Georgian Party and the latter became aware of the mentioned fact only after the Red Notice Application against the fugitive was annulled. Correspondingly, in the process of considering the matter, the Office of the Chief Prosecutor of Georgia

18 See https://pog.gov.ge/en/news/prokuraturis-gancxadeba-z-adeishvilis-mimarT-wiTeli-cirkulariT-saerTashoriso-Zebnis-gauqmebasTan-dak.

lacked the capacity to present its additional argumentation regarding the reasonability of continuing the search against Z. Adeishvili to the General Secretariat of Interpol.'

4.29

Interpol apparently relied on Mr Adeishvili's asylum status to delete his Red Notice. However, the decision (as reported by the Georgian authorities) does not indicate whether it was *the fact* of asylum status that led to the decision, or whether this was simply one factor considered by the CCF in determining whether the Red Notice conformed to Interpol's procedural rules. Later in 2015, however, Fair Trials International reported that Interpol had, in fact, adopted a new asylum policy but that the substance was not yet confirmed. The NGO's press release dated 29 May 2015 contained the following:

> 'We need written confirmation of the policy, but this is what we learned: Interpol has notified the policy to the National Central Bureaus, the national police contact points for Interpol, but has not disseminated it further. In substance, the policy is that Interpol will remove a Red Notice if it can verify that the person has been recognised as refugee under the 1951 Convention. It does not matter whether the criminal prosecution in question was the ground for the asylum or not; the grant of asylum suffices. Interpol will not reveal to the country behind the Red Notice which country granted asylum, to address confidentiality concerns. There are, however, important caveats: (A) Interpol must be able to verify the asylum grant, which asylum-granting countries may be slow to do for confidentiality reasons, and (B) the country issuing the Red Notice can revert to Interpol with further material asking it to revisit the decision.'[19]

4.30

Fair Trials International has posted on its website a document entitled 'Interpol Text on Refugee Policy Excerpts' which gives some limited detail about the policy. The text published by Fair Trials International reads as follows.[20]

> '**Interpol Text on Refugee Policy – Excerpts**:
>
> The objective of the policy is to support member countries in preventing criminals from abusing refugee status, while providing adequate and effective safeguards to protect the rights of refugees, as guaranteed under the 1951 Convention relating to the Status of Refugees and other applicable conventions.

19 Press release: 'Interpol announces new asylum policy at Council of Europe meeting' 29 May 2015. Available at: https://web.archive.org/web/20211128182626/https://www.fairtrials.org/node/779.

20 Available at: www.fairtrials.org/wp-content/uploads/INTERPOL-TEXT-ON-REFUGEE-POLICY.pdf. Words in square brackets inserted by authors.

In practice, according to the new policy, each Red Notice and [Wanted Person] Diffusion request against a refugee will be assessed by the General Secretariat or, where applicable by the Commission for the Control of Interpol Files (CCF), on a case-by-case basis along the following general guidelines:

In general, the processing of Red Notices and Diffusions against refugees will not be allowed if the following conditions are met:

(1) the status of refugee or asylum-seeker has been confirmed;

(2) the notice/diffusion has been requested by the country where the individual fears persecution;

(3) the granting of the refugee status is not based on political grounds vis-à-vis the requesting country.

In cases where the processing of Red Notices and Diffusions against refugees is denied, consideration will be given to sharing the information sent by the requesting country with the country of asylum so that the latter can reconsider its previous decision of granting the refugee status. If the country of asylum decides to revoke the refugee status based on the new information, the processing of Red Notices and Diffusions may be allowed if it otherwise complies with Interpol's rules.

With due respect for national laws, the General Secretariat will ensure the confidentiality of the information exchanged under that policy.

In addition, in accordance with this new policy, member countries are encouraged to systematically:

(1) check Interpol's databases (via the NCBs or by granting direct access to immigration authorities) when examining an application for asylum, in order to ensure that refugee status is not granted to dangerous criminals recorded in Interpol's databases;

(2) inform the General Secretariat and relevant member countries when a decision has been taken to refuse a person refugee status on the basis of that person's criminal background.

The policy was approved by the EC at its June 2014 session. It is therefore already in place and was implemented in a number of cases either directly by IPSG or based on CCF's recommendations.'

4.31

Fair Trials International does not provide any source for the new policy and it does not appear in any publicly available Interpol documentation. It has been suggested to the authors that the text is taken from an e-mail circulated by Interpol to NCBs. In any event, even if the text quoted by Fair Trials International does reflect current Interpol policy, its effect remains unclear.

4.32

The policy recognises the tension between Interpol's stated desire to uphold fundamental human rights while remaining politically neutral. The policy suggests that where a person sought by a particular member country enjoys asylum protection from that country the processing of Red Notices and Diffusions against refugees will generally not be allowed. However, the policy contains an important caveat: the use of Interpol will not be allowed as long as 'the granting of the refugee status is not based on political grounds vis-à-vis the requesting country'. This is ambiguous and potentially problematic.

4.33

It is unclear whether the caveat applies to cases concerning individuals who have been granted asylum status on political grounds (eg an individual who fears persecution on account of their political beliefs) or where the decision by the country granting asylum is of a political character (eg because the state granting asylum enjoys poor diplomatic relations with the requesting country). If it is the former, then the policy is likely to provide scant assistance to refuges and has the potential to seriously undermine the international asylum system. It is far from uncommon for individuals sought for prosecution in one country to be granted asylum in another country due to the fear they will be persecuted on account of their political beliefs. If it is the latter, then the policy has the potential to offer significant protection to refugees. However, no explanation is given as to how Interpol will approach the task of determining whether a decision to grant a particular individual is 'based on political grounds vis-à-vis the requesting country'. The lack of any such guidance poses great difficulties for practitioners when advising individuals with refugee status as to how Interpol would treat any request for a diffusion or Red Notice received from the country against which they have sought protection under international law.

4.34

It was not until 2017 that the refugee data processing policy was formally endorsed by the General Secretariat,[21] however this resolution gives no details about Interpol's policy beyond urging member countries to ensure that accurate data is shared on Interpol's systems, in particular confirmation of the grant of refugee status, and information of the outcome of the review of an asylum application. It appears that Interpol is carrying out ongoing work in this area, however the scope and progress of that work remains out of the public domain.

21 GA-2017-86-RES-09.

Current criticisms of Interpol Red Notices and Wanted Person Diffusions

4.35

Commentary on the Interpol reforms during the period 2014 to 2017 has broadly been positive, but always caveated with the need for further reforms. This section of the chapter will examine studies carried out by the Committee on Legal Affairs and Human Rights, subsequent resolutions of the Parliamentary Assembly of the Council of Europe (PACE), and reports from the European Parliaments Committee on Civil Liberties Justice and Home Affairs to highlight the criticisms made by these organisations of the Interpol Red Notice and Wanted Person Diffusion system.

2017 Committee on Legal Affairs and Human Rights Report

4.36

The Committee on Legal Affairs and Human Rights produced a report to PACE in March 2017 entitled 'Abusive use of the Interpol system: the need for more stringent legal safeguards.'[22]

4.37

The report welcomed the introduction of a separate Requests Chamber to deal solely with challenges, the introduction of time limits and dedicated specialist staff, and amendments to the statute of the CCF to permit disclosure of information so that applicants are able to know the allegations against them.

4.38

The report does express concern over the practical impact of these changes and identifies allegations of abuse on behalf of a number of individuals, including examples where the Refugee Policy should have prevented the circulation of Red Notices or Diffusions but failed to do so.

4.39

The report also highlighted the lack of resources to prevent abuses: both *ex ante* checks to filter out possible abuses; and *ex post* relief by the CCF. The report proposed that to counter abuse by member states more use be made of Articles 130 and 131 on the rules of processing of data. These Articles permit the General Secretariat to suspend or withdraw access rights to NCBs or international entities where rules have been infringed or impose corrective measures such as supervision of the processing operations of the

---

22 See https://pace.coe.int/en/files/23524/html.

NCB or international entity, or dispatching an assessment team to the NCB or international entity.

4.40

Whilst this recommendation was made in the 2017 Report from the Committee on Legal Affairs and Human Rights a subsequent study requested by the DROI Committee interviewed Interpol's Data Protection Officer who confirmed that no recommendations had been made as at the date of the interview on 24 September 2018[23] although the information now available on Interpol's web page indicates that:

> 'In INTERPOL's practice, since the entry into force of the RPD in 2012, interim and corrective measures have been applied with regard to different NCBs on different occasions.'[24]

4.41

PACE subsequently passed a resolution[25] 26 April 2017 acknowledging the important role that Interpol plays in international cooperation in the fight against transnational crime, and that the work that had been done since the 85th General Assembly in Bali was a step in the right direction. The PACE resolution however identified a number of areas of weakness and called upon Interpol to continue improving its Red Notice procedure in the following ways:

'8.1 further strengthening the preventive checks before Red Notices are circulated, in particular by:

8.1.1. increasing the capacity of Interpol's task force entrusted with such checks by bolstering the resources placed at its disposal;

8.1.2. ensuring that information on relevant cases made available by international or regional intergovernmental human rights bodies (in particular the United Nations High Commissioner for Refugees, the United Nations High Commissioner for Human Rights and the competent bodies of the Council of Europe) and, if appropriate, by non-governmental human rights organisations is duly taken into account;

8.1.3. publishing sufficiently detailed, authoritative interpretations ("repositories of practice") of Articles 2 and 3 of the constitution and of Interpol's policy in refugee and asylum cases;

23 See https://www.europarl.europa.eu/RegData/etudes/STUD/2019/603472/EXPO_STU(2019)603472_EN.pdf at p 26.

24 See https://www.interpol.int/en/How-we-work/Notices/Compliance-and-review.

25 See https://pace.coe.int/en/files/23714/html.

8.1.4. re-examining Red Notices periodically to ensure that they are deleted when they have not given rise to successful extradition within a reasonable amount of time;

8.1.5. examining with particular care repetitive Red Notice requests emanating from the same NCB targeting the same person after earlier requests were either rejected by Interpol or deleted following a decision of the CCF;

8.2. strengthening the CCF as an appeals mechanism by:

8.2.1. making it fully independent from Interpol, in particular by continuing to ensure that staff members dealing with preventive checks are not involved in assessing complaints against Red Notices which had passed these checks;

8.2.2. increasing its capacity, in particular by making sufficient staff available with expertise in the fields of human rights and criminal law and procedure;

8.2.3. ensuring that the CCF fulfils minimum procedural standards, in particular by enabling the targeted persons and their lawyers to be informed of and to comment on the reasons for the Red Notice request given by the requesting NCB;

8.2.4. ensuring that the CCF responds to and resolves appeals within a reasonable time, taking into account the gravity of the consequences of a Red Notice for a targeted person;

8.2.5. ensuring that the CCF publishes its decisions, provided the applicants agree; the decisions shall be sufficiently motivated in order to contribute to the development of consistent and predictable case law;

8.3. dealing appropriately with NCBs which have repeatedly abused the system for requesting publication of Red Notices, in particular by:

8.3.1. keeping statistics on Red Notices filtered out upstream by Interpol's preventive mechanism and downstream by successful challenges before the CCF;

8.3.2. subjecting new Red Notice requests by NCBs that have previously submitted a high number of abusive requests to more intensive prior scrutiny;

8.3.3. prioritising scrutiny by the CCF of complaints made against Red Notices requested by NCBs that have previously submitted a high number of abusive requests;

8.3.4. charging NCBs that submit a high number of abusive requests for the additional budgetary costs generated by the more intensive scrutiny of their requests and of complaints made against their requests;

8.4. setting up a compensation fund for victims of abusive or otherwise unjustified Red Notices financed by member States in proportion to the number of unjustified Red Notices emanating from their NCBs.'

4.42

In the immediate aftermath of Interpol's reforms, the reaction from the international community remained that more could and should be done to reduce the risk of abusive Red Notice and Diffusions being circulated.

2019 Committee on Legal Affairs and Human Rights Report

4.43

The Committee on Legal Affairs and Human Rights produced a further report in October 2019 entitled 'Interpol reform and extradition proceedings: building trust by fighting abuse'[26] which led to a PACE resolution on 29 November 2019.[27]

4.44

As part of its enquiry the Committee on Legal Affairs heard evidence from Interpol's General Counsel, Ms Rodriguez, and a representative from Fair Trials International, Mr Min (referred to above). Whilst Interpol's General Counsel informed the Committee that many of the 2017 recommendations had been implemented, the representative from Fair Trials International noted it was too early to tell whether the reforms had bedded in: in particular, whether the vetting process for Red Notices and Diffusions was effective. The primary concerns for the Committee were:

- resourcing, particularly as the CCF's budget had been reduced by 150,000 Euros between 2018 and 2019;
- transparency, although there had been a repository of practice on Article 3 of Interpol's Constitution since 2013, the repository of practice for Article 2 was long overdue. In addition, although there was an availability of extracts from written CCF decisions, these remained inadequate as they do not contain sufficient reasoning and do not always make it clear how a decision was reached;

26 See https://pace.coe.int/en/files/28090/html.
27 See https://pace.coe.int/en/files/28303/html.

- lack of statistics on requests rejected in the prior vetting process and notices found in violation by the CCF broken down by member states. It was pointed out that such statistics would help evaluate the success of measures taken to combat misuse of Interpol's systems by identifying bad actors.

4.45

The conclusion of the Committee on Legal Affairs and Human Rights was that although Interpol has made much progress in filtering our abusive Red Notices and wanted persons diffusions:

> 'The effectiveness of Interpol's instruments, as well as that of Council of Europe and EU tools designed to facilitate extradition, strongly depends on mutual trust. Such trust is severely undermined by the actions of a small number of States misusing these instruments in order to violate fundamental rights and freedoms. Fighting misuse of the instruments of international co-operation in the criminal field is thus clearly in the interest of the large majority of States wishing to co-operate effectively in the fight against impunity.'[28]

In particular the Committee's report noted that although the reform process at Interpol has prompted the introduction of stronger compliance checks for Red Notices, certain governments had reacted by using Wanted Person Diffusions instead of Red Notices.

4.46

Whilst this accords with anecdotal evidence, the number of Diffusions published by Interpol tells a mixed story. The data shows a peak of 22,753 diffusions published in 2015,[29] down to 15,763 published in 2018.[30] It is unclear whether this data would have been available to the Committee at the time of its report but it indicates a downwards trend in the total number of Diffusions issued each year. This downward trend has continued to 2022, the last year for which this data has been made available, when 12,478 Diffusions were published.[31] Whilst there appears to be a general reduction in the use of Diffusions this data does not identify breakdown use on a country-by-country basis, and therefore cannot confirm whether there has been a switch by certain member states to using Red Notices instead of Diffusions.

4.47

The concerns raised by the Committee were not new and repeat previously expressed criticisms around Interpol's ability to effectively vet and filter the

28 See https://pace.coe.int/en/files/28090/html.
29 Interpol Annual Report 2015.
30 See https://www.interpol.int/en/How-we-work/Notices/About-Notices.
31 See https://www.interpol.int/en/How-we-work/Notices/About-Notices.

number of requests it receives. As a result of the Committee's report the PACE passed a resolution on 29 November 2019 calling on Interpol to:

> '10.1.1 further improve transparency by disclosing data that would help to assess how effective its review mechanisms are, including yearly statistics on Red Notice requests received and refused, appeals to the CCF introduced and decided in favour or against the applicants, with a breakdown by country; and by publishing a "repository of practice" on the interpretation of Article 2 of Interpol's constitution;
>
> 10.1.2 further improve preventive and subsequent scrutiny of Red Notices and wanted person diffusions, by examining with particular care any repetitive requests, those that have not given rise to extraditions or extradition requests within a reasonable period of time and those submitted by NCBs which have previously submitted a high number of abusive requests; and by charging the countries responsible for the extra cost involved;
>
> 10.1.3 ensure more effective control over the information which flows through its communication system by requiring NCBs to delete data from national databases following a CCF or General Secretariat decision to delete a notice or wanted person diffusion and to provide confirmation of the deletion within a prescribed time limit;
>
> 10.1.4 further strengthen the appeals procedure before the CCF by making it speedier, more interactive and more transparent;
>
> 10.1.5 consider setting up an independent appeals body against the decisions of the CCF, such as an ombudsperson, who could also make recommendations for any further improvements of Interpol's working methods;
>
> 10.1.6 set up a compensation fund for victims of unjustified Red Notices and wanted person diffusions financed by member States in proportion to the number of such notices and diffusions emanating from their NCBs.'

Study Requested by the LIBE Committee published in February 2022

4.48

In February 2022 a paper commissioned by the European Parliament's Policy Department for Citizen's Rights and Constitutional Affairs at the request of the Committee on Civil Liberties, Justice and Home Affairs (LIBE) entitled 'Ensuring the rights of EU citizens against politically motivated Red Notices'[32] analysed Interpol's system of Red Notices.

4.49

The key findings of the paper are familiar and whilst some of the reforms have been implemented, others have yet to be addressed. The study identified that a number of legal tools are still missing and there continues to be a lack of transparency in the handling of notice requests.

4.50

The study also identified a number of systemic issues with the way in which Interpol operated and its reliance on NCBs. The first concern comes down to resourcing and how the number of submissions can possibly be reviewed (in 2022 11,282 new Red Notices where published[33]). The second being that decentralised National Central Bureaus under the control of domestic authorities represents a structural problem that is not addressed with knowledge management reforms.

4.51

The structural concern was more a problem of Interpol's membership than Interpol's procedures. Although Interpol has 196 member countries the LIBE Committee assessed that less than half are commonly described as 'strong democracies'.[34] The study also looked inwards to the structure of Interpol itself and expressed concern about the candidate for the Interpol Presidency, Major General Ahmed Naser Al-Raisi, of the United Arab Emirates who was elected to this post in November 2021 and the candidacy for the Executive Committee of a Chinese senior public security official. Both choices had garnered significant criticism from civil society, and it has been argued that their appointment risked undermining the integrity and neutrality of Interpol itself.

4.52

The study reached a damning conclusion that 'it is evident that the European Union cannot expect Interpol reforms to deliver required solutions to singularly safeguard EU citizens' rights.'[35]

32 See https://www.europarl.europa.eu/RegData/etudes/STUD/2022/708135/IPOL_STU(2022)708135_EN.pdf.
33 See https://www.interpol.int/en/How-we-work/Notices/About-Notices.
34 Ibid p 38.
35 Ibid p 46.

The future of Interpol

4.53

The recent criticisms of Interpol have all identified that certain member countries habitually abuse the Red Notice and Wanted Person Diffusion system and it may not be possible for Interpol to guard effectively against this risk given its existing structure and rules. Some of the more recent evaluations of the Red Notice and Wanted Person Diffusion systems summarised in this chapter have suggested that the system for international mutual cooperation in policing matters has already been undermined by the crisis in legitimacy to Interpol and its institutions caused by Red Notice and Diffusion abuse. A case in point is the refusal by some EU member states not to act upon Red Notices without conducting their own independent assessment of the reliability of the notice or Diffusion based on the Interpol member state sending the request. Equally the UK does not consider Red Notices as a basis for arrest in most cases and its NCB undertakes a risk assessment on cases outside the EU.[36] This risk has to be counterbalanced with the undoubted benefits that international co-ordination of police information confers.

4.54

At the 91st General Assembly in Vienna from 28 November 2023 to 1 December 2023 a number of resolutions were adopted that appear to signal an ongoing dedication to eliminating abuse of Red Notices and Wanted Person Diffusions, and to reestablish their integrity:

- Interpol tasked the Committee on the Processing of Data[37] to consider proposals regarding the settlement of disputes, improving the quality of the assessment of Interpol notices and diffusions and supervision measures for data processing;[38]
- Interpol:
  - emphasised the need for Red Notices and Wanted Persons Diffusions to confirm to the highest standards of data;
  - urged NCBs to take measures to ensure that Red Notices and Wanted Person Diffusions confirm to the highest standards including: specifying in the requests all necessary information to facilitate international police cooperation; and ensuring compliance with Interpol's Constitution and the Rules on the Processing of Data, in particular with Articles 2 and 3 of Interpol's Constitution;

36 See https://www.europarl.europa.eu/RegData/etudes/STUD/2019/603472/EXPO_STU(2019)603472_EN.pdf p.30.
37 Formerly the Working Group of the Processing of Information.
38 GA-2023-91-RES-09.

- requests all member countries to systematically inform the General Secretariat of the outcome of arrests and extradition proceedings with respect to wanted persons who have been arrested based on Red Notices and Wanted Person Diffusions;
- called upon all NCBs to encourage the appropriate authorities in their countries to recognise Red Notices and Wanted Person Diffusions as valid requests for provisional arrest pending extradition;[39]

- Interpol asked the Committee on the Processing of Data to consider the current rules regarding suspension of access to services and other interim or corrective measures;[40] and
- increased the CCF budget for 2024 to EUR 2,504,000[41] (this represents a significant increase from EUR 1,736,000 for 2023 and EUR 1,241,000 for 2022).

Interpol appears set for another period of significant reform; one that many commentators consider may be essential for the future of the organisation.

Conclusion

4.55

Red Notices and Diffusions are unquestionably some of the most important tools offered by Interpol to its members. They are correctly characterised as essential to combating serious international crime. It is also beyond sensible dispute that this area of Interpol's work has the greatest capacity to impact the individual and has the potential to contribute towards breaches of fundamental rights. However, Interpol has recognised this fact and has sought to adopt productive reforms.

4.56

Interpol has been making reforms steadily for a number of years now, and has addressed a number of the historical criticisms. For example, more data is now available on the number of Red Notices issued, CCF decision excerpts are now publicly available, and processes are in place, such as the NDTF to try to filter out abuses of the system. Whilst progress has been made, there remain concerns that it has been slow, and that a number of the recommendations highlighted above have yet to be implemented.

39 GA-2023-91-RES-10.
40 GA-2023-91-RES-06.
41 GA-2023-91-RES-14.

4.57

Despite the reforms, many international organisations and INGOs, as well as individual practitioners consider that there is still more work for Interpol to do in order to eliminate the abuses of its Red Notice and Wanted Person Diffusion systems. According to the Activity Report of the Commission for the Control of Interpol's Files for 2021, the CCF processed 651 complaints in 2021, of which 478 concerned admissible requests from applicants who were the subject of data recorded in Interpol's files. Of these 478 complaints the CCF concluded in 296 cases that the challenged cases should be deleted from Interpol's files as they did not comply with Interpol's rules. Therefore, despite the work of NDTF and repeated attempts to ensure more stringent checking of requests, 60% of complaints resulted in deletion of data from Interpol's files.

4.58

There will always be operational reasons why Interpol's procedures will necessarily be subject to a degree of confidentiality. However, the authors submit that its operational effectiveness would not be undermined on a case-by-case basis by affording a greater degree of clarity regarding the criteria it will follow when making operational decisions to publish Red Notices or to allow the publication of Diffusions on its databases. It is suggested that Interpol's approach to refugees provides an apposite example. A coherent published policy on its approach in cases concerning individuals with asylum protection would serve to increase public confidence that such issues are given appropriate weight by the organisation and conform to international legal norms. It would allow practitioners to provide accurate advice both to individuals and to requesting NCBs on the approach it will adopt in such cases. Interpol appears committed to making improvements to tackle the abuse of its Red Notice and WPD system, most recently at the 91st General Assembly in Vienna in November/December 2023. As Interpol has recognised, the stakes may be as high for the life of the organisation as for the refugees affected by the policy.

5 Finding out whether a Red Notice exists

1. **Introduction**
2. **Interpol**
3. **Diffusions**
4. **Requesting NCB**
5. **Other countries**
6. **Other NCBs**
7. **Other matters to consider**

Introduction

5.1

Finding out, with confidence, whether a client is the subject of a Red Notice or Diffusion is one of the most challenging tasks a lawyer can be instructed to undertake. It is not uncommon for a client who is aware of an overseas investigation to ask whether it is safe for them to travel internationally. The implications of getting this answer wrong can be serious: arrest, detention and extradition to a third country. These risks often need to be balanced against a client's need, whether for business or personal reasons, to be able to travel. So, what can be done?

5.2

This chapter will explore the three possible routes, both formal and informal, to consider when investigating whether a Red Notice or Diffusion exists:

- Interpol;
- Requesting NCB;
- Other NCBs (eg in a country where client is residing/has an intention to travel).

Interpol

5.3

Within Interpol itself there are two possible sources of information as to whether a Red Notice is in force: Public and Private.

Public Red Notices

5.4

A small proportion of Red Notices are published on Interpol's website. The listing generally details the individual's name, some basic personal information, a photograph and a broad indication of the offence that has resulted in the Red Notice. It is important to note that if an individual is not listed on this page, it does not mean that a Red Notice has not been published against them; the majority of Red Notices are available only on Interpol's restricted networks. These are visible only to national law enforcement authorities.

5.5

Any individual subject to a Diffusion will never feature on Interpol's website.

Private Red Notices

5.6

The majority of Red Notices are not published on Interpol's website and, in the normal course, the subject is not aware it exists until they are arrested. That said, where an individual believes they may be the subject of a Red Notice, it is sometimes possible to establish the position by way of a variety of different routes.

Commission for the Control of Files

5.7

The formal route and the route that most NCB's will direct you to in the first instance, is via the 'Requests Chamber' of the Commission for the Control of Files (CCF).

5.8

As explained in Chapter 2, the CCF ensures personal information is processed in compliance with relevant Interpol regulations. Individuals can therefore make a request to the CCF for disclosure of any information held by Interpol in relation to them.

5.9

The 'Statute of the Commission for the Control of Interpol's Files' sets out, under chapter 4, sub-chapter 1, the basic access conditions and procedures:

- Any person or entity shall have the right, free of charge, to submit directly to the CCF a request for access to data processed in the Interpol Information System and concerning them.
- A request shall be made in writing in one of Interpol's working languages (Arabic, English, French or Spanish) by the applicant or their duly authorised representative. Submission of the request is free of change.
- The Requests Chamber shall acknowledge receipt of any request at the earliest opportunity and inform the applicant of the applicable procedure and time frame.
- The Request Chamber shall inform the applicant at the earliest opportunity, and within one month, whether the request is admissible.
- A request will be declared inadmissible if: (i) the applicant fails to provide the necessary information within the deadline indication; (ii) it is considered incompatible with the Statute of the Commission for the Control of Interpol's Files or the Operating Rules; or (iii) it is clearly unreasonable.
- A request is deemed clearly unreasonable by taking into account the number or their repetitive/systematic nature.

5.10

In addition, the 'Operating rules of the Commission for the Control of Interpol's Files'[1] sets out in detail the further admissibility requirements for obtaining this information:

- the request includes a letter or a CCF application form, signed by the applicant sent by post or by email and explaining the purpose of the request;
- it is written in one of the organisation's working languages (Arabic, English, French or Spanish);
- the request comes from the person whom it concerns, or from that person's duly authorised representative or his/her legal representative;

1 See Appendix 5.

- where the applicant is an entity, the full name, date of incorporation or registration, the official registration number and the official address shall be provided;
- if the request comes from the duly authorised representative of the person who is the subject of the request, the request shall be accompanied by an original power of attorney signed by the said person authorising his/her representative to access any information about that person recorded in Interpol's files;
- if the request comes from the legal representative of the person who is the subject of the request, it shall be accompanied by a corresponding written declaration;
- the request shall be accompanied by a copy of a readable and non-redacted identity document belonging to the person who is the subject of the request, in order to prove his/her identity; and
- if the request calls into question the processing of information in Interpol's files, it shall set out the reasons, that is to say be accompanied by a summary of the arguments in support of the request, making specific reference to any relevant document attached. The Commission shall only be obliged to take into consideration those documents attached which have been translated into one of Interpol's official languages and certified if necessary.

5.11

In practical terms the request can be made either by letter or by filling in a CCF application form.[2] In the section of the form asking for reasons, the individual should state 'request for access as of right under Article 29 of Interpol's Statute of the Commission for the Control of Interpol's Files'.

5.12

Article 29 states that 'any person or entity shall have the right to submit directly to the Commission a request for access to, or correction and/or deletion of, data processed in the Interpol Information System and concerning that person or entity', guaranteed by the CCF. This means you do not have to justify or explain your interest in obtaining the information. The CCF is only obliged to consider a request if the person has reasonable grounds to think there may be information concerning them in Interpol's files. It is not necessary to provide a significant amount of detail in this section. That said, it can sometimes be beneficial to explain your client's reasons for the request (see **5.89** below).

5.13

Prior to any disclosure of information the CCF Requests Chamber will consult with the owner of that information, usually this is an NCB. The CCF may then

2 See Appendix 6.

restrict the communication of the data to the applicant for one or more of the following reasons:

- to protect public or national security or to prevent crime;
- to protect the confidentiality of an investigation or prosecution;
- to protect the rights and freedoms of the applicant or third parties; or
- to enable the CCF or Interpol to properly discharge their duties.

5.14

Any restriction must be justified and consideration should be given as to whether the information can be provided in a different way, for example, in a summary form. The CCF may also, where appropriate, direct the applicant to the relevant NCB who is the source of the data.

5.15

It is important to note that if the CCF does not provide any information, this does not mean that a Red Notice is not in place.

5.16

Under the Statute of the Commission for the Control of Interpol's Files, the Requests Chamber must make a decision on a request to access information within four months from the date on which the request was declared admissible. The applicant must be informed within one month of this decision.

5.17

Notwithstanding the above, if you are able to demonstrate that you know there is information on Interpol's files, the CCF may be able to provide access to that information even without the NCB's authorisation. Therefore, it is important that you explain in your letter how you know there is information and provide evidence to support what you say.

5.18

Trying to obtain information as to the existence of a Red Notice through the CCF is time consuming. The above detailed process has numerous stages which can result in delay or even refusal, but often yields useful results.

Diffusions

5.19

On occasion, the practitioner will not know whether there is a Red Notice or Diffusion in circulation. As dealt with elsewhere in this work, certain jurisdictions are more likely to issue Diffusions than requests for Red Notices.

Where the practitioner suspects that a Diffusion may have been sent, the process for finding out whether one exists is broadly similar to the process described in the preceding paragraphs, save that the application must include reference to the relevant Articles of Interpol's Rules on the Processing of Data (RPD) which concern Diffusions.

Requesting NCB

5.20

If your client has an idea which country has requested a Red Notice it may be quicker and more effective to confirm whether or not this is accurate directly with the requesting NCB. This can be done either formally or informally.

5.21

As with many aspects of the Red Notice process, perhaps the best route to getting confirmation is to build a relationship with the NCB and obtain informal confirmation as to the existence of the Red Notice process. This can be difficult if you do not know which officer(s) are conducting the investigation but, given in most cases the officers will want to speak to the subject of the Red Notice, they can often be amenable to beginning a dialogue with their legal representatives.

5.22

It should be noted that, as this is an informal approach, it is often the case that the national police forces may not be allowed to consult Interpol records or disclose information to an individual. A negative result from this type of enquiry should not be considered conclusive, not least because the relevant police forces may not have access to the relevant Interpol records. As noted above, depending on the position of a specific client, practitioners may want to consider whether it is strategically helpful to inform the police force that their client may be prepared to surrender at an agreed time and place. This has the benefit of establishing a semblance of control over what can be a very uncertain process. An offer of this nature may encourage a police force to disclose the existence of a Red Notice.

5.23

Where it is not possible to identify the relevant officer(s) or in the absence of reliable confirmation as to the existence of a Red Notice, it may be possible to make a request under data protection laws. In the UK, and other EU jurisdictions, an individual can make a 'Subject Access Request' in order to obtain a copy of any information an organisation holds in relation to them. It should, though, be noted that EU Member States often apply EU data protection laws in a different way depending on the local law.

United Kingdom

5.24

In the UK, the relevant legislation is the UK GDPR and the Data Protection Act 2018 (the DPA) and the following process should be followed:

- A valid Subject Access Request should be made in writing (including by e-mail, online form, fax or even by social media). Exceptions to this are available for those who find doing so impossible or unreasonably difficult due to a disability under the Equality Act 2010, where the organisation is required to make reasonable adjustments.
- In most cases, no fee will be charged. However a 'reasonable fee' for administrative costs can be charged for compliance with a request if it is manifestly unfounded or excessive.
- There is no requirement to mention the DPA specifically or to say that the communication is a Subject Access Request.
- The communication needs to make it clear that the individual is asking for their own personal data.
- A request is valid even if the individual has not sent it directly to the person that usually deals with such requests in the organisation.

5.25

The DPA does provide for a number of exemptions which restrict an individual's right to make a Subject Access Request when the personal data is processed for the following crime and taxation purposes:

- the prevention and detection of crime;
- the capture or prosecution of offenders; and
- the assessment or collection of tax or duty.

5.26

The Information Commissioner's Office (the ICO) provides the following by way of an example:

> 'A bank conducts an investigation into one of their customers for suspected financial fraud. During their investigation, the bank receives a subject access request for all of the personal data they hold from the customer in question. The bank decides that they will withhold information about the investigation, because it would be likely to prejudice the investigation as the individual may abscond or destroy evidence. However, the bank is able to provide other information in response to the request which would not prejudice the investigation (for example the individual's account details and transactions).'[3]

3 Available at: https://ico.org.uk/for-organisations/uk-gdpr-guidance-and-resources/individual-rights/right-of-access/what-other-exemptions-are-there/.

5.27

The exemption applies only if applying it would be likely to prejudice the investigation of crime and taxation offences.

5.28

A police force cannot have a blanket policy application for the exemption (eg 'for all Red Notice information requests' is not permitted) and each request must be considered individually.

5.29

The exemption does not justify withholding all personal data about an individual when only part of the personal data would be likely to prejudice the investigation. The degree of likelihood requires 'a degree of probability where there is a very significant and weighty chance to prejudice the identified public interests'.

Other countries

5.30

For the purpose of this section an individual is referred to as the 'data subject' in this context.

France

5.31

In France, right of access to personal information is governed by the *Loi Informatique et Libertés*, ('LIL'), in particular, Title III, articles 104 to 111. This includes transposition of the European directive of 27 April 2016, the 'Police-Justice Directive'.

5.32

An ad hoc decree of 22 May 2018 known as 'Gerrpol decree' (the 'Decree') specifically sets out the conditions for data processing in relation to the '[e]lectronic management of requests for provisional arrest with a view to extradition – INTERPOL' ('Interpol Processing'). This restricts the access rights of the individuals affected by Interpol Red Notices.

5.33

The common right to access information held by a data controller (Articles 104 and 105 of LIL) is not applicable to Interpol Processing. Article 6-III of the

Decree expressly provides that to avoid hindering research, investigations, prosecutions or the enforcement of criminal penalties, the right of access is limited. Data subjects may exercise their right of access, but such right is 'indirect' for the abovementioned reasons.

5.34

In France, Interpol data processing is managed by the Minister of the Interior (the 'Ministry'). In practice, it is the Department of the Police Direction Générale de la Police Nationale (DGPN), which carries out the processing on behalf of the Ministry. This police department is Interpol's National Central Bureau (NCB).

5.35

In order to access their data, data subjects must send their request to the relevant supervisory authority. In relation to information held by Interpol the relevant authority is the Commission Nationale Informatique et Libertés (CNIL). The request must include:

- the name of the processing operation concerned (in this case, Interpol);
- a clear request for copies of the data (or of the information needed, such as existence of a processing, the purpose of it, its duration, etc);
- a copy of both sides of an identity document showing the data subject's date and place of birth;
- a postal address for sending the results; and
- depending on the situation, any additional documents as requested by the CNIL.

5.36

Data subjects can submit their request for information online at https://services.cnil.fr/, or by post to Commission Nationale de l'informatique et des Libertés – 3 place de Fontenoy – 75007 PARIS.

5.37

The CNIL then appoints one of its members to carry out the relevant investigations. If the CNIL finds, in agreement with the data controller (here, the Ministry), that disclosure of the data does not jeopardise its purposes of state security, defence or public safety, the data may be disclosed to the applicant. If the request is accepted, the data will be provided to the data subject within six months, save for exceptional cases. No representation or payment is required, unless the requesting party abuses its right of request. It is for the data controller to prove this when alleged (Article 109 II of LIL).

5.38

The LIL provides several exemptions which restrict an individual's right to make the request. The restrictions under LIL are:

- to avoid interfering with ongoing investigations; enquiries, administrative or judicial proceedings;
- to avoid hindering the prevention or detection of criminal offences or the enforcement of their penalties;
- to protect public health;
- to protect national security; and
- to protect the rights and freedoms of others (Article 107 I° of LIL).

5.39

The restriction must be necessary and proportionate to the protected objective. The applicant must be informed of the reasons for the refusal or the limitations of the response unless to do so would hinder the protected objective (Article 107, I°, II° and III° of LIL).

5.40

The nature of the processing carried out does not allow for informal approaches. However, an acceptable less formal approach is to contact each of the intermediaries involved, starting with the Ministry and the Direction Générale de la Police Nationale, then the international relations division (DRI), and its operational cooperation section, the 'SCCOPOL', which ultimately manage the processing.

Germany

5.41

German law does not provide an individual with a direct right to access information held by Interpol. However, a request for information can be brought against Interpol itself, pursuant to Article 29 of the Statute of the CCF.

5.42

In Germany, the Federal Criminal Police Office (*Bundeskriminalamt, BKA*), as the National Central Bureau, is responsible for Interpol alerts in accordance with section 33 of the German Federal Criminal Police Act (*Bundeskriminalamtgesetz*, 'BKAG') and section 123, paragraph 4 of the Guidelines for dealings with foreign countries in criminal matters (*Richtlinien für den Verkehr mit dem Ausland in strafrechtlichen Angelegenheiten, RiVASt*). An individual can make a request for information to the German Federal Criminal Police Office, which receives and processes the information from Interpol, in accordance with the BKAG, section 84, para 1, sentence 1 and the German Federal Data Protection Act, section 57 (*Bundesdatenschutzgesetz*, 'BDSG'):[4]

- the right to information under German law, only applies to private individuals;
- the information provided is limited to that which relates solely to the data subject; and
- the information may only be provided to the actual person entitled, being the data subject themselves.

5.43

In order to make a request for information, the following documents and information must be sent by post to the German Federal Criminal Police Office:

- an informal request for information;
- a clearly legible copy of a valid identity document; and
- the residential address of the person to whom the application relates.

5.44

If the request for information is successful, the information will be sent by registered mail to the data subject's address. In principle, the right to information is free of charge.

5.45

If the data subject is represented by a lawyer:

- a current power of attorney is required which states the information which is requested. This must be signed by the person concerned; or
- assurance must be provided by a lawyer that a power of attorney exists which details the request for information.

5.46

Furthermore, a lawyer must provide assurance that their client is the same person to whom the request for information relates (the holder of the identity document submitted with the request).

5.47

The notice containing the requested information may be served on the lawyer if they confirm that the identity of the data subject accords with that of their client.

4 This states: 'The person responsible must provide data subjects with information on request as to whether he or she is processing data relating to them'.

5.48

An individual's right to information is restricted under section 57 paragraph 4, and sections 56, paragraphs 2(1) and 45 of the BDSG. The provision of information may be restricted or omitted if this would endanger the prevention, investigation, detection or prosecution or punishment of criminal offences.

5.49

In order to withhold information that would otherwise be provided under the BKAG, section 84, para 1, sentence 1, it is necessary that such disclosure of information would threaten the outcome of an ongoing criminal investigation. Even in such circumstances, the German Federal Criminal Police Office must ensure that they act proportionately. This requires them to consider whether the risk to the investigation can be negated by providing the requested information in part. This requirement that the German Federal Criminal Police act proportionately is expressly contained in the explanatory memorandum to the BDSG. From a legal point of view, requests for information cannot be denied absent these requirements.

5.50

There are no informal routes by which information can be requested.

Hong Kong

5.51

Interpol Hong Kong is part of the Hong Kong Police Force (HKPF), which operates as a sub-bureau of the Interpol National Central Bureau (NCB) in China.

5.52

A data subject may obtain personal information held by Interpol by making a Data Access Request (DAR), pursuant to section18(1)[5] of the Personal Data

5 Section 18(1) provides: '[a]n individual, or a relevant person on behalf of an individual, may make a request—
(a) to be informed by a data user whether the data user holds personal data of which the individual is the data subject;
(b) if the data user holds such data, to be supplied by the data user with a copy of such data.'
A 'data user' is defined under section 2(1) of the PDPO to mean 'a person who, either alone or jointly or in common with other persons, controls the collection, holding, processing or use of the data.' One does not qualify as a data user if it has no control on the content or data, but merely allowed or gave consent for disclosure (AAB No 4/1997, also *Eastweek Publisher Ltd v Privacy Commissioner for Personal Data* [2000] 1 HKC 692 (CA)).
For the avoidance of doubt, individual government bureaux and departments fall within the definition of 'person' referred to above: see the Interpretation and General Clauses Ordinance (Cap 1, Laws of Hong Kong).

(Privacy) Ordinance (Cap 486, Laws of Hong Kong) (PDPO). This right is available where the HKPF, in its capacity as a sub-bureau of the NCB, has control over the collection, processing and use of personal data, which is subsequently transferred to Interpol.

5.53

The data subject may fill out a 'Data Access Request Form' (the 'Form') and send it directly to the data user. While the use of the Form is not mandatory, it reduces the risks that the form employed did not contain the substance to qualify as a valid data access request. The requestor must provide true and accurate information to the data user in filing out the Form. A data user must either comply with the request, or inform the requestor that it does not hold the data, within 40 days after receiving the data request (section 19(1) of the PDPO). The Form can either be signed by the data subject himself or his legal representative who is authorised in writing (sections 2(1) and 17A of the PDPO).

5.54

A charge reflecting the direct and necessary costs for complying with the DAR will be levied by the data user. Section 28 of the PDPO prohibits the imposition of an 'excessive' fee. Examples of permissible items of charge include the time costs for locating, retrieving and reproducing the requested data, actual out-of-pocket expenses such as costs for utilising technical services, photocopying fees at a reasonable cost (eg HK$1 per page), postage fee for delivering the requested data, etc. It is noted that the costs for seeking legal advice to study the request in light of the PDPO may be considered excessive and/or not directly related to and necessary for the compliance with the request.

5.55

It is advisable that a data subject should specify the data requested and avoid making broad and generic requests (eg 'all personal data held by the HKPF'), as the data user may reasonably ask the requestor to provide further information to assist and locate the requested personal data, failing which the data user may be entitled to refuse to comply with the DAR.

5.56

A data user may refuse to comply with the DAR by relying on the exemptions under Part 8 of the PDPO. With regards to the nature of information HKPF usually holds (and which may be transferred to Interpol), the relevant exemptions include:

- safeguarding security, defence or international relations in Hong Kong (section 57 of the PDPO);[6]
- preventing or detecting a crime (section 58(1) of the PDPO): 'crime' is defined as an offence under Hong Kong laws or of a place outside Hong Kong, provided that personal data is held or used in connection with legal or law enforcement cooperation between Hong Kong and that jurisdiction.[7]

5.57

Alternatively, an individual may request information under the Code on Access to Information (the 'Code'), which provides the formal framework for the public's access to information held by government departments, including the HKPF. There is broad discretion and grounds available to the HKPF to refuse disclosure of the relevant information, such as the existence of a Red Notice or Diffusion against an individual, as detailed below.

5.58

Discretion is exercised under a 'harm or prejudice test'. The Access to Information Officer/department has to consider whether the public interest in disclosure outweighs any harm or prejudice that could result from disclosure[8]. It will be sufficient if there is a risk or reasonable expectation of harm in disclosure (Guidelines, paras 2.1.1, 2.2.2[9]).

6 In an unreported complaint lodged against a law enforcement agency, the Commissioner considered the data user to have rightly refused to confirm the existence or non-existence of records in its possession. Providing a reply would otherwise confirm their view or conclusion as to whether the data subject is linked to a triad society. The Commissioner found that exemptions under sections 57(1), 58(1)(a) and 58(1)(b) were engaged as there was substantial interest to protect their source of information. This would also allow members of the public to give information in confidence without fear and in full frankness. Therefore, the Commissioner opined that the data subject's entitlement to ascertain whether a data user holds his/her personal data under Data Protection Principle 6 was not contravened (*Personal Data (Privacy) Law in Hong Kong: A Practical Guide on Compliance* (2nd edn), paras 12.35–12.36).

7 The data user seeking to invoke the exemption has the burden to satisfy the court that all relevant pre-requisites have been met (*Cinepoly Records Co Ltd v Hong Kong Broadband Network Ltd* [2006] 1 HKC 433). In relying on an exempted ground, the HKPF may not divulge details of the investigation (eg nature of prosecution, progress etc) it is conducting, nor is it inclined to explain the relationship between the requested data and investigation at play. In that sense, although the HKPF does not appear to have a direct legal basis to impose a blanket refusal to comply with a DAR (as illustrated by its Personal Data Privacy Policy Statement (hyperlinked)), practically it may be difficult for an individual to challenge their rejection successfully.

8 The following categories of documents can be withheld under Part 2 of the Code: defence and security; external affairs; nationality, immigration and consular matters; law enforcement, legal proceedings and public safety; damage to the environment; management of the economy; management and operation of the public service; internal discussion and advice; public employment and public appointments; improper gain or advantage; research, statistics and analysis; third party information; privacy of the individual; business affairs; premature requests; and legal restrictions.

9 See https://www.access.gov.hk/filemanager/content/codeonacctoinfo/guidelines.pdf.

5.59

Aside from a blanket or wholesale refusal to provide any requested documents, the HKPF may decide to provide a summary of record(s), instead of a copy of the document(s) requested. The HKPF may also refuse to confirm or deny the existence of information and will be precluded from giving reasons of refusal if it would serve to confirm whether the information did or did not exist (Guidelines, para 2.1.2).

5.60

A data subject can challenge the failure to supply or produce requested data. This is provided for under the Code's following provisions:

- section 1.25 provides that any person who believes that a department has failed to comply with any provision of the Code may ask the department to review the situation; and
- section 1.26 provides that any person who believes a department has failed to properly apply any provision of the Code may also complain to the Ombudsman.

Italy

5.61

Italian law does not contain specific provisions governing access to information held by Interpol. As such Article 29 of the Statute of the Commission for the Control of Interpol's Files applies. The process for requesting information in Italy therefore follows international processes as set out in the CCF.

5.62

Whilst no specific exclusions or exemption to the provision of information apply in Italy, the Italian police can exercise discretion in line with specific rules and principles by which they are governed. The police could therefore refuse to disclose information based on privacy or security reasons or to avoid impairing ongoing investigations.

5.63

Whilst there are no specific informal channels by which to obtain information held by Interpol, is it always advisable to try contacting the Italian Police Offices first. In some instances, individuals who have been subject to a Red Notice have been able to discover this by asking the Italian police.

Netherlands

5.64

The relevant legislation regarding the processing of data belonging to individuals in the Netherlands is Directive (EU) 2016/680 (the 'Directive'). The Directive concerns the processing of personal data by competent authorities for the purposes of the prevention, investigation, detection or prosecution of criminal offences or the execution of criminal penalties, including the safeguarding against and the prevention of threats to public security. It also concerns the free movement of such data. Recital 25 of the Directive makes specific mention of its applicability to the processing of personal data by Interpol.[10]

5.65

The Dutch legislator has implemented the Directive in the Act on Police Data (*Wet Politiegegevens* (WPG)) and the Act on Judicial and Criminal Data (*Wet Justitiële en Strafvorderlijke Gegevens* (WJSG)). These provisions can be seen as a *lex specialis* deriving from the General Data Protection Regulation.

5.66

The WPG concerns data collected by the police and special investigative units. According to Article 25 (1)(c) of the WPG, an individual can request access to information that has been disclosed to an international organisation, such as Interpol.

5.67

The WSJG concerns data collected by the public prosecutor and the Central Judicial Collection Agency. An individual can request the Dutch Minister of Justice and Security provide access to judicial data in accordance with Article 18(c) of the WPG which has been transmitted to an international organisation, such as Interpol. Furthermore, based on Article 39i (1)(c) of the WJSG, the individual can request the Board of the Prosecutors General, a body of the Netherlands Public Prosecution Service (*College van procureurs-generaal*) to provide access to criminal data that have been transmitted to an international organisation, such as Interpol.

10 Recital 25 states: 'All Member States are affiliated to the International Criminal Police Organisation (Interpol). To fulfil its mission, Interpol receives, stores and circulates personal data to assist competent authorities in preventing and combating international crime. It is therefore appropriate to strengthen cooperation between the Union and Interpol by promoting an efficient exchange of personal data whilst ensuring respect for fundamental rights and freedoms regarding the automatic processing of personal data. Where personal data are transferred from the Union to Interpol, and to countries which have delegated members to Interpol, this Directive, in particular the provisions on international transfers, should apply.'

5.68

Article 25(1) of the WPG requires the data subject to make a written application to obtain the information held about them by Interpol. The written application can be directed towards the police unit of the region where the individual has its residence. Pursuant to Article 26(3) of the WPG, the application may also be made by a lawyer to whom the individual had granted special authorisation for the purpose of exercising their rights. The lawyer must make the request solely with the intention of representing the needs of the client and the communication in question shall be made to the lawyer. Article 24a(3) of the WPG states that there are no costs to the application.

5.69

Article 18 and 39i of the WJSG requires the data subject to make a written application to obtain information held about them by Interpol. This written request must be directed to the Dutch Minister of Justice and Security under Article 18 of the WJSG, and to the Board of the Prosecutors General under Article 39i of the WJSG.

5.70

Article 20 of the WJSG provides that the application may also be made by a lawyer to whom the individual had granted special authorisation for the purpose of exercising their rights. The lawyer must make the request solely with the intention of representing the needs of the client and the communication in question shall be made to the lawyer. In accordance with Article 25 of the WJSG, there are no costs to the application.

5.71

Neither the WPG, nor the WJSG make further reference of the information that must be included in the application. However, the website of the Dutch Data Protection Authority (*Autoriteit Persoonsgegevens*) provides further information on the application process, as well as an example application that individuals can use. It is recommended that anyone seeking to apply to the WPG or the WSJG specify as precisely as possible which data they wish to access. Furthermore, the individual must send a copy of their passport or ID-card with the application to prove their identity.

5.72

Article 27(1) of the WPG provides that a request for information can be declined as far as this is a necessary and proportionate measure. Article 27(1) also states the grounds on which the request of the individual can be declined. These grounds are:

- to avoid obstruction of judicial investigations or proceedings;

- to avoid adverse effects on the prevention, detection, investigation and prosecution of criminal offences or the execution of criminal penalties;
- to protect public safety;
- to protect the rights and freedoms of third parties;
- to protect national security; and
- in the event of a manifestly unfounded or excessive request.

5.73

A request for information can also be declined in accordance with Article 21(2) of the WJSG. The reasons for refusal are the same as apply under the WPG.

Spain

5.74

There is no Spanish legislation specifically regulating an individuals' right to request access to information about them from Interpol; there is also no legislation prohibiting such access either. As such, Article 29 of the Statute of the Commission for the Control of Interpol's Files applies. The process for requesting information in Spain therefore follows international processes as set out in the CCF.

United States of America

5.75

The Freedom of Information Act (FOIA) (5 USC § 552) governs public access to government records, including records held by Interpol Washington, US National Central Bureau (USNCB). Requirements for making requests are codified in section 16.3 of the FOIA regulations (28 CFR section 16.3).

5.76

A person requesting access to information may submit a request for records to USNCB FOIA Requester Service Centre (FRSC). The request must be made in writing and can be submitted electronically on FOIA.gov by clicking 'Create a Request' and selecting Interpol – United States National Central Bureau as the agency.

5.77

There are two requirements for making a request:

- the request must 'reasonably describe' the records sought; and

- the request must be made in accordance with the agency's published FOIA regulations.

5.78

The FOIA regulations require the requester to complete a Certification of Identify Form (DOJ Form 361) or a statement notarised or under penalty of perjury indicating the requester's full name, place of birth, date of birth, and current address. If a third party, ie not the subject of the Red Notice, is requesting records, the third party must obtain and submit the subject's written consent.

5.79

While there is no cost for submitting a FOIA request to USNCB, the applicant may incur fees for the processing and duplication of records depending on the category of requester and records at issue. The fee rates are currently five cents per page for duplication and an hourly search fee depending on the seniority of the personnel conducting the search. If the total fee does not exceed US$25, no fee will be charged. Depending on the circumstances, the applicant may seek a fee waiver.

5.80

FOIA provides that the government agency will provide access to identifiable documents within the agency's possession unless disclosure is prohibited by law or if one of three exclusions (5 USC section 552(c)) or nine exemptions applies.

5.81

These exclusions provide protection in three limited sets of circumstances where publicly acknowledging even the existence of the records could cause harm to law enforcement or national security interests. These exclusions are:

- the applicant is the subject of a criminal investigation or proceeding, is unaware that it is pending and disclosure of such records would interfere with the investigation or proceeding;
- requests for informant records maintained by a criminal law enforcement agency where the individual's status as an informant is not known by the applicant;
- requests for classified records maintained by the Federal Bureau of Investigation relating to foreign intelligence, counterintelligence, or international terrorism.

5.82

Nine exemptions include the following categories of documents:

- classified national defence and foreign relations information;
- internal agency personnel rules and practices;
- information that is prohibited from disclosure by another federal law;
- trade secrets and commercial or financial information obtained from a person that is privileged or confidential;
- inter-agency or intra-agency memoranda or letters that are protected by legal privileges;
- personnel, medical, financial, and similar files the disclosure of which would constitute a clearly unwarranted invasion of personal privacy;
- certain types of information compiled for law enforcement purposes;
- records that are contained in or related to examination, operating, or condition reports prepared by, on behalf of, or for the use of any agency responsible for the regulation or supervision of financial institutions;
- geological and geophysical information and data, including maps, concerning wells.

5.83

Unless disclosure would harm an interest protected by an exemption, or disclosure is prohibited by law, agencies should consider whether partial disclosure is possible and should make reasonable efforts to segregate and release non-exempt information.

5.84

There are no informal routes by which information can be requested.

Other NCBs

5.85

The final potential route in identifying whether a Red Notice is in existence is via any other NCB apart from the requesting NCB. In reality, this is likely to be the country in which the client either resides or where they intend to travel. As detailed above, in relation to the requesting NCB, again both a formal and/or informal approach can be used and the same considerations and legal avenues should be considered. It should be noted that an attempt is unlikely to be successful if there is no direct connection between the NCB and the client. This connection could be through citizenship or perhaps if the individual has been granted asylum in the requested country. Practitioners have reported some success by instructing reliable local counsel who have contacts with the relevant NCB and can sometimes obtain information as to the existence of a Red Notice.

5.86

One route that should certainly be considered is contacting the NCB of the country of which the target client is a citizen. Some countries, such as the USA, have specific Interpol liaison offices that may formally (as above) or informally assist a national who is trying to ascertain whether or not they are the subject of a Red Notice. It should be noted that these local offices often cannot provide any specific information but can be extremely useful in navigating the challenging procedures of the CCF or chasing up requests that have been ignored.

5.87

Finally, it is certainly worth local practitioners trying to build a relationship with their local Interpol representative office (if it exists) prior to any specific case request.

Other matters to consider

5.88

Two other potential matters should be considered in relation to finding out if a Red Notice is in existence.

Preventative requests

5.89

If you have a reasonable suspicion that a Red Notice may be issued against a client then a 'Preventative Request' should be made directly to the CCF. This can be made in conjunction with a Subject Access Request.

5.90

The purpose of a Preventative Request is to request that Interpol does not give effect to any application by a specific NCB for a Diffusion or Red Notice against specified individuals without a complete review of the underlying facts. The Preventative Request should clearly specify the requesting state and individuals (or classes of individuals, eg 'Bank Employee') who may be at risk. It should also clearly request a review of any application by Interpol's Office of General Counsel and invite representations from the target individual's legal team.

5.91

The Preventative Request should then provide as much detail as possible in support of the application. This should include relevant background information on the matter as well as the reasons why, as appropriate, the application for a Red Notice would be in breach of Interpol's Constitution or International Law. It is not uncommon for some countries to use Red Notices as a weapon of retaliation against individuals and businesses in relation to legitimate business practices. Alternatively, some countries use them to try and destabilise political opponents. Interpol's Constitution is clear: 'it is strictly forbidden for the Organisation to undertake any intervention or activities of a political … character'. Evidence should be provided as to why the suspected Red Notice is political in character.

5.92

In addition, international human rights law can provide a persuasive argument as to why a Red Notice should not be issued. Interpol is extremely sensitive about its network being abused by member countries in relation to politically motivated Diffusion and Red Notice requests. Under Article 2 of Interpol's Constitution, Interpol embeds the Universal Declaration of Human Rights therefore any Preventative Request should explain why a Red Notice would be a clear contravention of international human rights law.

5.93

It is important to ensure the preventative request has a clear explanation on how a Red Notice or any further application seeking a Red Notice may be in breach of Interpol's Constitution and operating rules. A properly, supported, preventative request can therefore be effective.

5.94

The preventative request should also include any exonerating evidence and corresponding documents to assist the CCF with its review. The CCF publishes anonymised decisions online and it may prove persuasive to refer to precedent decisions by the CCF with analogous fact patterns (if applicable).

5.95

It should be noted that there is a risk that a preventative request will be referred to the requesting NCB. This can result in increased scrutiny of the client and is particularly relevant when a client may be keeping a low profile.

5.96

Further arguments, similar to those identified in Chapter 6 should also be considered.

Informal police co-operation

5.97

Notwithstanding the above, it is important to note that, even where Interpol or a local NCB, states that a Red Notice has not been issued, there are still situations where someone can be detained in an overseas country. International police forces often have informal regional co-operation which can result in a police force in one country informally requesting the detention of an individual in another (eg this is common in South America). Often this co-operation may be limited to locating and maintaining surveillance whilst a formal extradition or mutual legal assistance request is made. In these circumstances it is not possible to identify this informal request via Interpol.

6 Interpol – Challenging Red Notices and Diffusions

1. Introduction

2. Procedure for challenging a Red Notice or Diffusion

3. Specific approach to Red Notices

4. Challenges based on Article 2 of the Interpol Constitution

5. Challenges based on Article 3 of the Interpol Constitution

6. Challenges based on breaches of the RPD

7. Challenges based on the 2017 Interpol Refugee Resolution

8. Challenges in domestic law – example jurisdictions

9. Conclusion

Introduction

6.1

It will be clear from earlier chapters that Interpol considers itself as a conduit between the law enforcement agencies of its member countries. Accordingly, an individual's first port of call in seeking to challenge a Red Notice or Diffusion should always be to consider all avenues to seek to persuade the authorities (be that the police or court of a member country) that has requested the Red Notice or sent a Diffusion to withdraw that request. Put succinctly, if an individual can persuade the authority that is pursuing them to end their pursuit there will no longer be a need or a legal basis for Interpol to maintain a Red Notice or Diffusion.

6.2

However, many individuals find themselves unable to persuade the authorities of a member country to end their pursuit. In such circumstances, what avenues are available to an individual (or his legal representative) who seeks to challenge a Red Notice or a Diffusion?

6.3

This chapter will seek to answer that question. The first part of the chapter considers the remedies offered by Interpol itself. The second part reviews the attempts that have been made in domestic courts either to challenge Red Notices or ameliorate their effects.

Procedure for challenging a Red Notice or Diffusion

The requests procedure

6.4

An individual or entity has the right to challenge the imposition of a Red Notice or Diffusion relating to them by making a formal 'request' that the information relating to them held in the Interpol Information System be deleted.[1] The effect of such deletion is that the Red Notice or Diffusion is deleted. There is no charge for the submission of a request.[2]

6.5

A request for deletion must be made to the Commission for the Control of Interpol's Files (CCF). The request is dealt with by the Requests Chamber. The Requests Chamber will consider whether the request is admissible (see **6.14–6.16** below) at the earliest opportunity and no later than one month from its receipt by the CCF.[3] If the request is admissible, it will examine whether the Red Notice or Diffusion was issued in compliance with Interpol's rules.

6.6

Before deciding whether to grant or refuse a request to delete a Red Notice or Diffusion, the Requests Chamber may seek additional information or clarification from the applicant, from the National Crime Bureau (NCB) of the state that asked the Red Notice or Diffusion to be issued, from the Interpol General Secretariat or from other entities concerned by the request (such as the NCBs of states that have been asked to extradite the applicant to the state seeking the applicant's surrender).[4]

1 Statute of the Commission for the Control of Interpol's Files, Article 29.
2 Ibid, Article 30(3).
3 Ibid, Article 32(1).
4 Ibid, Article 34.

6.7

The Requests Chamber shall examine a request on the basis of written submissions. There is no right to an oral hearing. Hearings may be held only if deemed necessary by the Requests Chamber for the examination of requests.[5]

6.8

The Requests Chamber shall then decide whether or not to grant the request to delete the Red Notice or Diffusion. If the request is granted, the Requests Chamber may also decide on other appropriate remedies to be granted by Interpol to the applicant. However, these remedies may only relate to Interpol's responsibilities in the particular case, and to the processing of data in the Interpol Information System.[6]

6.9

The Requests Chamber can make interim decisions. At any time during the proceedings, the Requests Chamber may decide on provisional measures to be taken by Interpol in relation to the processing of the data concerned in the request.[7]

6.10

Decisions of the Requests Chamber (whether a final decision on a request or an interim decision) will be provided to the General Secretariat within one month of the decision being made, and the General Secretariat shall implement the decision within one month of receiving it. A written copy of the decision will be provided to the applicant as well as the state that initially had the Red Notice or Diffusion issued.[8]

Pre-emptive requests

6.11

It can take a long time before the Requests Chamber decides whether to grant or refuse a request to delete a Red Notice or Diffusion. Article 32(1) of the Statute of the CCF states that the Requests Chamber shall decide whether a request is admissible at the earliest opportunity and no later than one month from its receipt by the CCF.[9] Article 40(2) states that the Requests Chamber shall decide on a request for the deletion of data within nine months from the

5 Ibid, Article 36.
6 Ibid, Article 39.
7 Ibid, Article 37.
8 Ibid, Article 41.
9 Ibid, Article 32(1).

date on which the request was declared admissible. The Requests Chamber does not meet frequently, but meets at least three times a year.

6.12

Because of this potential delay, many applicants prefer to make 'pre-emptive requests' to delete Red Notices. The term 'pre-emptive requests' is not used in the Statute of the CCF but is generally used to refer to requests not to issue a Red Notice or Diffusion in the event that a country seeks to have one issued. Interpol recognises the validity of such requests:

> 'Upon receipt of such requests, the Commission submits them, and any information provided, to the Interpol General Secretariat for its information and appropriate action, so that the information may be considered during future compliance reviews conducted by the Interpol General Secretariat if a request for police cooperation is received.'[10]

6.13

Individuals or entities who have made pre-emptive requests are free at any time to make an application for deletion of a Red Notice or Diffusion in the event that one is issued.

Admissibility

6.14

Rule 30(1) of the Operating Rules of the CCF makes clear that a request will only be admissible if the following conditions are met:

> '(a) the request includes a letter signed by the applicant, explaining the purpose of the request;
>
> (b) it is written in one of the Organization's working languages (Arabic, English, French and Spanish);
>
> (c) the request comes from the person whom it concerns, or from that person's duly authorized representative(s);
>
> (d) where the applicant is represented by a duly authorized representative, the request shall be accompanied by a power of attorney signed by the applicant authorizing his/her representative to access any information about him/her recorded in Interpol's files;

10 Interpol 2023, Interpol website, accessed 2 October 2023, https://www.interpol.int/en/Who-we-are/Commission-for-the-Control-of-INTERPOL-s-Files-CCF/How-to-submit-a-request.

(e) where the applicant is represented by a legal representative, the request shall be accompanied by the corresponding written declaration or certificate;

(f) where the applicant is an entity, the request shall be accompanied by documents showing that the individual who lodged the application on behalf of the entity has standing or authority to represent the entity, for example an extract from the Chamber of Commerce register or minutes of the governing body;

(g) the request shall be accompanied by a copy of a readable and non-redacted identity document belonging to the applicant in order to prove his/her identity. Where the applicant is an entity, the full name, date of incorporation or registration, the official registration number (if any), and the official address shall be provided;

(h) where the applicant submits a request for correction and/or deletion of information processed in the Interpol Information System, the request shall set out the reasons, and be accompanied by a summary of arguments in support of the request, making specific reference to any relevant attached document in the form provided for by the Secretariat. The Requests Chamber shall only take into consideration the attached documents which are or have been translated into one of Interpol's working languages, as described in paragraph 1(b) of the present Rule.'

6.15

The Operating rules of the CCF provide for the provision of further information by the applicant. Rule 30(2) states that:

> 'If, upon receipt of such request, further information is needed from the applicant to determine the admissibility of the request, the Requests Chamber shall invite the applicant to submit any missing or additional information within a given time limit. At the same time, the Commission shall inform the applicant that as a consequence of the failure to provide the information requested within the deadline that it specified, no admissibility decision nor further action will be taken in respect to the request concerned.'

6.16

Rule 30(4) of the Operating Rules of the CCF states that the Requests Chamber will not deal with requests where it considers them to be:

'(a) clearly unreasonable, for instance, because of their repetitive or systematic nature;

(b) not within the Requests Chamber's competence, as set out in the Statute.'

In these cases, the Requests Chamber is not obliged to grant the request or even reply to the applicant.

Revisiting a decision of the Requests Chamber

6.17

When a decision is made, it is final and binding on the applicant and on Interpol.[11] There is no appeal procedure.

6.18

However, in limited circumstances, an application can be made for a decision to be revisited. An application for a decision to be revisited will only be accepted where it is based on the discovery of facts which could have led the Requests Chamber to a different conclusion if that fact had been known at the time at which the request was being processed. Applications for revision must be made within six months after the discovery of the relevant fact(s).[12]

Interpol's general approach to the retention of data

6.19

Before considering the specific articles of the Rules on the Processing of Data (RPD) which relate to the removal of Red Notices and Diffusions from the Interpol database, it will be useful to consider Interpol's approach to the retention and deletion of 'data' in general. By so doing it is possible to identify general principles that are replicated in the specific provisions relating to Red Notices and Diffusions.

6.20

Article 51 of the RPD governs the deletion of data from Interpol's databases. 'Data' is defined in Article 1 of the RPD as:

> '... any item of information, irrespective of its source, pertaining to constituent elements of ordinary-law crimes, the investigation and prevention of such crimes, the prosecution of the offenders and punishment of the offences, and any information pertaining to missing persons and unidentified dead bodies.'

---

11 Statute of the Commission for the Control of Interpol's Files, Article 38.
12 Ibid, Article 40.

6.21

The deletion of 'data' is provided for in Article 51 of the RPD, which defines the circumstances in which data can be deleted. The circumstances can be divided into two categories: those that lead to automatic deletion and those where the General Secretariat may request a National Central Bureau (NCB) to delete data.

6.22

The circumstances that give rise to automatic deletion of data are as follows:

- Where the NCB that originally requested the data to be added requests for it to be removed. In such circumstances, deletion will be automatic (RPD Article 51(1)).
- Data will be deleted on expiry of the initial retention period if the NCB, national entity or international entity has not indicated the need to retain the data (RPD Article 51(2)).

6.23

RPD Article 51(1) is self-explanatory and – as already observed in the introduction to this chapter – any individual subject to a Red Notice or Diffusion (or his legal representative) must give careful consideration to whether there is any prospect of persuading the authority that has issued the Red Notice or Diffusion to withdraw their request.

6.24

RPD Article 51(2) requires a little further consideration. It is an important principle of the RPD that Interpol is not entitled to hold data arbitrarily or indefinitely. Article 10(1) of the RPD provides:

> 'The processing of data in the Interpol Information System may only be carried out for a given, explicit purpose which is in conformity with the Organization's aims and activities.'

6.25

The RPD seeks to ensure conformity with Article 10 by providing that data is only held in Interpol databases for the time required to achieve the purpose for which they were recorded. The RPD seeks to advance this goal by setting time limits on the initial period of retention and providing for periodic assessments. However, it is important to note that the focus of Article 51 is to encourage NCB's to actively consider whether the continued retention of data is justified. Furthermore, the RPD provide a high degree of flexibility allowing NCBs to retain data beyond the initial retention period (albeit with a requirement to provide reasons) and even retain data where the NCB believes retaining the data on the Interpol database to be 'of interest for the purposes of international police cooperation'.

General Secretariat's discretion to request the deletion of data

6.26

When the General Secretariat has reason to believe that the purpose for which data were recorded has been achieved or that the data no longer meet the minimum conditions for recording, it will merely request the NCB to 'examine the need' to retain the data.

6.27

At the very least in terms of Interpol's Constitution and procedural rules the organisation places a high degree of trust and responsibility in its member countries to ensure that data recorded in its databases is held to further the overarching aims of the organisation as defined in Article 2.

6.28

The next section of this chapter will examine the extent to which Interpol offers oversight and, where necessary, remedies to those affected by its important role in assisting NCBs to both locate and detain individuals sought for prosecution or to enforce outstanding sentences.

Specific approach to Red Notices

6.29

Article 81(3) of the RPD gives the General Secretariat the discretion to cancel a Red Notice. It provides as follows:

> '(3) The General Secretariat shall cancel a notice if:
>
> (a) the purpose of the cooperation request or the alert on the basis of which the notice was published has been achieved, and this information has been confirmed by the source National Central Bureau or international entity; or
>
> (b) if this request or alert is linked to one or several other requests or alerts whose purpose has been achieved and without which it cannot be maintained; or
>
> (c) the notice no longer meets the conditions for publishing a notice; or

(d) the National Central Bureau or international entity that requested the notice obtains data allowing it to carry out the required action but has not taken any steps to this end and, after being consulted, has not provided reasonable grounds for its lack of action.'

6.30

It is clear that the General Secretariat's discretion to cancel a notice is limited. Where the issuing NCB wishes to maintain the Red Notice, the only ground upon which the General Secretariat will intervene is pursuant to Article 81(3)(c). Such intervention is limited to a consideration of whether the necessary antecedent conditions for publishing a notice are present. Those conditions are defined by Article 83 of the RPD and were considered in Chapter 3.

6.31

The role of the General Secretariat in relation to Diffusions is even more limited. Article 100 of the RPD provides for the withdrawal or suspension of a Diffusion. However, the Article simply imposes upon the NCB an obligation to withdraw it once 'the purpose of the Diffusion has been achieved'.

Challenges based on Article 2 of the Interpol Constitution

6.32

It is clear that non-compliance with Article 2 of the Interpol Constitution is a valid ground of challenge. This is because Article 34(1) of the RPD states that 'the National Central Bureau, national entity or international entity shall ensure that the data are in compliance with Article 2 of [Interpol's] Constitution.'

6.33

Article 2(1) of the Interpol Constitution provides that Interpol's aims include:

> 'To ensure and promote the widest possible mutual assistance between all criminal police authorities within the limits of the laws existing in the different countries and in the spirit of the "Universal Declaration of Human Rights".'

6.34

Challenges to Red Notices and Diffusions under Article 2 of the Interpol Constitution must be based on the assertion that the Red Notice or Diffusion is not issued within the spirit of the Universal Declaration of Human Rights. This is because the Requests Chamber has made clear that:

> 'as a general practice, it does not enter into an inquiry designed to take decisions on application of national procedural law. The Commission does not function in a manner akin to that in which a domestic appellate court re-examines the actions of a domestic court of first instance.'[13]

Human rights violations that offend Article 2

6.35

The rights alleged to be at risk by the issuance of a Red Notice or Diffusion do not have to be contained within the Universal Declaration of Human Rights (UNDHR). The wording of Article 2 is wider than this, as a Red Notice or Diffusion will offend Article 2 if it is not 'within the spirit' of the UNDHR. Accordingly, challenges can be made to the Requests Chamber on the basis that the Red Notice or Diffusion offends a right enshrined in another international human rights agreement. This is clear because the Requests Chamber has quoted within the 'applicable framework' section of a number of its decisions rights contained within the International Covenant on Civil and Political Rights (ICCPR) and European Convention of Human Rights (ECHR) that enshrine rights not given equal protection by the UNDHR.[14]

6.36

The following paragraphs address examples of specific human rights that have been considered by the Requests Chamber when making decisions on challenges to Red Notices and Diffusions under Article 2.

6.37

Article 3 of the UNDHR states that 'We all have the right to life, and to live in freedom and safety.' In CCF Decision Excerpt Number 17 of 2018, the Requests Chamber deleted a Red Notice on the basis of the risk that an applicant's right to life (as well as their right to freedom from torture and right to a fair trial) would be infringed if they were returned to the country that sought the execution of the Red Notice.

6.38

It is not entirely clear how the Requests Chamber will deal with an allegation that an applicant's right to life will be infringed because they may be subject to the death penalty if returned to the country that issued the Red Notice. In CCF Decision Excerpt Number 6 of 2018, the Requests Chamber considered

---

13 CCF Decision Excerpt Number 12 of 2017.

14 See, for example, CCF Decision Excerpt Number 6 of 2019. In this decision, the Requests Chamber quoted the right of *non bis in idem* (ie double jeopardy) enshrined within Article 14(7) of the ICCPR and Article 4(1) of Protocol 7 of the ECHR, as part of the applicable framework to the case even though this right is not given equal protection by the UNDHR. The request was not granted on the facts of that case.

an argument that the applicant would be subject to the death penalty if returned to the country seeking execution of the Red Notice. In this decision, the Requests Chamber did not explicitly state one way or the other whether the death penalty offends Article 2 of the Interpol constitution (and in any event, the issue fell away in the decision because the country seeking execution of the Red Notice had previously provided an assurance that the applicant would not be subject to the death penalty). However, it is notable that the Requests Chamber relied on the following in its findings:

> 'The Commission carefully studied the Applicant's claims that he may be submitted to death penalty upon return. It underlined that further to international human rights standards, as expressed for instance in the General Comment No 6 of the United Nations Human Rights Committee on the right to life, death penalty may be applied by non-abolitionist states only for the most serious crimes and may never be applied to minor defendants, pregnant women, mentally retarded persons. Moreover, extradition should not take place from a country that abolished the death penalty to a country that still applies it, unless assurances have been given by the requesting country that such penalty will not be implemented.'[15]

6.39

This appears to suggest a nuanced approach to the issue. It suggests that whilst the death penalty does not offend Article 2 of the Interpol Constitution in and of itself, the death penalty may offend Article 2 if it is sought to be applied in particular circumstances (ie for a crime that is not 'most serious' and/or applied to children, pregnant women or those with mental impairments).

6.40

The authors question however whether a Red Notice or Diffusion concerning a case where the imposition of the death penalty is likely (and no assurance that the death penalty will be applied is forthcoming or likely to be forthcoming) can be challenged through Article 35 of the RPD. Article 35(1) of the RPD states that:

> 'In conformity with Article 5(3) of the present Rules, prior to any recording of data in a police database, the National Central Bureau, national entity or international entity shall ensure that the data are of interest for the purposes of international police cooperation.'

In CCF Decision Excerpt Number 1 of 2019, the Requests Chamber 'expressed strong concern' that a Red Notice concerning an offence of 'uttering unfunded

15 CCF Decision Excerpt Number 6 of 2018, §54.

cheques' 'may not be of interest for the purpose of international police cooperation' because:

> 'most Member Countries do not qualify the mere act of issuing an unfunded cheque as criminal, and an inability to repay a debt has been decriminalised in most national legal systems'.[16]

The consequence was that 'the lack of dual criminality would prevent most national authorities from entering into international police cooperation for such a case'.[17] This decision can arguably be applied to the death penalty. Most countries will not extradite an individual to a country for an offence where the death penalty could be imposed unless there is an assurance that the death penalty will not be applied in that individual's case. Therefore, in cases where the death penalty could be imposed and no assurance is forthcoming, it may be arguable that the Red Notice or Diffusion would be contrary to Article 35(1) of the RPD on the basis that most national authorities would be prevented from entering into international police cooperation for such a case.

6.41

Article 5 of the UNDHR states that 'No one shall be subjected to torture or to cruel, inhuman or degrading treatment or punishment.' The Requests Chamber has granted a number of requests to delete Red Notices on the basis that they are incompatible with the applicants' right to freedom from torture.

- In CCF Decision Excerpt Number 14 of 2018, the Requests Chamber deleted a Red Notice where it found that the applicant would be exposed to torture if he was returned to the country that had issued the Red Notice. The applicant had argued that he would be exposed to a high risk of torture in order to obtain forced confessions.
- In CCF Decision Excerpt Number 15 of 2018, the Requests Chamber deleted a Red Notice on the basis of the risk that the applicant would be subjected to torture. The applicant had argued that the conditions of his detention would constitute inhuman or degrading treatment, but the Requests Chamber did not specifically address these allegations.

6.42

If an applicant is sought pursuant to a Red Notice or Diffusion in a case where torture has been used to obtain evidence, this will be sufficient for a successful challenge pursuant to Article 2.

- In CCF Decision Excerpt Number 8 of 2018 concerned a Red Notice in respect of a case where the applicant alleged that his confession had been obtained as a result of torture. In considering that request, the Requests

16 CCF Decision Excerpt Number 1 of 2019, §28.
17 Ibid, §25.

Chamber confirmed that Article 2 'respects the fundamental rights of the data subjects, such as the right no[t] to face a trial tainted by the use of evidence obtained through torture'.[18]

6.43

Article 10 of the UNDHR states that:

> 'Everyone accused of a crime has the right to a fair and public trial, and those that try us should be independent and not influenced by others.'

There have been a number of decisions where the Requests Chamber has granted requests to delete Red Notices on the basis that the applicants' fair trial rights would be breached.

6.44

It appears that the threshold required for the Requests Chamber to grant a request to delete a Red Notice or Diffusion based on fair trial rights is very high. This is because the Request Chamber has stated in a number of decisions that the applicant needs to demonstrate a likelihood of 'flagrant denial' of those fair trial rights.[19]

6.45

Article 25 of the Universal Declaration of Human Rights states that:

> 'Everyone has the right to a standard of living adequate for the health and well-being of himself and of his family, including food, clothing, housing and medical care and necessary social services, and the right to security in the event of unemployment, sickness, disability, widowhood, old age or other lack of livelihood in circumstances beyond his control.'.

6.46

There is one decision where the Requests Chamber found that interference with this right constituted a breach of Article 2 of the Interpol Constitution. However, it is clear from that decision that the interference with the applicant's health must be extremely serious:

> '[T]he Commission noted that clear elements were presented by the Applicant and confirmed by the [...] Court (which had the power to weigh in all factors at hand) that an extradition proceeding could irreparably harm the Applicant and would be life-threatening according to medical professionals. It noted that added to the fact

18 CCD Decision Excerpt Number 8 of 2018, §43.

19 See, for example, CCF Decision Excerpt Number 5 of 2018, §35, and CCF Decision Excerpt Number 18 of 2018, §51.

that the individual is seriously facing death within the next five years, the prospective threat to the right to be prevented from treatments degrading one's health as a result of an extradition proceedings appears substantial to a point that cannot be safeguarded by Article 29(2) of the UDHR.

The Commission noted that though the NCB of […] proposed that the Applicant be provided with the assistance of a doctor and/or nurse in his journey to […], that no specific response appears to have been provided to explain palliative means or alternative avenues to prevent the potentially life-threatening irreparable harm that would be caused by the extradition procedure, according to medical professionals.'[20]

6.47

The right of *non bis in idem* (ie double jeopardy), enshrined within Article 14(7) of the ICCPR and Article 4(1) of Protocol 7 of the ECHR, is a right that the Requests Chamber engages with when determining whether a Red Notice or Diffusion is compatible with Article 2 of the Interpol Constitution.[21]

6.48

It should be noted however, that the Requests Chamber will only engage with the principle of double jeopardy if either: (a) the second prosecution occurs within the same country as the first prosecution; or (b) if the prosecutions occur in different states, that there is an international agreement between state A and state B setting out that the double jeopardy principle applies where one prosecution is in state A and the second prosecution is in state B. If two prosecutions that would engage the double jeopardy rule occur in different states and there is no such international agreement between state A and state B, the Requests Chamber will refuse to find that the potential double jeopardy amounts to a breach of Article 2 of the Interpol constitution. It will instead leave the application of the double jeopardy principle to the relevant national courts to be decided either at trial or in extradition proceedings.[22]

6.49

There are a number of qualified rights that applicants may seek to rely on when challenging a Red Notice or Diffusion under Article 2. For example, in CCF Decision Excerpt Number 9 of 2017, the applicant sought to argue that the Red Notice was incompatible with his right to travel (ie his right 'to leave any country, including his own, and to return to his country') under Article 13 of the UNDHR. However, the Requests Chamber gave this argument short shrift, simply noting the following:

20 CCF Decision Excerpt Number 5 of 2019, §30–31.
21 See, for example, CCF Decision Excerpt Number 6 of 2019.
22 CCF Decision Excerpt Number 9 of 2017, §30.

'[The right to travel] can be subject to lawful, necessary, and proportionate limitations as envisioned in UDHR Article 29. Sovereign states are therefore not prevented for instance from enacting legal requirements regarding access to their territory or from issuing an order to request the arrest of an individual suspected or convicted of having committed a crime.'[23]

6.50

It is clear that the Requests Chamber will be very slow to find that the existence of a Red Notice or Diffusion is a disproportionate interference with a right that can be qualified by a lawful, necessary and proportionate limitation. The Requests Chamber has already stated that 'as a general practice, it does not enter into an inquiry designed to take decisions on application of national procedural law',[24] and so it seems to follow that as a general practice it will be very slow to take decisions on the proportionality of decisions taken by competent national bodies. In any event, the public interest in ensuring that criminals are bought to justice is very high, and so the maintenance of a Red Notice or Diffusion will in the vast majority of cases be a proportionate interference with qualified rights. It appears therefore, that an argument that the maintenance of a Red Notice or Diffusion is a disproportionate interference with a qualified right such that there is a violation of Article 2 of Interpol's Constitution must require truly exceptional features to be successful.

Approach taken by the Requests Chamber in assessing Article 2 challenges

6.51

The Requests Chamber has made clear that in an Article 2 challenge the burden is on the applicant to convincingly demonstrate, with evidence, the likelihood that a flagrant denial of their human rights has taken place (or would take place if they were returned to the country seeking execution of the Red Notice or Diffusion):

'In order to respect the spirit of the UDHR while at the same time respecting the limited role of the Commission, the simple assertion of a violation of rights cannot rise to the level of an Article 2 violation. Rather, in carrying out an Article 2 analysis, the Commission considers all relevant information to determine whether the Applicant has convincingly demonstrated the likelihood that flagrant denial of her human rights took place.'[25]

---

23 CCF Decision Excerpt Number 9 of 2017, §34.
24 See **6.34** and CCF Decision Excerpt Number 12 of 2017.
25 CCF Decision Excerpt Number 13 of 2017, §46.

6.52

The evidence that the applicant's human rights would be breached must be specific to the applicant:

> 'The Commission recalled that it is not its role to assess a Country's law enforcement or judicial system in abstracto. Hence, it does not rely on general statements concerning the situation in a country and only examines the compliance of data with INTERPOL's rules on the basis of specific information related to the case under study or to the person who is the subject of the request'.[26]

6.53

In most successful Article 2 challenges, numerous sources of evidence are deployed to persuade the Requests Chamber that the maintenance of the Red Notice or Diffusion would be contrary to Article 2. The Requests Chamber has, in its decisions, relied on a number of different sources of evidence to find that a flagrant breach of an applicant's human rights is likely. These sources include:

(1) **Detailed statements from applicants:** The Requests Chamber will take into account statements from applicants setting out in detail the alleged human rights violations against them. For example, in CCF Decision Excerpt Number 8 of 2018, the Requests Chamber referred to a document in which the applicant 'meticulously detailed the alleged torture acts he claimed were imposed on him in custody in order to extract accusatory statements from him'.

(2) **Expert evidence relating to the applicant's case:** The Requests Chamber has considered specific expert report tailored to the applicant's case. For example, in CCF Decision Excerpt Number 5 of 2019, the Requests Chamber considered whether a Red Notice was compatible with an applicant's right to security in the event of sickness. In deciding that the Red Notice would be incompatible with this right, the Requests Chamber considered a medical report of his treating physician. Expert evidence that an applicant may wish to rely on might include, for example, reports addressing the likelihood that the applicant would be tortured, the likelihood of a fair trial and the conditions of detention the applicant could expect to face.

(3) **Findings of the UN Human Rights Council (UNHRC):** The UNHRC is an intergovernmental body that aims to promote and protect human rights around the glove. The UNHRC has a complaints procedure whereby any individual, group of individuals or non-governmental organisation can submit a complaint against any of the member states of

26 CCF Decision Excerpt Number 3 of 2018, §50.

the UN. When deciding on requests to delete Red Notices and Diffusions, the Requests Chamber has taken into account findings made by the UNHRC relating to the case at hand. For example, in CCF Decision Excerpt Number 14 of 2018, the Requests Chamber 'paid particular attention' to a UNHRC report analysing the possible human rights violations the applicant would be subjected to if returned to the country seeking execution of the Red Notice.

(4) **Decisions of competent national courts:** Decisions of competent national courts indicating that the applicant's human rights would be breached if they were surrendered to the country seeking execution of the red notice have been taken into account by the Requests Chamber. Typically, such decisions arise in the course of extradition proceedings. Where an applicant seeks to rely on a decision of a national court refusing extradition, the Requests Chamber will only give weight to it if extradition was refused on human rights grounds.

In CCF Decision Excerpt Number 3 of 2018, the Requests Chamber stated:[27]

> '[I]n the present case, the decision of Country B's court, authenticated by the NCB of Country B, denies the extradition of the Applicant to Country A, on the basis of the risks that he would be submitted to inhuman/degrading treatment in the context of his detention and that he would face an unfair trial. These fundamental human rights are enshrined in Articles 3 and 6 of the ECHR, to which the decision directly refers, and they are equally protected through Articles 5 and 10 of the UDHR. Moreover, the decision highlights that the Applicant would face heightened individual risks on account of his race, religion, and nationality, due to systemic discriminations towards … and individuals of … origin in the justice and prison systems of Country A. The Commission noted that this decision is built upon on a comprehensive analysis of supporting evidence, …
>
> Although this decision is not legally binding on other States, who remain at liberty to decide sovereignly to cooperate on this case and extradite the Applicant should he be later apprehended on their territories, the conclusions drawn by Country B's independent judicial body on the risks faced by the Applicant in case of extradition cannot be ignored by the Commission in the course of its own review.'.

Similarly, in CCF Decision Excerpt Number 5 of 2019, the Requests Chamber stated:[28]

27 CCF Decision Excerpt Number 3 of 2018, §51–52.
28 CCF Decision Excerpt Number 5 of 2019, §26–31.

'When assessing extradition refusals, the Commission recalled its position that the mere existence of an extradition refusal by another member states does not necessarily mean that the purpose of the data is no longer valid. In cases where this situation arises, the Commission pays specific attention as to the grounds for the extradition refusal, and whether it is purely procedural or connected to issues linked with analogous principles which are part of INTERPOL's rules.

In light of the terms of Article 2 of INTERPOL's Constitution, the Commission noted that the matter indeed raised issues related to the right to health and security in the event of sickness (Article 25 of the UDHR) and also with the right to be prevented from degrading treatment (Article 5 of the UDHR). At the same time, it recalled that the UDHR also provides that all human rights set forth in this document may be limited for reasons of public order (Article 29(2) of the UDHR).

As such, the Commission recalled the decision (also cited by [...] Court), *N v United Kingdom*, which called to: "search for a fair balance between the demands of the general interest of the community and the requirements of the protection of the individual's fundamental rights'" and noted that "neither the decision to remove an alien who was suffering from a serious illness to a country where the facilities for the treatment of that illness were inferior to those available in the Contracting State, nor the fact that the individual's circumstances, including his or her life expectancy, would be significantly reduced, constituted in themselves 'exceptional' circumstances sufficient to give rise to a breach of Article 3."

The Commission found that though distinct from the matter at hand, it concurred with the approach taken to assess the risks of degrading treatments, and found that it could shed some light as to the approach to take in the present matter. It noted that other decisions had followed in the footsteps of this one at the European level, including in *Paposhvili v Belgium*.

Therefore, the Commission noted that clear elements were presented by the Applicant and confirmed by the [...] Court (which had the power to weigh in all factors at hand) that an extradition proceeding could irreparably harm the Applicant and would be life-threatening according to medical professionals. It noted that added to the fact that the individual is seriously facing death within the next five years, the prospective threat to the right to be prevented from treatments degrading one's health as a result of an extradition proceedings appears substantial to a point that cannot be safeguarded by Article 29(2) of the UDHR.'

(5) **General reports from international and national bodies:** Applicants can support their case by reference to general reports from international and national bodies, if these reports are numerous, reliable, and consistent. However, the Requests Chamber has indicated that because of the general nature of such reports, their main use to an applicant will be to bolster evidence that has already been submitted:

> 'The Commission underlined that it is not its role to assess a country's law enforcement or judicial system *in abstracto*, and that therefore it does not usually rely on general statements concerning the situation in a country to ground its findings. It rather examines the compliance of data with INTERPOL's rules based on specific information related to the case under study or to the person who is the subject of the request. Yet in some instances where multiple international and national reliable sources all present a consistent, documented, and concurring account of a situation characterized by serious human rights violations, the Applicant's individual allegations echoing such a context may then appear as reinforced and be seen as additionally supported.'[29]

(6) **Unsatisfactory explanations from countries seeking execution of a Red Notice or Diffusion:**

If a country seeking execution of a Red Notice is unable or unwilling to provide a satisfactory answer to an applicant's allegations of human rights abuses, the Requests Chamber may take this into account in support of the applicant's case.

In CCF Decision Excerpt Number 8 of 2018, the Requests Chamber was not satisfied that it had a sufficient answer regarding the evidence the case against the applicant was based on (other than a confession allegedly obtained through torture) and why there had been delays in the case. The Requests Chamber gave weight to this.[30]

> 'The Commission recalled that although its function is not to evaluate the reliability or the quality of evidence in a manner that should be undertaken at trial or during extradition hearings, its role is nonetheless to review whether the NCB provided sufficient information linking the wanted individual to the charges against him. In this case, the Commission held that the fact that the prosecution appears to rely mostly – if not only – on a confession which has been recanted due to its alleged extraction under torture, raise strong concerns as to the legality, adequacy and sufficiency of the evidence adduced. Considering this, along with the long and unaccounted delays in the investigation before

29 CCF Decision Excerpt Number 6 of 2019, §32.
30 CCF Decision Excerpt Number 8 of 2018, §44.

the inclusion of the Applicant, the Commission concluded that the flaws identified in the case and their impact on the Applicant's fundamental rights raised doubts regarding the compliance of the data with Article 2 of INTERPOL's Constitution'.

By contrast however, a satisfactory explanation from the country seeking execution of the Red Notice will often be given significant weight by the Requests Chamber. For example, in CCF Decision Excerpt Number 2 of 2018, the applicant submitted that the maintenance of the Red Notice was incompatible with his right to a fair trial. In dismissing the request, the Requests Chamber relied heavily on the explanations provided by the country seeking execution of the Red Notice:[31]

> 'In this case, as a result of its review of the above mentioned elements, the Commission finds that the information provided by the NCB of Country A, through the provision of copies of all the court decisions, is sufficient to indicate:
>
> - the possible effective and personal participation of the Applicant to the acts for which he has been accused in all five cases,
> - the appropriate implementation of national procedures, which led to the Applicant's conviction in absentia in all five cases,
> - the possibility for the Applicant to be tried again in his presence, with the assistance of a lawyer of his choosing, for all five cases.'

Challenges based on Article 3 of the Interpol Constitution

6.54

Many successful applications for the deletion of Red Notices and Diffusions are based on the submission that the Red Notice or Diffusion offends Article 3 of Interpol's Constitution.

6.55

Article 3 of the Interpol Constitution provides as follows:

> 'It is strictly forbidden for the Organization to undertake any intervention or activities of a political, military, religious or racial character.'

31 CCF Decision Excerpt Number 2 of 2018, §38.

Development of Article 3

6.56

At the 1951 General Assembly in Lisbon a short but important resolution was passed signalling Interpol's attempt to maintain its political neutrality. The resolution included a recommendation that Interpol members (and specifically heads of NCBs) should:

> 'see that no request for information, notice of persons wanted and, above all, no request for provisional arrest for offences of a predominantly political, racial or religious character, is ever sent to the International Bureau or to the National Central Bureaus, even if – in the requesting country – the facts amount to an offence against the ordinary law'.

6.57

However, the resolution went further than simply relying on Interpol members or the heads of NCBs to uphold their obligations under the Constitution. It empowered the President of Interpol (known at the time as the 'Chief of the International Bureau') to intervene where there was any doubt with regard to the political, racial or religious character of a request. The resolution indicated that, in such cases, the President, in conjunction with the Secretary General, could suspend any request whilst further enquiries were made of the requesting authority.

6.58

This was an important development in Interpol's procedures. Firstly, it strengthened Article 3 of Interpol's Constitution by introducing the principle of 'predominance'. This ensures that requests by NCBs must be considered contextually to determine whether they are of a political, racial or religious character – an important safeguard as regimes with scant regard for fundamental rights are likely to describe even the most naked political persecution as an ordinary criminal prosecution. Secondly, the resolution signalled a willingness on behalf of the organisation itself not to simply act as a conduit but to provide some (albeit limited) oversight of the use of its databases.

6.59

A further resolution was adopted by the General Assembly in 1984 which gave guidance as to how Interpol would interpret Article 3. The resolution afforded Interpol greater flexibility to allow its databases to be used to combat terrorism. It drew a distinction between offences which are 'by their very nature political' (eg membership of a particular prohibited organisation or the expression of particular political views) and offences which are politically motivated but have 'no direct connection with the political life of the offender's country or cause for which they are fighting'. The resolution indicated that offences falling into the former category would fall within the scope of Article 3 (and thus not be suitable for Interpol involvement) whereas the latter category may fall outside the scope of Article 3. The resolution further stated that offences were more likely to fall into this latter category where offences are committed outside the area of the political dispute and constitute a serious threat to personal freedom, life or property.

6.60

This more nuanced approach to the scope of Article 3 was clearly intended to provide the organisation with sufficient flexibility to allow its resources to be used to combat terrorism. The resolution provided even more flexibility by drawing a further distinction between situations where an NCB is seeking to prevent terrorist activity (as compared to investigating or prosecuting terrorist offences). The resolution states that:

> 'When prevention is involved there is nothing to hinder the circulation of technical information, even if this has been obtained in connection with politically motivated cases.'

6.61

Notwithstanding the necessary steps that Interpol has taken to reduce the scope of Article 3, it remains an important procedural protection and can be invoked successfully to cause a Red Notice to be lifted or a Diffusion to be deleted.

Predominance test

6.62

The test for whether a Red Notice of Diffusion violates Article 3 is called the 'predominance test'. The test, which is highly factually specific, requires the Requests Chamber to:

> 'evaluate all relevant information and pertinent elements, as provided by the rules, to determine whether the offense is of a predominantly political character.'[32]

6.63

There must be predominance. The Requests Chamber has acknowledged that in some cases, there may be some political elements around a case, but not sufficient to establish any predominance over the substantive ordinary criminal law dimension of the case.[33]

32 CCF Decision Excerpt Number 2 of 2017.
33 CCF Decision Excerpt Number 9 of 2019.

6.64

Article 34(3) of the RPD provides a non-exhaustive list of factors that the Requests Chamber will consider in determining whether the case is of a predominantly political character:

> '(3) To determine whether data comply with Article 3 of the Constitution, all relevant elements shall be examined, such as:
>
> (a) nature of the offence, namely the charges and underlying facts;
>
> (b) status of the persons concerned;
>
> (c) identity of the source of the data;
>
> (d) the position expressed by another NCB or another international entity;
>
> (e) obligations under international law;
>
> (f) implications for the neutrality of the Organization;
>
> (g) the general context of the case.'

(a) Nature of the offence, namely the charges and underlying facts

6.65

In relation to the nature of the offence, Interpol has made clear that it is essential to verify two particular features of any case: 'first, that the underlying facts match the charges in the particular case; and secondly, that the facts link the individual concerned to the charges'. In order for it to be able to carry out the assessment of whether an offence is predominantly political, Interpol requires that the activities and/or role of an individual should be explained, and that it is not sufficient for a state simply to assert that the individual 'was involved in [insert crime]'.[34]

6.66

As stated at **6.59** above, a resolution adopted by the General Assembly in 1984 draws a distinction between offences which are 'by their very nature political' (eg membership of a particular prohibited organisation or the expression of particular political views) and offences which are politically motivated but have 'no direct connection with the political life of the offender's country or cause for which they are fighting'. The resolution indicated that offences falling into the former category would fall within the scope of Article 3 (and thus not be suitable for Interpol involvement) whereas the latter category may fall outside the scope of Article 3.

---

34 Interpol Repository of Practice: Application of Article 3, 3.13.

6.67

Whether an offence is political in nature will require an examination of the facts. However, particular categories of offences which, depending on the facts, may be seen by the Requests Chamber to be predominantly political include:

(a) offences concerning freedom of expression;

(b) offences concerning freedom of assembly and freedom of association;

(c) offences against the security of the state;

(d) offences committed in the context of an unconstitutional seizure of power;

(e) membership of a terrorist organisation;

(f) election crimes;

(g) illegal emigration;

(h) purely military offences;

(i) purely religious or racial offences, such as membership of a prohibited religious organisation.

(b) Status of the persons concerned

6.68

The status of the person concerned refers to a person's occupation or role within a particular group (eg a protest group), as well as the question of whether they are acting in a professional or purely private capacity.

6.69

An individual's status as a politician is a very significant factor that the Requests Chamber will take into account. In a case where a politician or former politician is sought by their own country, the country requesting execution of a Red Notice may be asked to provide evidence, such as evidence of personal gain or that the offence is considered an ordinary law crime. A Red Notice alleging a failure by politicians to comply with administrative or political procedurals will generally be considered predominantly political.[35]

6.70

Where politicians or former politicians are sought by other countries, Interpol considers a number of criteria:

35 Ibid, 3.1.

> 'This scenario may raise a number of difficulties such as possible application of immunity under international law. In application of the principles enumerated in the ICJ Yerodia case, and based on INTERPOL practice, the following criteria are to be examined: (1) The position of the wanted person. Here, a general distinction is made between Head of State/Government and Minister of Foreign Affairs, on the one hand, and other State officials on the other. In general, only the former enjoy full immunity under international law; (2) Whether the person is currently in office; (3) The identity of the source of data, ie whether it was an NCB or an international tribunal (in the latter case, the individual may not enjoy immunity under international law); (4) Whether the country where the individual served as a politician objects to the processing of data.'[36]

(c) Identity of the source of the data

6.71

Insofar as the source of the data is concerned, the main distinction is between NCBs and international organisations. This is because international organisations are often politically neutral, whereas NCBs will not be:

> 'If an international tribunal such as the International Criminal Tribunal for the Former Yugoslavia (ICTY) requests the publication of a red notice for person Y on a charge of "genocide", the Organization would usually conclude, on the basis of another element (identity of the source of data) that Article 3 does not apply unless there is any specific doubt in relation to a particular item of data. The rationale for such a determination is the independence of the International Tribunal and its status under international law (eg in the case of ICTY, the fact that it was established by the United Nations Security Council acting under Chapter VII of the United Nations Charter), which guarantees its political neutrality, combined with the nature of the offence (element 1) as serious international crimes (see General Assembly Report AGN/63/RAP No 13 (1994) adopted by Resolution AGN/63/RES/9).'[37]

6.72

Accordingly, applicants may wish to bolster their cases under Article 3 with evidence that demonstrates, where appropriate, a state's political motivation in seeking execution of the Red Notice or Diffusion.

---

36 Ibid, 3.1.

37 Ibid, paragraph 30.

(d) The position expressed by another NCB or another international entity

6.73

The Requests Chamber will pay particular attention to the position expressed by another NCB or other international entity. However, this does not mean that any protest to the Red Notice or Diffusion expressed by such bodies will have decisive weight: the Requests Chamber will need to scrutinise the specific arguments raised by the body.[38]

(e) Obligations under international law

6.74

Depending on the specific obligation, obligations under international law can either lead the Requests Chamber to conclude that a specific case is predominantly political, or conclude that it is not.

6.75

For example, it is a norm of international law that Heads of State benefit from immunity whilst in office (see **6.70** above). Therefore, the Requests Chamber would likely conclude in such a situation that the case is predominantly political.

6.76

On the other hand, if there is an international agreement seeking to limit particular behaviour, then a case concerning an offence designed to combat this behaviour may help persuade the Requests Chamber to decide that the case is not predominantly political. Interpol gives the following example:

> 'If NCB X seeks the arrest with a view to extradition of person Y on a charge of "exporting controlled commodities without a licence" and the summary of facts states that the products illegally exported had both civilian and military applications, particularly in the case of nuclear weapons, the Organization would usually conclude, on the basis of another element (obligations under international law) that Article 3 does not apply. The rationale for such a determination is that the international community, by means of various international instruments, has undertaken to effectively control and combat the illegal transfer of weapons and dual use goods/technology that pose a particular risk to international security (eg United Nations Security Council Resolution S/RES/1540 adopted under Chapter VII of the United Nations Charter, calling upon States to "adopt and enforce appropriate effective laws which prohibit any non-State actor to [sic]

38 Ibid, paragraph 30.

manufacture, acquire ... nuclear, chemical or biological weapons ...").'.[39]

(f) Implications for the neutrality of the Organization

6.77

Interpol will refuse to intervene in a particular case where it is clear that the matter has become an international dispute which requires two States to either come to an agreement or litigate a case under International Law. If Interpol did intervene in such a case, Interpol would be seen to be taking sides, which is obviously incompatible with its neutrality.

6.78

One example of this approach is the *Rainbow Warrior* case. In that case, the French foreign intelligence agency (DGSE) sank the Greenpeace ship 'The Rainbow Warrior' when it was docked in a port in New Zealand. As a result of the incident, New Zealand asked Interpol to issue Red Notices against the French individuals involved, for crimes including murder and arson. Initially, Interpol complied with these requests. However, Interpol ceased to cooperate further once the dispute became a matter for negotiation and settlement by the two states involved.[40]

(g) The general context of the case

6.79

The last factor listed in Article 34(3) is the general context of the case. Often, this refers to key political events that have taken place in a state or an ongoing political situation. Interpol gives two examples demonstrating this:[41]

> 'A red notice was requested by an NCB for the former President of the country, on charges of embezzlement. The individual was accused of approving a series of economic decisions that severely undermined the national treasury. The General Secretariat denied publication after concluding that the measures taken by the individual were of a political nature, adopted in the context of a difficult economic situation. This conclusion was reached after considering the general context of the case (eg previous occurrence of a coup d'état which deposed the individual, and the support of international financial institutions for the measures he adopted), and the fact that the individual derived no personal benefit.'

39 Ibid, paragraph 30.
40 Ibid, paragraph 30.
41 Ibid, 3.1, p 13.

> 'A red notice request and an IPCQ diffusion were sent by an NCB seeking the arrest and extradition of an individual wanted for financial crimes. The individual concerned was the former prime minister of the country, who had recently lost the election to the presidency and remained a major opponent to the current regime. In addition, at the time when the data were processed, the political situation in the country was volatile and demonstrations for and against the government were common. Considering the status of the individual concerned, and bearing in mind the general context of the case, notably the ongoing political situation in the country, it was concluded that the case was of a predominantly political nature as understood in Article 3 of the Constitution.'

6.80

The general context of the case may include whether the state that seeks execution of the Red Notice or Diffusion has a reputation for disguising political attacks on individuals as Red Notices for seemingly legitimate offences. In CCF Decision Excerpt Number 13 of 2019, a Red Notice was deleted after the applicant claimed that the Red Notice was issued as a politically motivated attack against him.

Challenges based on breaches of the RPD

6.81

The RPD contains 135 Articles with appendices. Many of the rules are inward facing in the sense that they provide relatively precise, technical guidance as to how data is to be processed by NCBs and Interpol. The majority of these rules do not lend themselves to being deployed on behalf of applicants who seek the deletion of their data processed by Interpol, including the deletion of Red Notices or Diffusions.

6.82

Additionally, a review of all 135 Articles is plainly beyond the scope of this work. Nonetheless, the authors have found that Articles 12 and 82 (and by extension Article 99) of the RPD can provide practitioners with a helpful template for making representations on the basis that the request for or circulation of a Red Notice or Diffusion is, in any given case, defective and in breach of the RPD for a wide variety of fact sensitive reasons.

6.83

Rules based challenges to Red Notices and Diffusions can only realistically be made once the CCF has made a relevant disclosure of the content of the request received by the NCB, which will usually contain most, if not all of the information contained in the Red Notice or Diffusion which is the subject of challenge, including:

(a) reference to and details of the domestic warrant or order upon which the request for the Red Notice is based;

(b) the description of the charge(s);

(c) the 'status' of the person, ie whether they are wanted for the purpose of extradition;

(d) the maximum sentence of imprisonment (if the request is an accusation case) or the sentence imposed (if the request is a conviction case); and

(e) a summary of the facts.

6.84

In relevant part, Article 12(1) provides as follows:

> 'Data processed in the INTERPOL Information System must be accurate, relevant, not excessive in relation to their purpose, an up to date, to allow them to be used by National Central Bureaus, national entities and international entities.'

6.85

This overarching requirement of accuracy, relevance and contemporaneity is the context in which the more precise requirements of Article 83 must be viewed. Article 83 sets out the minimum *cumulative* criteria that a Red Notice must meet, which include:

- the offence must be a *serious* ordinary law crime;
- the offence must not raise controversial issues relating to cultural or behavioural norms;
- the offence must not relate to family or private matters or 'derive from private disputes';
- the offence must not originate from a violation of laws or regulations of an administrative nature.

6.86

The minimum, cumulative criteria set out in Article 83(1) should be carefully considered by the practitioner, as it stands in the stead of the more familiar 'dual criminality' provisions that appear in extradition treaties and domestic extradition law. There is reference to a 'non-exhaustive list' of specific offences which fall within these categories, which is kept with the General Secretariat but is not publicly available.

6.87

Whilst the majority of requests for Red Notices which obviously do not meet this minimum criteria are likely to be filtered out by the General Secretariat, there is scope for full representations to be made on those that are circulated, but which relate to a private matter or derive from a private dispute. For example, in many jurisdictions it is not uncommon for criminal proceedings to be brought at the same time as a claim for damages in a civil court, with the issues litigated in both proceedings arising from a private or commercial dispute. In such cases, an applicant may have access to information that was not made available by the NCB to Interpol when the request for a Red Notice was made, such as court orders or judgments in the related civil proceedings, which might assist in persuading the Requests Chamber that the offence described in the Red Notice does not meet the minimum criteria in Article 83.

6.88

The other minimum criteria are set out in detail in Article 83 and include the minimum penalty threshold, which is two years in accusation cases, reflecting that the offence must be a *serious* ordinary law crime; and 'at least six months' in conviction cases. Extradition practitioners will note that the minimum penalties are significantly higher than is the norm on most extradition arrangements, including the Framework Decision of 2002 which governs the European arrest warrant scheme.

6.89

The requirements of Article 83(2)(b) (and Article 12(1)) in particular are likely to be engaged in most cases where there is a concern over the quality of the information contained in the Red Notice. Albeit expressed in language which suggests the General Secretariat and/or the Requests Chamber of the CCF retain a measure of discretion, the overall tenor of the Article is that the following minimum 'judicial data' is required for a Red Notice to be published:

- a summary of the facts of the case, 'which shall provide a succinct and clear description of the criminal activities, including the time and location';
- the charge(s);
- reference to a valid arrest warrant or judicial decision having the same effect, and where possible, a copy of the same.

6.90

In this regard, note also the mandatory language of Article 8(3) of the RPD, which provides: 'The publication of INTERPOL notices and the transmission of diffusions shall be in accordance with Articles 73 et seq of the present Rules'.

6.91

Decisions of the Requests Chamber of the CCF helpfully refer to the 'IPSG standards for the application of the RPD', which to the authors' knowledge, is not a publicly available document. The relevant standard provides valuable guidance as to how the General Secretariat and the CCF apply Articles 12, 83 and 99 (in the case of Diffusion requests). It reads as follows:

> '[…] For red notice requests and diffusions seeking the arrest of a person, it is important to provide sufficient facts that link the wanted individual to the charges against him/her. Providing such facts is crucial for facilitating international police cooperation.'

6.92

It follows that the practitioner should be alive to arguments as to the inadequacy or sufficiency of particulars of the allegation(s), which can provide a fertile ground of challenge. In particular, where there are multiple allegations of criminal conduct imputed to more than one accused, the request must not only describe with sufficient clarity what acts are attributed to each person sought in connection with the alleged criminal conduct, but provide a sufficient factual basis for that attribution. In the event that such particulars are not disclosed on the fact of the request for a Red Notice or Diffusion, the applicant will have strong grounds to contest the request on the basis that it does not comply with the RPD.

6.93

There are only a few rules that relate to the circulation of Diffusions in contrast to the number that apply to requests for and the publication of Red Notices. Nonetheless, Article 99(2) of the RPD is something of a catch-all gateway through which all relevant Articles of the RPD can be relied on when making representations to delete a Diffusion. Article 99(2) provides as follows:

> 'Before circulating a diffusion, the National Central Bureau or international entity shall ensure:
>
> (a) the quality and lawfulness of the data it provides in support of its diffusion;
>
> (b) that its diffusion complies with the general conditions for recording data;
>
> (c) that the data is of interest for the purpose of international police cooperation;
>
> (d) that its request complies with INTERPOL's rules, specifically with Articles 2(1) and 3 of the Constitution, as well as with the obligations imposed on the requesting entity under international law.'

6.94

In the author's experience, the Requests Chamber of the CCF approaches the 'quality and lawfulness' criteria for Diffusions in the same manner as the accuracy, relevance and contemporaneity requirements imposed by Article 12 of the RPD and the sufficiency of particulars of the allegation requirement imposed by Article 83 of the RPD. This is evidenced by the relevant extract from the IPSG standards reproduced above. It follows that although all representations to delete a Diffusion will be fact sensitive, similar arguments can be advanced based on the inadequacy of particulars and defects in the request.

6.95

The request for a Red Notice or Diffusion and the data that the NCB has asked to be processed in Interpol's Information System must also be of interest for the purpose of 'international police cooperation'. This rather nebulous phrase appears throughout the RPD and is a foundational concept that underpins Interpol. Nonetheless, it does beg the question as to whether in certain cases, the publication or circulation of Red Notice or Diffusion is in the interests of international police cooperation. Importing the data protection principles from elsewhere in the RPD, the processing of a person's data is only for the purpose of international police cooperation if it is necessary to advance that aim. It is not uncommon for Red Notices and Diffusions to remain in place not only long after either extradition proceedings have been concluded, but when the person who is sought has made contact with the authorities in the requesting state and engaged in the domestic proceedings. In such circumstances, there is a strong argument that the continued processing of that person's data is no longer necessary and accordingly is not compliant with the RPD.

Challenges based on the 2017 Interpol Refugee Resolution

6.96

In 2017, Interpol's General Assembly adopted resolution GA-2017-86-RES-09, regarding the processing of data related to individuals who have been granted refugee or asylum seeker status. The Resolution formally adopted the following policy introduced by the Interpol Executive Committee in June 2014:

> 'In general, the processing of red notices and diffusions against refugees will not be allowed if the following conditions are met:
>
> - the status of refugee or asylum-seeker has been confirmed;
> - the notice/diffusion has been requested by the country where the individual fears persecution;
> - the granting of the refugee status is not based on political grounds vis-à-vis the requesting country.'

Accordingly, individuals or entities may seek to challenge Red Notices or Diffusions on the basis that these conditions are met.

Challenges in domestic law – example jurisdictions

France

6.97

It is possible for an applicant to challenge the NCB's decision not to disclose (certain) information in France. The data subject must first refer the matter to the CNIL. If there is no response, or if the response is unsatisfactory, they can then appeal to France's highest administrative court, the Conseil d'Etat.

6.98

On the basis of Articles 4 and 5 of LIL, applicants may argue that:

- the processing is lawful and fair;
- the data is collected for specified, explicit and legitimate purpose; and
- the data is adequate, relevant and limited to what is necessary in relation to the purposes for which they are processed.

6.99

Despite the fact that the CNIL centralises all requests, data subjects can, in theory, try to appeal to the administrative courts on grounds of ultra vires ('*recours en excès de pouvoir*'). To do so, they should first send their request for access to the data to the Ministry of the Interior. They could then challenge the Ministry of the Interior's unsatisfactory response by arguing that it is an administrative act adversely affecting them. The rights of rectification and deletion can be exercised indirectly through the CNIL, in the same way as requests for access.

Germany

6.100

In Germany, individuals can lodge a complaint where they consider that their data has been unlawfully processed by the German Federal Criminal Police Office as NCB. Pursuant to section 60 of the BDSG, the person concerned can appeal to the German Federal Commissioner for Data Protection and Freedom of Information (*Bundesbeauftrager für den Datenschutz und die Informationsfreiheit*, BfDI) and issue a complaint about unlawful data processing contrary to the principles of the GDPR.

6.101

Pursuant to section 61, paragraph 1 of the BDSG, it is possible to initiate legal proceedings where the data subject disagrees with the the decision of the BfDI. The German Federal Criminal Police Office's website includes reference to this right of appeal.

6.102

However, to date, no known individuals have defended themselves against unlawful data processing by the German Federal Criminal Police Office by lodging a complaint with the BfDI pursuant to section 60, paragraph 1 of the BDSG.

6.103

In 2017, the Wiesbaden Administrative Court (*Verwaltungsgericht*) was called upon by German citizen who had been wanted by the US law enforcement authorities on bribery charges since 2012. However, investigation proceedings were also conducted against him in Germany because of these allegations, which were discontinued pursuant to section 153a, paragraph 1 of the German Code of Criminal Procedure (*Strafprozessordnung*, 'StPO'). He received a discontinuance payment (*Geldauflage*) which generally excludes further investigation and punishment for the same alleged offence. The person concerned claimed that the USA's action of initiating an Interpol search against him violated the Interpol provisions on double jeopardy and interfered with his right to freedom of movement.

6.104

He therefore turned to the Wiesbaden Administrative Court and demanded that the German Federal Criminal Police Office, as the NBC for INTERPOL, take measures to have the Red Notice deleted. The danger of being arrested restricted his right to freedom of movement under Article 21 of the Treaty on the Functioning of the European Union (TFEU). The Wiesbaden Administrative Court referred questions to the European Court of Justice (ECJ) on the application of the double jeopardy rule, in particular on provisional arrest in the case of a Red Notice.

6.105

In its verdict, the ECJ decided that the question as to whether the double jeopardy rule applies, must be judicially established. Until this has been established, the processing of the data and the provisional arrest is permissible and does not violate Article 54 of the Schengen Convention (*Schengener Durchführungsübereinkommen*, SDÜ) and Article 21, paragraph 1 of the TFEU, each in conjunction with Article 50 of the EU Charter of Fundamental Rights.

In cases where it is still necessary to verify whether the double jeopardy rule applies, the provisional arrest for verification is a necessary step.

6.106

Furthermore, it is possible to appeal alerts issued by Germany to Interpol itself. The issuance of a Red Notice by the German Federal Criminal Police Office is a search measure within the meaning of section 130 of the StPO and can be challenged before the competent Local Court (*Amtsgericht*) pursuant to section 98, paragraph 2, sentence 2 of the StPO. As a result, this is can be the subject of judicial review.

Hong Kong

6.107

DPP3 governs the use of personal data in Hong Kong. It provides that 'personal data shall not, without the prescribed consent of the data subject, be used for a new purpose'. The transfer of data amongst bureaux or departments is subject to restrictions under DPP3. Neither HKPF nor Interpol's processing of data has been a subject of challenge in Hong Kong courts and limited means of challenging a Red Notice or the effects of a Red Notice exist in Hong Kong.

Italy

6.108

Limited means of challenging the processing of personal data, a Red Notice or the effects of a Red Notice exist in Italy. However, a small number of Italian individuals have sought preventive remedies in order to avoid being extradited in the event that an extradition request was made in connection with a known Red Notice in their name.

6.109

In one known case an individual requested the Italian Ministry of Justice grant him a guarantee against extradition to the USA as a result of a request for extradition which had not been issued yet. The Ministry declined to answer the application and the individual filed an appeal with the Italian Administrative Court of the Region of Lazio (TAR Lazio) against the lack of ruling by the Ministry. The TAR concluded, in accordance with the Ministry's ruling, that Public Administrations (such as the Ministry of Justice) have no obligation to rule on pre-emptive requests of such kind. The Consiglio di Stato (the supreme administrative Court in Italy) confirmed the TAR decision.[42]

42 See Consiglio di Stato, Division III, Judgment, 23/11/2022, n 10309.

Netherlands

6.110

In the Netherlands it is possible to challenge the *Wet Politiegegevens* (WPG) and the *Wet Justitiële en Strafvorderlijke Gegevens* (WJSG) in connection with potential unlawful data processing.

- In accordance with Article 31a of the WPG, the individual can file a complaint at the Dutch Data Protection Authority (*Autoriteit Persoonsgegevens*) for breaches of GDPR data protection principles. Subsequently, pursuant to Article 29 of the WPG, an individual can challenge the processing of their data for breaches of GDPR data protection rules via a judicial administrative route.
- According to Article 26a of the WJSG, the individual can file a complaint at the Dutch Data Protection Authority (*Autoriteit Persoonsgegevens*) for breaches of GDPR data protection principles. A decision of the Dutch Data Protection Authority regarding such a complaint constitutes an order within the meaning of the Dutch General Administrative Law Act (Article 26a(5) of the WJSG), and is thus subject to a challenge through the judicial administrative route.

6.111

At present, no individuals have challenged the use of their data by Interpol before the Dutch domestic courts, particularly in relation to the issuance of Red Notices.

6.112

Whilst no individuals have specifically challenged a Red Notice based on a human rights obligation, some Dutch nationals have sought to challenge the human rights consequences of a Red Notice if acted upon. In a case which was brought before the Dutch Supreme Court, a suspect was arrested in Venezuela after the Netherlands issued an international Red Notice. The suspect argued that Article 3 of the European Convention on Human Rights (ECHR) (prohibition of torture) had been breached because the detention conditions in Venezuela were such that it constituted an 'inhumane treatment' within the meaning of Article 3 of the ECHR. According to the Advocate General in this case, the fact that the detention conditions in Venezuela did not meet what is considered 'acceptable' in the Netherlands (and many Western European countries) did not consequentially mean that the Netherlands should have refrained from taking any action leading to the detention of the defendant in Venezuela.

6.113

In another case which was brought before the District Court of the Hague, the judicial authorities of Curaçao issued a Red Notice which led to the arrest of a suspect in the Netherlands. Subsequently, the suspect tried to prevent the Dutch State of transferring him to Curaçao if no guarantee was provided by the State that the detention conditions in Curaçao complied with Article 2 (right to life) and Article 3 (prohibition of torture) of the ECHR. According to the suspect, the detention conditions in Curaçao involved torture and inhuman treatment, and therefore would constitute a breach of Article 3 of the ECHR. Furthermore, the suspect argued that there was a risk to life should he be extradited due to violence and tension between two rival drug gangs in Curaçao. Notwithstanding the applicant's arguments, the District Court of the Hague rejected the case concluding that the arguments put forth by the suspect in relation to Article 2 and 3 of the ECHR did not prevent their transfer to the judicial authorities of Curaçao.

Spain

6.114

Limited means of challenging a Red Notice, or the effects of a Red Notice, or to challenge decisions by the NCB in relation to the provision of information held by Interpol exist in Spain. In one case brought by Google before the Spanish National Court, Google appealed a resolution from the Spanish Data Protection Agency in relation to the 'digital right to be forgotten'. Google claimed that the fact that information in relation to a person's Red Notice of Interpol was still publicly available on the internet, but not on the Interpol data bases, despite the notice being terminated, did not constitute a data protection breach. The court ruled in favour of Google, on the grounds that it was truly confirmed that an international arrest warrant had been duly processed, and that a legitimate interest of internet users in having access to the information in question, which is neither inaccurate nor obsolete, exists.

6.115

Information contained in the data bases of Interpol are commonly included in the Schengen Information System (SIS). The SIS consists of a central system ('Central SIS II Regulation'), a national system (the 'N SIS II') in each member state and a communication infrastructure connecting the central system with the different national systems. In accordance with data protection principles, all individuals whose data are processed in the Central SIS II Regulation have specific rights granted by the Central SIS II Regulation. Any individual exercising any of these rights may apply to any of the competent authorities of the state of their choice where the Central SIS II Regulation is operated. This option is possible because all national databases (N SIS II) are identical to the central system database. Therefore, these rights can be exercised in any country operating the Central SIS II Regulation, regardless of the member state that issued the alert.

6.116

When an individual exercises their right of access, rectification of inaccurate data and erasure in respect of unlawfully stored data, the competent authorities must comply with such requests within a strict time limit. In general, the individual shall be informed as soon as possible, and in any case no later than 60 days after the date on which access was requested, or earlier if national law so provides. The individual shall also be informed about the follow-up given to the exercise of their correction and deletion rights as soon as possible and, in any case, no later than three months after the date on which the rectification or deletion was requested, or earlier if national law so provides.

6.117

Articles 67 and 68 of the Central SIS II Regulation set out the remedies available to individuals when their request for the exercise of a right has not been satisfied. Any person may bring an action before the courts or the competent authority under the law of any member state for access, rectification, erasure or for compensation in relation to an alert relating to him.

6.118

In case they have to deal with a complaint with a cross-border element, national data protection authorities must cooperate with each other to ensure the rights of data subjects.

United States of America

6.119

There is no federal domestic data protection law with which an individual has challenged USNCB's processing of data. USNCB data is exempt from provisions of the Privacy Act of 1974. Individuals have challenged arrests/detention pursuant to Red Notices on the basis of an unconstitutional violation of due process and/or the Fourth Amendment. Further, a number of non-US citizens with an outstanding Red Notice sought asylum and/or relief under the Convention Against Torture (CAT), but US courts have generally denied these claims.[43] Some examples of these cases are described below.

43 By way of example: *El Omari v Interpol*, 35 F 4th 83 (2nd Cir 2022): A US citizen brought a claim against Interpol alleging negligent infliction of emotional distress and violation of his right to due process of law under the New York State Constitution after Interpol refused to delete a Red Notice identifying him as a convicted criminal in the United Arab Emirates. Both lower and appellate courts dismissed the case for lack of subject matter jurisdiction, concluding that Interpol was immune from suit under the International Organizations Immunities Act (IOIA). The courts did not decide the due process claim.
Villalobos Sura v Garland, 8 F 4th 1161 (9th Cir 2021): an El Salvadorian citizen with an outstanding Red Notice applied for 'withholding of removal and relief' under CAT after entering the United States without appropriate documentation. The petitioner was placed in a withholding-only proceeding before an immigration judge who denied the application because the Red Notice, an arrest warrant, and various factual concessions by the petitioner supported a fair probability that the petitioner committed a serious non-political crime before arriving in the US which is a bar to relief. The Board of Immigration Appeals (BIA) and 9th Circuit affirmed.

6.120

Though the bar for successful CAT relief based on a Red Notice is high, US courts have granted petitions to review the BIA's denial of CAT relief on the basis of probable commission of a serious non-political crime when solely supported by a Red Notice.[44]

6.121

In 2021, in support for Interpol institutional reforms, the US government passed the Transnational Repression Accountability and Prevention (TRAP) provision as part of the National Defense Authorization Act (NDAA) for Fiscal Year 2022 (22 USC § 263b). The TRAP provision prohibits government agencies from extraditing an individual based solely on a Red Notice or Diffusion. The provision also includes various public policy efforts, such as a biannual report on abuse. US focus on human rights abuses through Interpol is a developing area.

6.122

Under the fourth amendment of the US Constitution, individuals can only be arrested for probable cause. The US Department of Justice takes the position that a Red Notice alone cannot establish probable cause. As a result, individuals may challenge an arrest on this basis. Similarly, the US Immigration and Customs Enforcement (ICE) recently issued Directive 15006.1, which prohibits ICE personnel from relying exclusively on a Red Notice to justify law enforcement actions.

6.123

However, while a Red Notice on its own is not dispositive, when it is accompanied by other evidence, the government may rely on it alongside corroborating documents for enforcement action.

Conclusion

6.124

Dr Rutsel Silvestre J Martha, an academic and former General Counsel of INTERPOL, delivered an address to the European Criminal Bar Association in 2007 in which he said:[45]

> 'I should like to observe that very often such requests [for deletion of material held by Interpol] are motivated by the lawyers concerned

44 See for example, *Gonzalez-Castillo v Garland*, 47 F 4th 971 (9th Cir 2022).

45 See https://www.ecba.org/extdocserv/conferences/lyon2007/remedies_against_interpol.pdf at paras 40–41.

with the argument that there is no evidence that their clients have committed the crime of which they are accused or are being sought.

This argument, I must say, is not the right argument to submit to Interpol.'

6.125

Dr Martha went on to explain that such arguments were not effective for two reasons. Firstly, because such matters are considered to be the concern of the individual NCBs, so there is no provision for such considerations either in Interpol's Constitution or processing rules. Secondly, those rules establish a presumption of consistency in favour of the NCBs that have provided the information to Interpol. Dr Martha suggests, correctly in the view of the authors, that:[46]

'for a request for modification, blocking and destruction of items of information to be successful it must by supported by arguments derived from those rules'.

46 Ibid, at para 47.

7 Red Notices – practical guidance

1. **Introduction**
2. **First steps**
3. **Identifying the existence of a Red Notice**
4. **Preventative Requests**
5. **Challenging a Red Notice**
6. **Contents of representations**
7. **Litigation PR and the media**
8. **Conclusion**

Introduction

7.1

Being instructed to represent a client in relation to either a confirmed or suspected Red Notice can be an interesting, but strategically challenging, task. Every decision needs to be considered against a complex backdrop which can include a myriad of issues: legal, reputational, logistical and, often, political. While no two cases are the same and there is no prescriptive way to approach a Red Notice, there are a number of consistent themes to consider. Drawing on the authors' own experience, as well as feedback helpfully provided by experienced practitioners in this area, we set out in this chapter some practical guidance which may be considered when being instructed in relation to a Red Notice.

First steps

7.2

The first call or meeting with your client is, in many cases, critical. Whilst perhaps seemingly obvious, it is important to obtain as much information as possible from the client, not least why they believe they are the subject of a Red Notice. There may be occasions where the client's concern stems from paranoia based around ongoing politically exposed litigation or other ancillary issues. In such cases, action may be premature and potentially counter-productive. Conversely, the client may have well-placed sources within a requesting country's government who have indicated the likelihood of a Red Notice. Whatever the source of the concern, it is generally recommended that any information provided by the client is critically evaluated and validated, if possible, by way of publicly available information.

7.3

This first meeting is also an important opportunity to manage a client's expectations. Red Notices are usually difficult and costly to challenge; it is important that a client fully appreciates how long the process can take, how frustrating it can be and the likelihood of success. This cost–benefit analysis can be a challenging conversation to have due to the high-stakes, but often opaque, nature of the process. It is helpful to discuss and agree a strategy before making any concrete decisions. Careful thought should be given at this early stage as to whether *anything* should be done: sometimes, the best strategy is to maintain a low profile and wait for more, potentially helpful, information to become available. It is also important to establish whether the client intends to travel; if they intend to do so whilst the existence of a Red Notice is uncertain, they should be made aware of the risks and advised on how those risks might be mitigated. In particular, the client should be informed that in many Member States, unlike the UK and the United States, Red Notices effectively operate as arrest warrants which can be executed by law enforcement officers, either at border control or freely within the territory of the executing state, without the need to obtain an arrest warrant from a domestic court.

Identifying the existence of a Red Notice

7.4

Before taking any proactive action to determine whether a Red Notice exists, it is important to assess what risk to the client may flow from these initial enquiries. One potential reaction to a request to Interpol for information about a Red Notice is that the authorities in the requesting state may be galvanised into action. Whilst the client is likely to be outside of that jurisdiction, they may have family members or business interests that could be impacted by a renewed interest in their case. It is possible that a request for information may prioritise or speed up an investigation. Concurrent to any police action, there is also the risk that a previously confidential Red Notice could be made public, with the subsequent reputational damage to your client; this can have a significant effect on both their personal life and their business. For example, it could result in an individual being suspended from work or result in commercial damage if customers decide to no longer engage with a business that is subject to a Red Notice. In particular, the subjects of public Red Notices frequently experience closure of their bank accounts, as part of financial institutions 'de-risking'.

7.5

As set out in Chapter 5, a variety of routes may be used to identify whether a Red Notice has been issued. The most common means for ascertaining the existence of a Red Notice is a formal request to the Commission for the Control of Interpol's Files (CCF). The process is set out in detail in Chapter 5 and a sample application form is contained in Appendix 6. As previously indicated, the CCF process imposes a strict set of requirements. Failure to follow these can result in the request not being approved for processing or in the language of the rules declared 'admissible'. Notwithstanding these bureaucratic hurdles, there are other, more practical issues. For example, how much information should be contained in any request for information? The answer to this is case specific but, in general terms, it may be strategically sensible to include only publicly available information and keep any sensitive evidence in reserve, for a potential challenge later, for the reasons set out at **7.6** below. Typically, practitioners will include a high-level description of the alleged conduct and the underlying criminal proceedings that have given rise to the request for the circulation of the suspected Red Notice.

7.6

The second issue to consider is that the CCF will almost always consult with or look to obtain the consent of the requesting NCB. It is essential that a client understands from the outset that any information provided to the CCF is likely to be shared with the relevant NCB. As indicated above, this may not be in the best interests of your client, as it could trigger a reaction in relation to the underlying investigation. It should also be noted that just because the CCF does not confirm the existence of a Red Notice does not mean that one does not exist; in fact, some practitioners consider a non-committal answer from the CCF to indicate support for the existence of a Red Notice. Whilst this should not be considered a definitive approach, it is certainly worth bearing in mind if you have received an unhelpful reply.

7.7

Some lawyers, particularly in the United States, have indicated that the NCB of the country of which the target is a citizen can be helpful in confirming the existence of a Red Notice. This route rarely identifies the underlying information but can be useful in identifying whether there is anything that actually needs to be investigated. In other jurisdictions, including the UK, a direct approach to the NCB would be unusual and it is more common for practitioners to go through Interpol's formal channels.

7.8

A side point to consider at this stage is that well-resourced clients may want to use third-party sources such as private investigators to try and confirm the existence of a Red Notice. Feedback from practitioners uniformly advised against this and suggested there was a high degree of risk in this approach as companies may, for the right price, act unlawfully to obtain details of a Red Notice. While this may have professional consequences if instructed directly by the lawyer, it can also cause problems for the client if they are ultimately responsible for instruction of the investigator. Again, clients should be advised that dealing with Red Notices – frustratingly – often requires patience.

7.9

It may be possible to use data protection law to make a subject access request to the NCB. Example processes in relation to the UK, US and Germany are set out in Chapter 5, but practitioners indicate that this route is rarely successful as most legislation provides a 'prevention and detection of crime' exemption which can be used to resist Red Notice subject access requests.

7.10

The final, general, point to remember in relation to all the possible routes in identifying the existence of a Red Notice is that investigations and local police forces can move quickly and circumstances can change. Just because a Red Notice was not in existence at the time of checking, does not mean this cannot change; one can be put in place 24 hours later and the client is exposed. For example, if the CCF has confirmed on 1 January that no Red Notice exists, it will not write respond proactively if one is circulated on 2 January. As such, the value of any confirmation is necessarily limited. Given the length of time it takes to receive a reply from the CCF (typically several months), this can be an extremely frustrating aspect of the process for challenging a Red Notice.

Preventative Requests

7.11

One area in which practitioners across the world have had success is a Preventative Request, especially in relation to politically based Red Notices. As explained in Chapter 5, a Preventative Request is sent to the CCF and, in some cases, the General Secretariat, requesting that Interpol does not give effect to an application by a specific NCB for a Diffusion or Red Notice against a specified individual without a complete review of the underlying facts.

7.12

In terms of the content of any Preventative Request, there is a strategic decision to be made about how much detail is included. Lawyers have a natural tendency to 'keep the powder dry', it is worth remembering that it can take considerable time for Interpol to consider a request and it may be desirable to ensure that any relevant evidence is before it when it finally does so. It is a judgment call and one worth carefully considering.

7.13

Less risky, is using publicly available information. Any Preventative Request should clearly and concisely set out the nature of the request, the factual background as well as the reasons why Interpol should not give effect to a Red Notice request. Interpol has been receptive to arguments which are focused on its constitutional duty to act neutrally: Article 3 of its Constitution states that it should not become involved in 'activities of a political … character'. There has been a significant amount of governmental, via the EU, and non-governmental organisation (NGO) pressure on Interpol in relation to the use of political Red Notices; consequently, it may be suggested that it is particularly sensitive to this approach. Reference should be made, as appropriate, to any potential burden on the rights of individuals under the Universal Declaration of Human Rights. As much relevant supporting material as possible should be included, such as press articles, civil judgments or any other evidence that supports either the political or unfair nature of the application.

7.14

Finally, in terms of suggested possible arguments, it is worth comparing, to the extent possible, other similar cases that may have been reported in the press or the courts which can be used as a non-binding precedent. In recent years, the CCF has published anonymised decision excerpts on its website, which can provide a useful reference.

Challenging a Red Notice

7.15

Once the existence of a Red Notice is confirmed a decision must be made as to whether to challenge it. We set out the available routes for challenging a Red Notice in Chapter 6, but, in the first instance, clients should be asked why they want to challenge it. A common, and understandable, response is the need for personal and/or business travel or reputational reasons but these must form part of a wider risk assessment and cost benefit analysis. A broader strategy should be considered and discussed and, at least in the short term, the client may be better advised to stay where they are rather than risk arrest and detention by travelling. As set out below, it may be better both to focus on and target the underlying reason for the Red Notice and to make sure the client is well prepared for this, rather than potentially getting distracted about their inability to travel. Even if a decision to challenge the Red Notice is taken, it is likely that the client will need to be advised to avoid travel in the intervening period, which will last many months.

7.16

Without doubt, the best way to remove the threat of a Red Notice is by addressing the underlying investigation and/or proceedings against a client. This will be achieved with the assistance of local counsel. However, in some cases, particularly where politics are at play, this may not be realistic. In those circumstances, the next best way addressing the risk to the client is likely to be by way of a successful asylum application or extradition decision on behalf of the client. Both offer long-term protections, which will not be achieved by simply securing the deletion of a Red Notice. Again, however, these are often not available options therefore a formal challenge under the Interpol Constitution and Rules on the Processing of Data (RPD) may be required.

7.17

As a starting point, like all formal engagement with Interpol, it is essential to be fully aware of the published rules (see Appendices 1–5). Often similar arguments as may be deployed in relation to a Preventative Request may be used under the RPD, specifically, in relation to alleged breaches of Article 3 of Interpol's Constitution. As is a constant theme in this chapter, there is a judgment call to be made in terms of what supporting evidence is used. Often, a brief summary of the underlying facts is sufficient, with a then-greater focus as to how these facts demonstrate a breach of Interpol's Constitution and RPD. It may be necessary to remind the client, who will likely be eager to 'defend' themselves, that Interpol will not engage in a debate around the facts of the case and alleged conduct; it is concerned only with its own function and obligations as an information sharing organisation.

7.18

Practitioners also report that it is receptive to challenges based on demonstrating that the alleged conduct which is the reason for the Red Notice is, in fact, a civil dispute that is being presented as criminal proceedings. This has certainly been effective in circumstances where a state is involved in acrimonious civil litigation with a privately owned foreign company and uses a Red Notice to target in-country employees and directors.

7.19

Another potentially successful area for challenge is where there is evidence that the requesting NCB knows the whereabouts of the target individual yet has decided not to make a formal extradition request. In cases like this, Interpol may be persuaded that the Red Notice is unnecessary and is not 'effectively' preventing or suppressing crime (as required under its Constitution).

7.20

A final practical point worth considering in terms of challenging a Red Notice is whether it is possible, in circumstances where the client is particularly high-profile and/or well connected, to get government support. It may be possible to use the national state of the client to support the removal of the Red Notice through Interpol. There may be political and diplomatic issues which prohibit public government support, but it may be possible to utilise informal, 'back channel', routes to help an application for removal of a Red Notice.

Contents of representations

7.21

Representations to Interpol challenging a Red Notice are subject to a ten-page limit, not including appendices. It is, of course, worth being mindful of this limit, but the authors experience is that representations slightly in excess of this limit will still be considered.

7.22

As noted above, Interpol is not concerned with the facts of the underlying case, except to the extent that they provide necessary context or illustrate breaches of its constitution and RPD. Breaches of the RPD will be fact sensitive.

7.23

When considering whether there has been a breach of the constitution, the test applied by the CCF in its assessment as to whether data is processed in conformity with the rights guaranteed by the Universal Declaration of Human Rights (UDHR) appears to be whether there is a 'real risk' or 'likelihood' of a breach of the relevant article, following the decisions of the European Court of Human Rights in the cases following *Soering v United Kingdom*.[1]

7.24

When assessing a potential breach of Article 10 of the UDHR (fair trial) the authors experience is that the CCF will consider whether there has been a 'flagrant denial of justice' or is a 'real risk' of such a breach.

7.25

Finally, in relation to Article 3 cases, as discussed in Chapter 6 of this work, the authors note that the CCF's interpretation of 'political … character' is broader than that adopted in UK extradition courts and is more akin to the test applied in asylum proceedings. It is not necessary, for example, to illustrate that a client

1 [1989] ECHR 14.

is a political figure; it may be sufficient to show that they are in opposition to the state for commercial or other reasons and that the criminal proceedings against them are being used for an improper purpose.

7.26

As outlined out in Chapter 6, practitioners will wish to consider numerous sources of potential evidence when making submissions to the CCF, including press reports, decisions of competent national courts, reports from international bodies and (where relevant to breaches of Interpol's Constitution and RPD) evidence relating to the applicant's case. In some cases, expert evidence will provide significant weight, including evidence on prison conditions, the relevant legal system and/or the political background. Any evidence provided to the CCF will need to be in one of their four working languages, which are Arabic, English, French or Spanish.

Litigation PR and the media

7.27

Whilst the main focus of this publication is the various legal processes and procedures available in relation to Interpol, the use of the media and litigation PR should not be underestimated. Like any kind of engagement with the media in relation to ongoing or potential legal proceedings, a cautious approach should be adopted. That said, in certain cases it may be appropriate to use the media to convey your client's point of view and exert pressure either on Interpol or the requesting NCB. If resources are available, then it is worth instructing a suitable litigation PR company, as they will have direct access to journalists and media organisations. They can also assist with the presentation of any message that your client is trying to get across. It should be noted that any contact with the press should be carefully assessed against the legal risk; nothing should be done without the client being aware of such risks. Similar to creating a strategic legal plan, it is worth creating and agreeing a media plan which covers a period of time and maintains pressure as opposed to a single effort which then disappears and is less effective. In terms of practical recommendations, it is vital that the basis of any discussions with a journalist is agreed at the outset (eg what is on the record, what is for background and what is off the record). It is also helpful to request quote approval in advance of any article being published.

Conclusion

7.28

This chapter is not intended to be a definitive guide to identifying and challenging Red Notices but rather, to provide the reader with practical suggestions that have successfully been used by practitioners in this field. Engagement with Interpol can undoubtedly be frustrating and it is not to say these suggestions will work every time but, in the right circumstances, they could well be successful.

7.29

The impact of a Red Notice on an individual is often extremely onerous, but so is the process for challenging one. Expectation management from the outset and a realistic assessment of the likely outcome and length of time to resolution are, accordingly, a practitioner's greatest assets when conducting these cases.

Appendix 1 Constitution of the ICPO–Interpol

REFERENCES

The Constitution of the ICPO-INTERPOL adopted by the General Assembly at its 25th session (Vienna, Austria, 1956).

Articles 35 and 36 amended by the General Assembly at its 31st session (Madrid, Spain, 1962).

Articles 2, 15, 16 and 19 amended by the General Assembly at its 33rd session (Caracas, Venezuela, 1964).

Article 17 amended by the General Assembly at its 46th session (Stockholm, Sweden, 1977).

Article 1 amended by the General Assembly at its 53rd session (Luxembourg, 1984).

Articles 11 and 12 amended by the General Assembly at its 66th session (New Delhi, India, 1997).

Article 5 amended; Articles 34-37 concerning the Advisers combined in Articles 34 and 35; new heading "THE COMMISSION FOR THE CONTROL OF FILES" added and certain provisions concerning the Commission inserted in Articles 36 and 37. Amendments adopted by the General Assembly at its 77th session (St Petersburg, Russia, 2008).

Articles 28 and 29 amended by the General Assembly at its 86th session (Beijing, China, 2017).

Articles 15, 16, 17, 19, 23 and 24 amended by the General Assembly at its 89th session (Istanbul, Türkiye, 2021).

Article 12 amended by the General Assembly at its 91st session (Vienna, Austria, 2023).

CONSTITUTION OF THE INTERNATIONAL CRIMINAL POLICE ORGANIZATION-INTERPOL

CONTENTS

GENERAL PROVISIONS 3

STRUCTURE AND ORGANIZATION 3

THE GENERAL ASSEMBLY 3

THE EXECUTIVE COMMITTEE 4

THE GENERAL SECRETARIAT 5

NATIONAL CENTRAL BUREAUS 6

THE ADVISERS 6

THE COMMISSION FOR THE CONTROL OF FILES 7

BUDGET AND RESOURCES 7

RELATIONS WITH OTHER ORGANIZATIONS 7

APPLICATION, MODIFICATION AND INTERPRETATION OF THE CONSTITUTION 7

TEMPORARY MEASURES 8

APPENDIX 1: LIST OF STATES TO WHICH THE PROVISIONS OF ARTICLE 45 OF THE CONSTITUTION SHALL APPLY 9

CONSTITUTION OF THE INTERNATIONAL CRIMINAL POLICE ORGANIZATION-INTERPOL

GENERAL PROVISIONS

Article 1

The Organization called the "INTERNATIONAL CRIMINAL POLICE COMMISSION" shall henceforth be entitled: "THE INTERNATIONAL CRIMINAL POLICE ORGANIZATION-INTERPOL". Its seat shall be in France.

Article 2

Its aims are:

(1) To ensure and promote the widest possible mutual assistance between all criminal police authorities within the limits of the laws existing in the different countries and in the spirit of the "Universal Declaration of Human Rights";

(2) To establish and develop all institutions likely to contribute effectively to the prevention and suppression of ordinary law crimes.

Article 3

It is strictly forbidden for the Organization to undertake any intervention or activities of a political, military, religious or racial character.

Article 4

Any country may delegate as a Member to the Organization any official police body whose functions come within the framework of activities of the Organization.

The request for membership shall be submitted to the Secretary General by the appropriate governmental authority. Membership shall be subject to approval by a two-thirds majority of the General Assembly.

STRUCTURE AND ORGANIZATION

Article 5

The International Criminal Police Organization-INTERPOL shall comprise:

- The General Assembly
- The Executive Committee
- The General Secretariat
- The National Central Bureaus
- The Advisers
- The Commission for the Control of Files

THE GENERAL ASSEMBLY

Article 6

The General Assembly shall be the body of supreme authority in the Organization. It is composed of delegates appointed by the Members of the Organization.

Article 7

Each Member may be represented by one or several delegates; however, for each country there shall be only one delegation head, appointed by the competent governmental authority of that country.

Because of the technical nature of the Organization, Members should attempt to include the following in their delegations:

(a) High officials of departments dealing with police affairs,

(b) Officials whose normal duties are connected with the activities of the Organization,

(c) Specialists in the subjects on the agenda.

Article 8

The functions of the General Assembly shall be the following:

(a) To carry out the duties laid down in the Constitution;

(b) To determine principles and lay down the general measures suitable for attaining the objectives of the Organization as given in Article 2 of the Constitution;

(c) To examine and approve the general programme of activities prepared by the Secretary General for the coming year;

(d) To determine any other regulations deemed necessary;

(e) To elect persons to perform the functions mentioned in the Constitution;

(f) To adopt resolutions and make recommendations to Members on matters with which the Organization is competent to deal;

(g) To determine the financial policy of the Organization;

(h) To examine and approve any agreements to be made with other organizations.

CONSTITUTION OF THE INTERNATIONAL CRIMINAL POLICE ORGANIZATION-INTERPOL

Article 9

Members shall do all within their power, in so far as is compatible with their own obligations, to carry out the decisions of the General Assembly.

Article 10

The General Assembly of the Organization shall meet in ordinary session every year. It may meet in extraordinary session at the request of the Executive Committee or of the majority of Members.

Article 11

(1) The General Assembly may, when in session, set up special committees for dealing with particular matters.

(2) It may also decide to hold regional conferences between two General Assembly sessions.

Article 12

The General Assembly shall determine the arrangements for holding each of its sessions, including when circumstances make it impossible or inadvisable to hold a session as initially decided.

Article 13

Only one delegate from each country shall have the right to vote in the General Assembly.

Article 14

Decisions shall be made by a simple majority except in those cases where a two-thirds majority is required by the Constitution.

THE EXECUTIVE COMMITTEE

Article 15

The Executive Committee shall be composed of the President of the Organization, the three Vice-Presidents and nine Delegates.

The thirteen members of the Executive Committee shall belong to different countries, due weight having been given to geographical distribution.

Elected Executive Committee members shall hold official positions within a national administration throughout their term of office on the Executive Committee.

Article 16

The General Assembly shall elect, from among nominations put forward by the competent governmental authorities, the President and three Vice-Presidents of the Organization.

A two-thirds majority shall be required for the election of the President; should this majority not be obtained after the second ballot, a simple majority shall suffice.

The President and Vice-Presidents shall be from different continents.

Article 17

The President shall be elected for four years. The Vice-Presidents shall be elected for three years. They shall not be immediately eligible for re-election either to the same posts or as Delegates on the Executive Committee.

If, following the election of a President, the provisions of Article 15 (paragraph 2) or Article 16 (paragraph 3) cannot be applied or are incompatible, a fourth Vice-President shall be elected so that all four continents are represented at the Presidency level.

If this occurs, the Executive Committee will, for a temporary period, have fourteen members. This exceptional situation shall come to an end as soon as circumstances make it possible to apply the provisions of Articles 15 and 16.

Article 18

The President of the Organization shall:

(a) Preside at meetings of the Assembly and the Executive Committee and direct the discussions;

(b) Ensure that the activities of the Organization are in conformity with the decisions of the General Assembly and the Executive Committee;

(c) Maintain as far as is possible direct and constant contact with the Secretary General of the Organization.

Article 19

The General Assembly shall elect from among nominations put forward by the competent governmental authorities, the nine Delegates on the Executive Committee.

The Delegates shall be elected for a period of three years. They shall not be immediately eligible for re-election to the same posts.

Article 20

The Executive Committee shall meet at least once each year on being convened by the President of the Organization.

Article 21

In the exercise of their duties, all members of the Executive Committee shall conduct themselves as representatives of the Organization and not as representatives of their respective countries.

Article 22

The Executive Committee shall:

(a) Supervise the execution of the decisions of the General Assembly;

(b) Prepare the agenda for sessions of the General Assembly;

(c) Submit to the General Assembly any programme of work or project which it considers useful;

(d) Supervise the administration and work of the Secretary General;

(e) Exercise all the powers delegated to it by the Assembly.

Article 23

The term of office of an Executive Committee member is deemed to end when this member resigns, or ceases to hold an official position within his or her national administration, or can no longer perform his or her duties as an Executive Committee member.

The competent governmental authority shall immediately notify the Secretary General of the termination of the Executive Committee member's term of office before it is due to expire.

The General Assembly shall elect a new Executive Committee member for a full term of office.

Article 24

In exceptional circumstances, on the proposal of the Executive Committee, the General Assembly may terminate an Executive Committee member's term of office before it is due to expire.

THE GENERAL SECRETARIAT

Article 25

The permanent departments of the Organization shall constitute the General Secretariat.

Article 26

The General Secretariat shall:

(a) Put into application the decisions of the General Assembly and the Executive Committee;

(b) Serve as an international centre in the fight against ordinary crime;

(c) Serve as a technical and information centre;

(d) Ensure the efficient administration of the Organization;

(e) Maintain contact with national and international authorities, whereas questions relative to the search for criminals shall be dealt with through the National Central Bureaus;

(f) Produce any publications which may be considered useful;

(g) Organize and perform secretariat work at the sessions of the General Assembly, the Executive Committee and any other body of the Organization;

(h) Draw up a draft programme of work for the coming year for the consideration and approval of the General Assembly and the Executive Committee;

(i) Maintain as far as is possible direct and constant contact with the President of the Organization.

Article 27

The General Secretariat shall consist of the Secretary General and a technical and administrative staff entrusted with the work of the Organization.

Article 28

The appointment of the Secretary General shall be proposed by the Executive Committee and approved by the General Assembly for a period of five years. The Secretary General may be re-appointed only once, for a further period of five years, but must lay down office on reaching the age of sixty-five. The Secretary General may be allowed to complete the term of office on reaching the age of sixty-five but shall not hold office beyond the age of seventy.

The Secretary General must be chosen from among persons highly competent in police matters.

In exceptional circumstances, the Executive Committee may propose at a meeting of the General Assembly that the Secretary General be removed from office.

Article 29

The Secretary General shall engage and direct the staff, administer the budget, and organize and direct the permanent departments, according to the directives decided upon by the General Assembly or Executive Committee.

The Secretary General shall submit to the Executive Committee or the General Assembly any propositions or projects concerning the work of the Organization.

The Secretary General shall be responsible to the Executive Committee and the General Assembly.

The Secretary General shall have the right to take part in the discussions of the General Assembly, the Executive Committee and all other dependent bodies.

In the exercise of his or her duties, the Secretary General shall represent the Organization and not any particular country.

Article 30

In the exercise of their duties, the Secretary General and the staff shall neither solicit nor accept instructions from any government or authority outside the Organization. They shall abstain from any action which might be prejudicial to their international task.

Each Member of the Organization shall undertake to respect the exclusively international character of the duties of the Secretary General and the staff, and abstain from influencing them in the discharge of their duties.

All Members of the Organization shall do their best to assist the Secretary General and the staff in the discharge of their functions.

NATIONAL CENTRAL BUREAUS

Article 31

In order to further its aims, the Organization needs the constant and active co-operation of its Members, who should do all within their power which is compatible with the legislations of their countries to participate diligently in its activities.

Article 32

In order to ensure the above cooperation, each country shall appoint a body which will serve as the National Central Bureau. It shall ensure liaison with:

(a) The various departments in the country;

(b) Those bodies in other countries serving as National Central Bureaus;

(c) The Organization's General Secretariat.

Article 33

In the case of those countries where the provisions of Article 32 are inapplicable or do not permit of effective centralized co-operation, the General Secretariat shall decide, with these countries, the most suitable alternative means of co-operation.

THE ADVISERS

Article 34

On scientific matters, the Organization may consult "Advisers". The role of the Advisers shall be purely advisory.

Article 35

Advisers shall be appointed for three years by the Executive Committee. Their appointment will become definite only after notification by the General Assembly.

They shall be chosen from among those who have a world-wide reputation in some field of interest to the Organization.

An Adviser may be removed from office by decision of the General Assembly.

THE COMMISSION FOR THE CONTROL OF FILES

Article 36

The Commission for the Control of Files is an independent body which shall ensure that the processing of personal information by the Organization is in compliance with the regulations the Organization establishes in this matter.

The Commission for the Control of Files shall provide the Organization with advice about any project, operation, set of rules or other matter involving the processing of personal information.

The Commission for the Control of Files shall process requests concerning the information contained in the Organization's files.

Article 37

The members of the Commission for the Control of Files shall possess the expertise required for it to accomplish its functions. Its composition and its functioning shall be subject to specific rules to be laid down by the General Assembly.

BUDGET AND RESOURCES

Article 38

The Organization's resources shall be provided by:

(a) The financial contributions from Members;

(b) Gifts, bequests, subsidies, grants and other resources after these have been accepted or approved by the Executive Committee.

Article 39

The General Assembly shall establish the basis of Members' subscriptions and the maximum annual expenditure according to the estimate provided by the Secretary General.

Article 40

The draft budget of the Organization shall be prepared by the Secretary General and submitted for approval to the Executive Committee.

It shall come into force after acceptance by the General Assembly.

Should the General Assembly not have had the possibility of approving the budget, the Executive Committee shall take all necessary steps according to the general outlines of the preceding budget.

RELATIONS WITH OTHER ORGANIZATIONS

Article 41

Whenever it deems fit, having regard to the aims and objects provided in the Constitution, the Organization shall establish relations and collaborate with other intergovernmental or non-governmental international organizations.

The general provisions concerning the relations with international, intergovernmental or non-governmental organizations will only be valid after their approval by the General Assembly.

The Organization may, in connection with all matters in which it is competent, take the advice of non-governmental international, governmental national or non-governmental national organizations.

With the approval of the General Assembly, the Executive Committee or, in urgent cases, the Secretary General may accept duties within the scope of its activities and competence either from other international institutions or organizations or in application of international conventions.

APPLICATION, MODIFICATION AND INTERPRETATION OF THE CONSTITUTION

Article 42

The present Constitution may be amended on the proposal of either a Member or the Executive Committee.

Any proposal for amendment to this Constitution shall be communicated by the Secretary General to Members of the Organization at least three months before submission to the General Assembly for consideration.
All amendments to this Constitution shall be approved by a two-thirds majority of the Members of the Organization.

Article 43

The French, English and Spanish texts of this Constitution shall be regarded as authoritative.

CONSTITUTION OF THE INTERNATIONAL CRIMINAL POLICE ORGANIZATION-INTERPOL

Article 44

The application of this Constitution shall be determined by the General Assembly through the General Regulations and Appendices, whose provisions shall be adopted by a two-thirds majority.

TEMPORARY MEASURES

Article 45

All bodies representing the countries mentioned in Appendix I shall be deemed to be Members of the Organization unless they declare through the appropriate governmental authority that they cannot accept this Constitution. Such a declaration should be made within six months of the date of the coming into force of the present Constitution.

Article 46

At the first election, lots will be drawn to determine a Vice-President whose term of office will end a year later.

At the first election, lots will be drawn to determine two Delegates on the Executive Committee whose term of office will end a year later, and two others whose term of office will end two years later.

Article 47

Persons having rendered meritorious and prolonged services in the ranks of the ICPC may be awarded by the General Assembly honorary titles in corresponding ranks of the ICPO.

Article 48

All property belonging to the International Criminal Police Commission are transferred to the International Criminal Police Organization.

Article 49

In the present Constitution:

- "Organization", wherever it occurs, shall mean the International Criminal Police Organization;
- "Constitution", wherever it occurs, shall mean the Constitution of the International Criminal Police Organization;
- "Secretary General" shall mean the Secretary General of the International Criminal Police Organization;
- "Committee" shall mean the Executive Committee of the Organization;
- "Assembly" or "General Assembly" shall mean the General Assembly of the Organization;
- "Member" or "Members" shall mean a Member or Members of the International Criminal Police Organization as mentioned in Article 4 of the Constitution;
- "delegate" (in the singular) or "delegates" (in the plural) shall mean a person or persons belonging to a delegation or delegations as defined in Article 7;
- "Delegate" (in the singular) or "Delegates" (in the plural) shall mean a person or persons elected to the Executive Committee in the conditions laid down in Article 19.

Article 50

This Constitution shall come into force on 13 June 1956.

****

APPENDIX 1:

LIST OF STATES TO WHICH THE PROVISIONS OF ARTICLE 45 OF THE CONSTITUTION SHALL APPLY

Argentina, Australia, Austria, Belgium, Brazil, Burma, Cambodia, Canada, Ceylon, Chile, Colombia, Costa Rica, Cuba, Denmark, Dominican Republic, Egypt, Eire, Finland, France, Federal German Republic, Greece, Guatemala, India, Indonesia, Iran, Israel, Italy, Japan, Jordan, Lebanon, Liberia, Libya, Luxembourg, Mexico, Monaco, Netherlands, Netherlands Antilles, New Zealand, Norway, Pakistan, Philippines, Portugal, Saar, Saudi Arabia, Spain, Sudan, Surinam, Sweden, Switzerland, Syria, Thailand, Turkey, United Kingdom of Great Britain and Northern Ireland, United States of America, Uruguay, Venezuela, Yugoslavia.

****

Appendix 2 Interpol's Rules on the processing of data

REFERENCES

51st General Assembly session, Resolution AG/51/RES/1, adopting the "Rules on International Police Cooperation and on the Internal Control of INTERPOL's Archives".

55th General Assembly session, Resolution AGN/55/RES/2, delegating to the Executive Committee the adoption of the "Rules on the Deletion of Police Information Held by the General Secretariat", and the decision taken by the Executive Committee at its 84th session (Saint Cloud, France, 4-6 March 1987) adopting these Rules.

59th General Assembly session, Resolution AGN/59/RES/7, adopting the "Rules Governing the Database of Selected Information at the ICPO-INTERPOL General Secretariat and Direct Access by NCBs to that Database".

70th General Assembly session, Resolution AG-2001-RES-08, adopting the "Rules Governing Access by an Intergovernmental Organization to the INTERPOL Telecommunications Network and Databases".

72nd General Assembly session, Resolution AG-2003-RES-04, adopting the "Rules on the Processing of Information for the Purposes of International Police Cooperation".

76th General Assembly session, Resolution AG-2007-RES-09, adopting the "Implementing Rules for the Rules on the Processing of Information for the Purposes of International Police Cooperation".

80th General Assembly session, Resolution AG-2011-RES-07 approving the Rules on the Processing of Data and abrogating, on 30 June 2012, the "Rules on the Processing of Information for the Purposes of International Police Cooperation", the "Implementing Rules for the Rules on the Processing of Information for the Purposes of International Police Cooperation", and the "Rules Governing Access by an Intergovernmental Organization to the INTERPOL Telecommunications Network and Databases".

The English version of the rules was corrected by the General Secretariat on 14 March 2013, in application of the provisions of Article 33(3) of the Rules of Procedure of the ICPO-INTERPOL General Assembly.

83rd General Assembly session, Resolution AG-2014-RES-18 adopting amendments to INTERPOL's Rules on the Processing of Data.

85th General Assembly session, Resolution AG-2016-RES-06 adopting amendments to INTERPOL's Rules on the Processing of Data.

88th General Assembly session, Resolution AG-2019-88-RES-02 adopting amendments to INTERPOL's Rules on the Processing of Data.

91st General Assembly session, Resolution GA-2023-91-RES-08 adopting amendments to INTERPOL's Rules on the Processing of Data.

CONTENTS

PREAMBLE 7
Article 1: Definitions..7
Article 2: Aim..8
Article 3: Subject..9
Article 4: Scope..9

TITLE 1: GENERAL PRINCIPLES..9

CHAPTER I: PRINCIPLES CONCERNING INTERNATIONAL POLICE COOPERATION..9
Article 5: Compliance with the principles of governance and responsibilities associated with the processing of data..9
Article 6: Access to the INTERPOL Information System..9
Article 7: Control of data processing..10
Article 8: Use of INTERPOL notices and diffusions..10
Article 9: Direct communication using messages..10

CHAPTER II: PRINCIPLES CONCERNING INFORMATION PROCESSING.........10
Article 10: Purposes of international police cooperation..10
Article 11: Lawfulness..11
Article 12: Quality..11
Article 13: Transparency..11
Article 14: Confidentiality..12
Article 15: Security..12
Article 16: External processing for police purposes..13
Article 17: Effective implementation..13
Article 18: Rights of access, correction and deletion of data..13

TITLE 2: PARTICIPANTS..14

CHAPTER I: ROLE OF THE NATIONAL CENTRAL BUREAUS..14
Article 19: Coordination of data flow..14
Article 20: Coordination of criminal inquiries..14
Article 21: Granting authorizations to directly access the INTERPOL Information System at the national level..14

CHAPTER II: ROLE OF THE GENERAL SECRETARIAT..14
Article 22: Administration of the system..14
Article 23: Additional measures to enhance cooperation..15
Article 24: Recording data..15
Article 25: Coordination..15
Article 26: Emergency measures..15

CHAPTER III: RELATIONS WITH THE INTERNATIONAL ENTITIES AND PRIVATE ENTITIES....16
Article 27: Conditions relating to the processing of data by international entities....16
Article 28: Conditions relating to the processing of data by private entities....17

TITLE 3: PROCEDURES FOR PROCESSING DATA....18

CHAPTER I: POLICE DATABASES....18

SECTION 1: AUTHORIZATION....18
Article 29: Creation of a database....18
Article 30: Modification of an existing database....18
Article 31: Deletion of an existing database....19
Article 32: Authorizations granted by the Executive Committee....19
Article 33: Register of existing databases....19

SECTION 2: FUNCTIONING....19
Article 34: Compliance with the Organization's Constitution....19
Article 35: Interest of the data for the purposes of international police cooperation....19
Article 36: General characteristics of databases....20
Article 37: Minimum conditions for recording data in the databases....20
Article 38: Additional conditions for recording data on persons....20
Article 39: Additional conditions for recording data on deceased persons....21
Article 40: Additional conditions for recording data on persons who are victims or witnesses....21
Article 41: Additional conditions for recording data on minors....21
Article 42: Additional conditions for recording particularly sensitive data....21
Article 43: Additional conditions for recording copied or uploaded data....21
Article 43A: Additional conditions for temporarily processing large data sets....22
Article 44: Status of persons....22
Article 45: Definition of specific conditions of use when recording data....23
Article 46: Updates....23
Article 47: Recording of data at the initiative of the General Secretariat....23
Article 48: Supplementary information and corrections....23
Article 49: Retention period....23
Article 50: Periodic assessments....24
Article 51: Deletion of data....24
Article 52: Temporary retention of criminal history....25
Article 53: Retention of data for purposes of redirecting enquiries....25

SECTION 3: CONSULTATION....25
Article 54: Direct access....25
Article 55: Interconnection....25
Article 56: Downloading for the purposes of international police cooperation....26
Article 57: Indirect access....27

Article 58: Access restrictions 28
Article 59: Disclosure of data subject to restrictions 28
Article 60: Access by third parties 28
Article 61: Disclosure of data to the public 28

SECTION 4: USE OF DATA 29
Article 62: Conditions of use 29
Article 63: Verification of the accuracy and relevance of data 29
Article 64: Use of data for a criminal investigation purpose other than the initial purpose or for an administrative purpose 29
Article 65: Use of data for administrative purposes *[deleted]* 30
Article 66: Special conditions for use 30
Article 67: Forwarding data 30

SECTION 5: SPECIFIC RULES RELATING TO CRIME ANALYSIS FILES 31
Article 68: Analysis files 31
Article 69: Use of analysis files 31
Article 70: Additional conditions for recording data on criminal analysis purposes 32
Article 71: Crime analysis reports 32
Article 72: Completion of crime analysis projects 32

CHAPTER II: NOTICES AND DIFFUSIONS 33

SECTION 1: PROVISIONS COMMON TO NOTICES 33
Article 73: INTERPOL notices system 33
Article 74: Role of the General Secretariat 33
Article 75: Structure of INTERPOL notices 33
Article 76: Requests for the publication of notices 33
Article 77: Examination of requests by the General Secretariat 34
Article 78: Incomplete or non-compliant requests for notices 34
Article 79: Publication of notices 34
Article 80: Implementation of notices 34
Article 81: Suspension, withdrawal or cancellation of a notice 35

SECTION 2: PROVISIONS SPECIFIC TO RED NOTICES 35
Article 82: Purpose of red notices 35
Article 83: Specific conditions for publication of red notices 35
Article 84: Assurances provided by the requesting National Central Bureau or international entity ..36
Article 85: Provision of documents that could support extradition or surrender proceedings 36
Article 86: Legal review by the General Secretariat 36
Article 87: Steps to be taken following the location of the person 37

SECTION 3: PROVISIONS SPECIFIC TO OTHER NOTICES 37
Article 88: Blue notices 37
Article 89: Green notices 37

Article 90: Yellow notices.....38
Article 91: Black notices.....38
Article 92: Purple notices.....38
Article 93: Orange notices.....39
Article 94: Stolen work of art notices.....39
Article 95: INTERPOL-United Nations Security Council Special Notices.....39
Article 96: Other special notices.....39

SECTION 4: DIFFUSIONS.....39
Article 97: Diffusions system.....39
Article 98: Diffusion forms.....40
Article 99: Circulation of diffusions.....40
Article 100: Suspension or withdrawal of a diffusion.....40
Article 101: Recording of cooperation requests or alerts circulated in messages.....40

SECTION 5: NOTICES AND DIFFUSIONS PUBLISHED AT THE INITIATIVE OF THE GENERAL SECRETARIAT.....41
Article 102: Requests for information.....41
Article 103: Publication of notices.....41

SECTION 6: POSITIVE QUERY RESULTS.....41
Article 104: Generation of positive query results.....41
Article 105: Procedure for managing positive query results.....41
Article 106: Record of positive query results.....42

CHAPTER III: DATA SECURITY.....42

SECTION 1: MANAGEMENT OF RIGHTS OF ACCESS TO THE INTERPOL INFORMATION SYSTEM.....42
Article 107: Designation of a new National Central Bureau.....42
Article 108: Granting a right of access to a new national entity.....42
Article 109: Granting a right of access to a new international entity.....42
Article 110: Register of rights of access to the INTERPOL Information System.....42
Article 111: Individual rights to access the INTERPOL Information System.....42

SECTION 2: CONFIDENTIALITY.....43
Article 112: Confidentiality levels.....43
Article 113: Additional measures taken by the General Secretariat.....43
Article 114: Respecting confidentiality in the INTERPOL Information System.....44

SECTION 3: MANAGEMENT OF THE SECURITY SYSTEM.....44
Article 115: Security rules.....44
Article 116: Implementation by the National Central Bureaus and entities.....44
Article 117: Appointment of a security officer.....44

SECTION 4: SECURITY INCIDENTS 45

Article 118: Information on security incidents 45

Article 119: Partial or complete restoration of the INTERPOL Information System 45

TITLE 4: SUPERVISION AND MONITORING 45

CHAPTER I: TYPES OF SUPERVISION 45

Article 120: Supervision of users 45

Article 121: Designation of a data protection officer within National Central Bureaus and national and international entities 45

Article 121A: Designation of a data protection officer within the General Secretariat 46

Article 122: Monitoring the use of data 46

Article 123: Evaluation of national entities 47

Article 124: Evaluation of National Central Bureaus 47

CHAPTER II: SUPERVISORY TOOLS 47

Article 125: Compliance management database 47

Article 126: Register of processing operations 47

Article 127: Comparison of data for verification purposes 48

CHAPTER III: SUPERVISION MEASURES 48

Article 128: Examination procedure 48

Article 129: Interim measures 49

Article 130: Measures applicable to users 49

Article 131: Corrective measures applicable to National Central Bureaus and international entities 49

TITLE 5: FINAL PROVISIONS 50

CHAPTER I: PROCESSING FOR ANY OTHER LEGITIMATE PURPOSE 50

Article 132: Definition of processing for any other legitimate purpose 50

Article 133: Processing conditions 50

Article 134: Retention of data 50

CHAPTER II: SETTLEMENT OF DISPUTES 50

Article 135: Settlement of disputes 50

APPENDIX: CHARTER RELATING TO ACCESS TO THE INTERPOL INFORMATION SYSTEM BY NATIONAL ENTITIES 51

PREAMBLE

The General Assembly of the International Criminal Police Organization – INTERPOL,

CONSIDERING Article 2, paragraph 1 of the Organization's Constitution,

HAVING CONSULTED the Commission for the Control of INTERPOL's Files in accordance with Article 36, paragraph 2 of the Constitution,

CONSIDERING that it is the responsibility of the General Assembly, in accordance with Article 8(d) of the Constitution, to determine the operating rules for the INTERPOL Information System regarding data processing,

HAS ADOPTED THE FOLLOWING RULES:

Article 1: Definitions

For the purposes of the present Rules:

(1) "Ordinary-law crime" means any criminal offences, with the exception of those that fall within the scope of application of Article 3 of the Constitution and those for which specific rules have been defined by the General Assembly.

(2) "Data" means any item of information, irrespective of its source, pertaining to constituent elements of ordinary-law crimes, the investigation and prevention of such crimes, the prosecution of the offenders and punishment of the offences, and any information pertaining to missing persons and unidentified dead bodies.

(3) "Personal data" means any data about an identified natural person or a person who may be identified by means that may reasonably be used.

(4) The "INTERPOL Information System" means all the structured material resources and software used by the Organization – databases, communications infrastructure, advanced sensor technology and other services – to process data through its channels in the context of international police cooperation.

(5) "Processing" means any operation or set of operations performed on data, whether or not by automatic means, such as collection, recording, consultation, transmission, use, disclosure and deletion.

(6) "Source" means any National Central Bureau which processes data in the INTERPOL Information System, and which is ultimately responsible for those data, or any international entity or private entity whose data are processed in the INTERPOL Information System, or on behalf of which data are recorded in the System, and which is ultimately responsible for them.

(7) "National Central Bureau" means any body designated by a country to perform the liaison functions provided for under Article 32 of the Organization's Constitution.

(8) "National entity" means an entity legally authorized to fulfil the role of a public institution that has specifically been authorized by the National Central Bureau of its country, through an agreement and within the limits determined by that National Central Bureau, to directly consult data processed in the INTERPOL Information System or to directly provide data for one or more of the processing purposes listed in Article 10 of the present Rules.

(9) "International entity" means any international, intergovernmental or non-governmental organization which fulfils an international public interest mission, which has concluded an agreement with the Organization on the exchange of data and which has been granted direct or indirect access to a part of the INTERPOL Information System by the Organization.

(10) "Private entity" means any legal person governed by private law such as a business, company, commercial association or a not-for-profit organization, not covered by the category of international entities, which has concluded an agreement with the Organization on the exchange of data, and in particular, on the processing of data in the INTERPOL Information System.

(11) "Request for international cooperation" means any steps taken by a National Central Bureau, an international entity or the General Secretariat via the INTERPOL Information System to send a request for assistance to one or more of the Organization's Members to carry out a specific action in conformity with the Organization's aims and activities.

(12) "International alert" means any steps taken by a National Central Bureau, an international entity or the General Secretariat via the INTERPOL Information System to send a notification to one of more of the Organization's Members about specific threats to public safety, persons and property.

(13) "Notice" means any request for international cooperation or any international alert published by the Organization at the request of a National Central Bureau or an international entity, or at the initiative of the General Secretariat, and sent to all the Organization's Members.

(14) "Diffusion" means any request for international cooperation or any international alert from a National Central Bureau or an international entity, sent directly to one or several National Central Bureaus or to one or several international entities, and simultaneously recorded in a police database of the Organization.

(15) "Message" means any request for international cooperation, any international alert or any data that a National Central Bureau or international entity with powers of investigation and prosecution in criminal matters chooses to send directly to one or several National Central Bureaus or to one or several international entities through the INTERPOL Information System but that it chooses, unless otherwise indicated, not to simultaneously record in a police database of the Organization.

(16) "Direct access" means entering and obtaining data in the INTERPOL Information System by expressly authorized persons using automatic means and without assistance from the General Secretariat.

(17) "Indirect access" means entering and obtaining data in the INTERPOL Information System with assistance of the General Secretariat.

(18) "Particularly sensitive data" means any personal data revealing racial or ethnic origin; political opinions; religious or philosophical convictions; trade-union membership; or concerning health or sexuality.

(19) "Interconnection" means any electronic link which involves connecting a part of the INTERPOL Information System to a part of another information system.

(20) "Download" means any operation involving the exportation of data from the INTERPOL Information System into another information system.

(21) "Upload" means any operation involving the importation of data from another information system into the INTERPOL Information System.

(22) "Crime analysis" means the methodical identification and provision of insight into the relationship between data carried out in the context of international police cooperation.

(23) "Status of a person" means information about a person in connection with an event which warrants the processing of data in the INTERPOL Information System.

(24) "Positive query result" means a presumed match between data already recorded in the INTERPOL Information System and other data that are entered in this system.

(25) "Advanced sensor technology" means technology which facilitates the identification of persons and objects through automated data processing and may allow semi-automated decision-making, which requires human intervention for verification purposes.

(26) "Large data set" means a collection of structured or unstructured data shared by a source of data with the General Secretariat, which is not verified or categorized and which, due to its volume or complexity, cannot be assessed in accordance with all the requirements of the present Rules when initially processed by the General Secretariat.

(27) "Permanent operational police database" means a permanent police database created by the General Secretariat, irrespective of the particular data processing technology used, according to the requirements specified in Article 29 of the present Rules.

(28) "Recording" means inserting data or other items of information into a police database or a crime analysis file, according to the conditions for recording outlined in the present Rules.

Article 2: Aim

The aim of the present Rules is to ensure the efficiency and quality of international cooperation between criminal police authorities through INTERPOL channels, with due respect for the basic rights of the persons who are the subject of this cooperation, in conformity with Article 2 of the Organization's Constitution and the Universal Declaration of Human Rights to which the said Article refers.

Article 3: Subject

The present Rules lay down the general principles, the responsibilities and the arrangements for the functioning of the INTERPOL Information System.

Article 4: Scope

(1) The processing of data through INTERPOL channels shall be done exclusively in the INTERPOL Information System.

(2) The present Rules shall apply to all data-processing operations performed in the INTERPOL Information System.

(3) Notwithstanding the applicable provisions of the present Rules, the General Assembly may adopt a separate legal framework whereby the Organization's Members agree to follow rules governing the processing of data for purposes of international judicial cooperation.

TITLE 1: GENERAL PRINCIPLES

CHAPTER I: PRINCIPLES CONCERNING INTERNATIONAL POLICE COOPERATION

Article 5: Compliance with the principles of governance and responsibilities associated with the processing of data

(1) International police cooperation through INTERPOL channels shall take place in accordance with the basic rules governing the Organization's operations, in particular its Constitution.

(2) The processing of data in the INTERPOL Information System shall be performed in conformity with, in particular, Articles 2, 3, 26, 31, 32, 36 and 41 of the Constitution.

(3) The Organization's Members shall endeavour to exchange a maximum of information of interest for the purposes of international police cooperation, with due observance of the Organization's political neutrality, independence and mandate, and of their respective national legislations and international conventions to which they are parties.

(4) At the national level, the National Central Bureaus shall play a central role concerning the processing of data in the INTERPOL Information System.

(5) The source shall be fully responsible for the data it processes in the INTERPOL Information System, regardless of the method used for such processing, and for the consequences directly resulting from such processing, and shall take appropriate measures to correct any incorrect processing of data.

(6) INTERPOL shall be fully responsible for any unauthorized or incorrect use and/or storage of data by INTERPOL and for the consequences directly resulting from such unauthorized or incorrect use and/or storage of data, and shall take appropriate measures to correct any incorrect processing of data by the Organization.

(7) Recipients of data processed in the INTERPOL Information System shall be fully responsible for:

   (a) any action taken at the national level based on data they have received;

   (b) taking the appropriate measures so that data received are immediately updated at the national level once they have been informed of any modification or deletion.

Article 6: Access to the INTERPOL Information System

(1) National Central Bureaus are entitled to direct access to the System in the performance of their functions pursuant to the Constitution. This access shall include:

   (a) the recording, updating, and deletion of data directly in the Organization's police databases, as well as the creation of links between data;

   (b) direct consultation of the Organization's police databases, subject to specific conditions determined for each database and to restrictions and confidentiality rules laid down by their sources;

   (c) use of INTERPOL's notices and diffusions allowing the transmission of requests for cooperation and international alerts;

   (d) following up on positive query results;

   (e) transmission of messages.

(2) Access by national entities and international entities to the INTERPOL Information System is subject to authorization, and to the conditions provided for in Articles 21 and 27, respectively, of the present Rules.

Article 7: Control of data processing

(1) National Central Bureaus and international entities shall retain, at all times, control over the processing of their data, in accordance with the present Rules. Any National Central Bureau or international entity shall be free, in particular, to restrict the access to or the use of its data in one of the Organization's police databases, under the conditions provided for in Article 58 of the present Rules.

(2) Data processed in the INTERPOL Information System shall be those provided by National Central Bureaus, national entities and international entities. Nevertheless, data supplied by private entities in application of Article 28 of the present Rules or those recorded by the General Secretariat in application of Article 24(2) of the present Rules, may also be processed in the System.

Article 8: Use of INTERPOL notices and diffusions

(1) Requests for cooperation and international alerts through INTERPOL channels shall be sent by means of INTERPOL notices or diffusions.

(2) National Central Bureaus are entitled to use INTERPOL notices and diffusions in the performance of their functions pursuant to the Constitution. For international entities, entitlement shall be subject to authorization.

(3) The publication of INTERPOL notices and the transmission of diffusions shall be in accordance with Articles 73 et seq. of the present Rules.

(4) National Central Bureaus may send requests for cooperation and international alerts by means of messages, in accordance with Article 9 below. For international entities with powers of investigation and prosecution in criminal matters, this option shall be subject to authorization.

Article 9: Direct communication using messages

(1) The INTERPOL Information System enables direct communication between National Central Bureaus by means of messages.

(2) National Central Bureaus are entitled to send messages in the performance of their functions pursuant to the Constitution. For international entities, entitlement shall be subject to authorization.

(3) National Central Bureaus or international entities shall, prior to sending a message, ensure that it is in conformity with the present Rules.

(4) The General Secretariat may not record a message in one of the Organization's police databases without the prior consent of the National Central Bureau or international entity that sent the said message. The National Central Bureau or international entity is presumed to have given prior consent if the General Secretariat is one of the recipients of the said message.

(5) Further entitlements to communicate directly by means of messages may be granted in the context of specific projects or initiatives. In exceptional circumstances, a National Central Bureau may entitle expressly authorized persons who are not members of its staff to send such messages.

CHAPTER II: PRINCIPLES CONCERNING INFORMATION PROCESSING

Article 10: Purposes of international police cooperation

(1) The processing of data in the INTERPOL Information System may only be carried out for a given, explicit purpose which is in conformity with the Organization's aims and activities.

(2) Data shall be processed in the INTERPOL Information System for at least one of the following purposes:

(a) to search for a wanted person with a view to his/her detention, arrest or restriction of movement;

(b) to locate a person or an object of interest to the police;

(c) to provide or obtain information related to a criminal investigation or to the criminal history and activities of a person;

(d) to warn of a person, an event, an object or a modus operandi related to criminal activities;

(e) to identify a person or a dead body;

(f) to carry out forensic analyses;

(g) to carry out security checks that directly pertain to international police cooperation and are aimed at preventing or detecting crime;

(h) to carry out border management and border control activities;

(i) to identify threats, crime trends and criminal networks, including for crime analysis.

(3) The National Central Bureaus, national entities and international entities shall be responsible for determining the purpose of processing their data and for performing regular reviews, particularly once this purpose may have been achieved.

(4) The General Secretariat shall put in place mechanisms and tools to guarantee compliance with the said purpose at all times, under the conditions provided for in Articles 125 to 127of the present Rules.

(5) The National Central Bureaus, national entities and international entities shall comply with this purpose when using data.

(6) National Central Bureaus, national entities and international entities shall only be allowed to process data for other purposes of international police cooperation or for administrative purposes if the processing is in conformity with the Organization's aims and activities, and is not incompatible with the purpose for which the data were initially processed in the INTERPOL Information System. The source shall be notified of such processing and shall retain the right to oppose it, under the conditions provided for in Article 64 of the present Rules. Such processing shall be the sole responsibility of the National Central Bureau, national entity or international entity choosing to process the data for purposes other than those for which the data had initially been processed.

(7) Data may also be processed for any other legitimate purpose distinct from international police cooperation, under the conditions provided for in Articles 132 et seq. of the present Rules.

Article 11: Lawfulness

(1) Data processing in the INTERPOL Information System should be authorized with due regard for the law applicable to the National Central Bureau, national entity or international entity and should respect the basic rights of the persons who are the subject of the cooperation, in accordance with Article 2 of the Organization's Constitution and the Universal Declaration of Human Rights to which the said Article refers.

(2) The National Central Bureaus, national entities and international entities shall be responsible for ensuring lawfulness of the collection and entry of their data in the INTERPOL Information System.

(3) The National Central Bureaus, national entities and international entities shall also be responsible for ensuring the lawfulness of the consultation of the data entered in the INTERPOL Information System.

Article 12: Quality

(1) Data processed in the INTERPOL Information System must be accurate, relevant, not excessive in relation to their purpose and up to date, to allow them to be used by National Central Bureaus, national entities and international entities.

(2) The National Central Bureaus, national entities and international entities shall be responsible for the quality of the data they record and transmit in the INTERPOL Information System.

(3) The General Secretariat shall put in place the mechanisms and tools to guarantee compliance with the aforementioned quality at all times.

(4) The National Central Bureaus, national entities and international entities are required to check the quality of data before using them, under the conditions provided for in Article 63 of the present Rules.

Article 13: Transparency

(1) The processing of data in the INTERPOL Information System should guarantee at all times that the processing rights of National Central Bureaus, national entities and international entities are respected in accordance with the present Rules.

(2) The General Secretariat shall be responsible for ensuring the transparency of data-processing operations and of the functioning of the Organization's databases:

  (a) It shall request the opinion of the Commission for the Control of INTERPOL's Files if it intends to carry out any operations involving the processing of personal data referred to in Articles 27 to 31, 55, 56, 61, 68(4,d), 73(2) and 97(3) of the present Rules;

  (b) It shall inform the Commission for the Control of INTERPOL's Files of any steps taken in application of Articles 51(7), 59, 118 and 125(2,b) of the present Rules;

(c) It shall submit to the Executive Committee any project or request relating to the processing of data in the INTERPOL Information System for which its prior authorization is required in accordance with Articles 17(5), 22(3), 23, 29, 30, 31, 55(3), 68(8), 97(3) and 131(3) of the present Rules, and shall attach the opinion of the Commission for the Control of INTERPOL's Files whenever so required by the present Rules. The Executive Committee shall report to the General Assembly on the authorizations it grants under the conditions provided for in Article 55(6) of the present Rules;

(d) It shall inform the Executive Committee of the measures taken in application of Articles 59, 68(4) and 118 of the present Rules;

(e) Under the conditions provided for in Article 126 of the present Rules, it shall keep up-to-date registers of the following:

(i) National Central Bureaus, national entities and international entities to which access has been granted to the INTERPOL Information System or which have supplied the data processed in the system;

(ii) the Organization's police databases, including analysis files;

(iii) interconnection operations;

(iv) the downloading and uploading operations performed;

(v) the data-processing operations recorded in the databases;

(vi) the data-management tools implemented by the General Secretariat;

(vii) comparison operations carried out for verification purposes.

These registers shall be available at all times to the National Central Bureaus. They shall also be available to international entities according to the access rights they have been granted, as well as to national entities through their National Central Bureaus.

(f) The General Secretariat shall keep an up-to-date list of the maximum data retention periods as defined by the Executive Committee in accordance with these Rules, and shall make this list publicly available.

Article 14: Confidentiality

(1) The confidentiality of data processed in the INTERPOL Information System should be determined according to the risks linked to their disclosure for those who are the subject of cooperation, the sources and the Organization. Data should only be accessible to persons authorized to know such information.

(2) National Central Bureaus, national entities and international entities are responsible for attributing levels of confidentiality to the data they enter in the INTERPOL Information System and for observing the confidentiality of the data they consult, transmit or use for external processing purposes, under the conditions provided for in Articles 112 et seq. of the present Rules.

(3) The General Secretariat shall ensure that all data are processed in the INTERPOL Information System according to the confidentiality level attributed by the National Central Bureau, national entities or international entities which carried out the processing.

(4) The General Secretariat shall take, in accordance with the present Rules, all necessary and appropriate measures to increase the confidentiality level attached to data to protect against risks that their disclosure may have for those who are the subject of cooperation, the sources of data and the Organization.

Article 15: Security

(1) The data processed in the INTERPOL Information System should be protected against risks violating their integrity and confidentiality, and remain available at all times to the National Central Bureaus, national entities and international entities having direct access to the INTERPOL Information System.

(2) The General Secretariat shall be responsible for setting up an information security management system. To that end, in consultation with the National Central Bureaus or with their representatives on the advisory bodies set up for the purpose, it shall establish and regularly update a security policy based on internationally accepted standards and on a risk assessment.

(3) The General Secretariat shall be responsible for developing the communication infrastructure and databases in order to preserve the security of data, in compliance with the security policy established.

(4) The General Secretariat shall be responsible for defining authorization or security-clearance procedures for its staff for each level of data confidentiality, under the conditions provided for in Articles 112 et seq. of the present Rules.

(5) National Central Bureaus and international entities shall be responsible for the access they grant to the INTERPOL Information System, the security of the facilities which enable them to access that system, compliance with the established rules of security and for maintaining data at a level of security at least equivalent to that laid down by the General Secretariat in cases of external processing.

(6) The General Secretariat shall take, in accordance with the present Rules, all appropriate measures to protect the security of data processed in the INTERPOL Information System.

Article 16: External processing for police purposes

(1) The data initially processed in the INTERPOL Information System may be processed outside the system if this processing is necessary and carried out for police purposes. Any external processing must be in compliance with the above-mentioned data-processing principles.

(2) The National Central Bureaus and international entities shall be responsible for implementing the arrangements for external processing, under the conditions provided for in Articles 114(4) and 116 of the present Rules.

(3) The General Secretariat shall advise the National Central Bureaus and international entities in implementing these arrangements.

Article 17: Effective implementation

(1) The present Rules must be effectively implemented.

(2) National Central Bureaus, national entities and international entities shall be responsible for defining and establishing effective and appropriate measures to guarantee the compliance of their operations with the principles and obligations laid down in the present Rules, in particular through staff training.

(3) National Central Bureaus shall be responsible for defining and establishing procedures to guarantee the compliance of the operations of their national entities with the principles and obligations laid down in the present Rules, prior to granting them authorization to directly consult data processed in the INTERPOL Information System or to directly provide data for processing purposes in the System.

(4) The National Central Bureaus shall be responsible for regularly evaluating the operation of each of their national entities in the light of the present Rules, and shall, within the limits set by the present Rules, take all necessary and appropriate corrective measures vis-à-vis these national entities to terminate any non-compliant processing of data. They may take all necessary precautionary measures to take account of the risk inherent in any clearly non-compliant use of data.

(5) The General Secretariat shall be responsible for regularly evaluating the operation of the National Central Bureaus in the light of the present Rules. It shall take all necessary and appropriate corrective measures to terminate any non-compliant processing of data, under the conditions provided for in Article 131 of the present Rules. Any measures which may result in the long-term suspension of the processing rights of a National Central Bureau shall be submitted to the Executive Committee for prior approval.

(6) The General Secretariat shall be responsible for regularly evaluating the operation of the international entities in the light of the present Rules, and shall adopt any necessary and appropriate corrective measures to terminate any non-compliant processing of data, under the conditions provided for in Article 131 of the present Rules.

Article 18: Rights of access, correction and deletion of data

(1) Any person or entity shall be entitled to submit directly to the Commission for the Control of INTERPOL's Files a request for access to, or correction and/or deletion of data processed in the INTERPOL Information System concerning that person or entity.

(2) These rights of access to, or correction and deletion of data shall be guaranteed by the Commission for the Control of INTERPOL's Files and be governed by separate rules. Unless otherwise specified in those rules, requests for access to, or correction and/or deletion of data may not be processed in the INTERPOL Information System.

TITLE 2: PARTICIPANTS

CHAPTER I: ROLE OF THE NATIONAL CENTRAL BUREAUS

Article 19: Coordination of data flow

(1) The National Central Bureaus shall be responsible for coordinating at the national level the processing in the INTERPOL Information System of data provided by their countries.

(2) The National Central Bureaus shall be responsible, with due respect for the present Rules, for providing the institutions of their countries with data processed in the INTERPOL Information System and necessary for the performance of their duties.

Article 20: Coordination of criminal inquiries

(1) Matters relating to criminal inquiries shall be coordinated in conjunction with the National Central Bureaus.

(2) The National Central Bureaus shall be responsible for coordinating at the national level the processing of requests for cooperation and international alerts sent to them by means of INTERPOL notices, diffusions and messages. As such, they shall be free to determine the most appropriate means, at the national level, for effective international cooperation.

(3) The National Central Bureaus shall be responsible for following up on requests for cooperation and international alerts that they have sent at the request of the institutions of their respective countries, by means of INTERPOL notices, diffusions and messages.

Article 21: Granting authorizations to directly access the INTERPOL Information System at the national level

(1) The National Central Bureaus alone shall be entitled to authorize the entities of their countries to access the INTERPOL Information System and determine the extent of their access and processing rights.

(2) Prior to granting authorizations for direct access, the National Central Bureaus must ensure that all the following conditions are met:

(a) the entity to which it intends to grant direct access to the INTERPOL Information System is a national entity as defined in Article 1(8) of the present Rules;

(b) the nature of the activities and tasks of this entity do not violate the aims or the neutrality of the Organization;

(c) the national laws do not prohibit such access by this entity;

(d) the entity will be able to observe the present Rules;

(e) the access and processing rights it intends to grant are limited, strictly necessary and proportionate to the execution of the tasks and functions of this entity.

(3) When a National Central Bureau grants an authorization to directly access the INTERPOL Information System, it shall be subject to a prior agreement between the National Central Bureau and the new national entity. The agreement must comply with the "Charter relating to access to the INTERPOL Information System by national entities" appended to the present Rules.

(4) When a National Central Bureau grants authorization to a new national entity, it shall immediately notify the General Secretariat and all National Central Bureaus and international entities.

(5) National entities shall process their data in the INTERPOL Information System within the limits of the processing rights granted to them.

(6) National Central Bureaus shall communicate to their national entities the necessary information for them to exercise these processing rights.

(7) National Central Bureaus shall be responsible for the processing of data by the national entities they authorize to access the INTERPOL Information System.

CHAPTER II: ROLE OF THE GENERAL SECRETARIAT

Article 22: Administration of the system

(1) The General Secretariat shall be responsible for the general administration of the INTERPOL Information System.

(2) It shall design, organize and administer the INTERPOL Information System and decide upon which technologies it should be based. When implementing data processing technologies, the General Secretariat shall ensure that the requirements of these Rules are integrated by design and by default as early as possible through appropriate technical and organizational measures.

(3) It shall examine and process, under the Executive Committee's supervision and with due respect for the present Rules, downloading and interconnection requests submitted by the National Central Bureaus, under the conditions laid down in Articles 55 and 56 of the present Rules.

(4) It shall house the Organization's databases.

(5) It shall manage the processing of data in the INTERPOL Information System and ensure that the conditions for processing data in the Organization's databases are duly observed. It shall put in place the tools for managing data and access to the System. It shall perform a management role when conducting spot checks and resolving processing incidents.

Article 23: Additional measures to enhance cooperation

(1) The General Secretariat shall be entitled to propose to the General Assembly the conclusion of agreements relating to data processing, and to propose to the Executive Committee the establishment of databases, INTERPOL notices or diffusions under the conditions laid down in Articles 27, 28, 29, 73 and 97 respectively of the present Rules.

(2) The General Secretariat may, within the limits set by the present Rules, carry out tests to examine and draw up the above proposals.

Article 24: Recording data

(1) In accordance with the present Rules, the General Secretariat shall record, update and delete data in the Organization's police databases:

   (a) on behalf of sources which do not have direct access to the INTERPOL Information System;

   (b) on its own initiative, when the data are obtained from publicly accessible sources that it has directly consulted or from persons who have contacted the General Secretariat or the National Central Bureaus, or when the data are the result of crime analyses conducted by the General Secretariat, under the conditions set forth in Article 47 of the present Rules;

   (c) in exceptional circumstances, at the request or on behalf of a National Central Bureau, national entity or international entity with direct access to the INTERPOL Information System.

(2) The General Secretariat may only record data on behalf of sources which do not have access to the INTERPOL Information System or on its own initiative if procedures for updating and deleting the information have been established beforehand.

Article 25: Coordination

(1) The General Secretariat shall facilitate cooperation between the National Central Bureaus. It shall request from them or forward to them, in accordance with the present Rules and the restrictions and rules of confidentiality laid down by the source, all the data that it believes may improve the coordination of international cooperation.

(2) If the purposes of international cooperation so require, the General Secretariat may exercise a role of direct coordination with the national entities, subject to express authorization by their respective National Central Bureaus.

(3) The General Secretariat shall, whenever necessary, facilitate cooperation between the National Central Bureaus and international and private entities.

(4) In order to improve international coordination, the General Secretariat may publish notices on its own initiative, under the conditions laid down in Article 103 of the present Rules.

Article 26: Emergency measures

(1) If the cooperation mechanisms established by the Organization, its independence or the fulfilment of its commitments are under serious and imminent threat and the proper functioning of the INTERPOL Information System is likely to be interrupted, the Secretary General shall take, with regard to data processing, the appropriate measures required under these circumstances after official consultation with the President of the Organization. He shall notify the National Central Bureaus and the Commission for the Control of INTERPOL's Files. These measures should be prompted by the desire to ensure, within the shortest possible time, that the National Central Bureaus have the means of performing their functions pursuant to the Constitution.

(2) When there is a real and imminent threat to people or property, and the data allowing a National Central Bureau, a national entity or an international entity to prevent this threat are subject to access restrictions placed against them, the General Secretariat shall be authorized to apply the emergency procedure provided for in Article 59 of the present Rules.

CHAPTER III: RELATIONS WITH THE INTERNATIONAL ENTITIES AND PRIVATE ENTITIES

Article 27: Conditions relating to the processing of data by international entities

(1) Whenever it considers it desirable, and when it is consistent with the aims and objects provided in its Constitution, the Organization may establish relations with international entities in order to collaborate with them on data processing on a regular basis. The establishment of regular relations between the Organization and an international entity shall be laid down in an agreement.

(2) The General Secretariat shall request the opinion of the Commission for the Control of INTERPOL's Files about all draft agreements that involve the processing of personal data.

(3) The General Secretariat shall submit all draft agreements to the General Assembly for approval. To justify its request, the General Secretariat shall provide:

(a) the purposes, conditions and implications of the agreement;

(b) the outcome of any tests conducted by the General Secretariat;

(c) the opinion of the Commission for the Control of INTERPOL's Files if the draft agreement concerns the processing of personal data;

(d) the text of the draft agreement.

(4) Data processing by international entities shall be subject to all the following conditions:

(a) The international entity is an international, intergovernmental or non-governmental organization performing a public-interest role at the international level;

(b) Such processing is strictly limited to the purposes of cooperation envisaged between the international entity and INTERPOL;

(c) The processing of personal data is strictly limited to the entity's need to know about such data;

(d) The international entity undertakes, in the agreement, to observe the processing principles and the general obligations incumbent upon any source, as set out in the present Rules;

(e) The international entity and INTERPOL have concluded an agreement on the procedures for processing data transmitted between both parties.

(5) Direct access by international entities to part of the INTERPOL Information System shall be subject to the following additional conditions:

(a) The international entity accepts and agrees to comply with the present Rules and the specific provisions of the agreement;

(b) The international entity accepts and agrees to comply with such security rules and administrative procedures as may be established by the INTERPOL General Secretariat pursuant to the present Rules to allow access to and use of the INTERPOL Information System;

(c) The international entity accepts that regular checks may be performed, either remotely or on the premises, on its processing of data transmitted by INTERPOL;

(d) Access shall only be granted to one unit or department within the said entity;

(e) Access may not result in the interruption or delay of the transmission of requests for cooperation and alerts, or access to such requests and alerts by the National Central Bureaus;

(f) The international entity wishing to be able to transmit data by means of a message to one or several National Central Bureaus or one or more international entities has powers of investigation and prosecution in criminal matters;

(g) The international entity wishing to request the publication of INTERPOL notices or to transmit diffusions has powers of investigation and/or prosecution in criminal matters. However, the use of the special notice system shall be examined on a case-by-case basis.

(6) The Organization's decision to authorize a new international entity to access the INTERPOL Information System shall be notified to the National Central Bureaus and other international entities by the General Secretariat. Access shall only become effective after completion of a procedure to safeguard the control by the other National Central Bureaus and other international entities over the rights granted to the new entity to process their data, under the conditions laid down in Article 109 of the present Rules.

(7) The list of agreements concluded shall be forwarded each year to the Executive Committee, to the Commission for the Control of INTERPOL's Files and to the General Assembly.

Article 28: Conditions relating to the processing of data by private entities

(1) Insofar as it is relevant to the accomplishment of its aims, the Organization may establish relations with private entities wishing to cooperate with it in data-processing matters. The establishment and conduct of relations between INTERPOL and a private entity shall be laid down in an agreement.

(2) The General Secretariat shall request the opinion of the Commission for the Control of INTERPOL's Files about all draft agreements that involve the processing of personal data.

(3) The General Secretariat shall submit all draft agreements to the General Assembly for approval. To justify its request, the General Secretariat shall provide:

(a) the purposes, conditions and implications of the agreement;

(b) the outcome of any tests conducted by the General Secretariat;

(c) the opinion of the Commission for the Control of INTERPOL's Files if the draft agreement concerns the processing of personal data;

(d) the text of the draft agreement.

(4) Cooperation with a private entity must:

(a) respect INTERPOL's Constitution and in particular the principle of national sovereignty. Any National Central Bureau which has recorded data in the INTERPOL Information System or on whose behalf data have been recorded in the system may oppose the forwarding of that data to a private entity;

(b) be subject to agreements, the conclusion of which has previously been authorized by the Executive Committee and then approved by the General Assembly.

(5) Such cooperation may only be considered if:

(a) the private entity is a legal person governed by private law;

(b) the processing is in conformity with the Organization's aims and activities;

(c) the purpose of the cooperation is clearly stated and corresponds to one of the prevention activities related to ordinary-law crimes;

(d) it is of interest for the purposes of international police cooperation in relation to the purpose concerned;

(e) durable cooperation is envisaged;

(f) the type of data to which access is made possible is identified in a specific manner;

(g) the data supplied by the private entity are identified as such and cannot be confused with the data obtained from other sources;

(h) the independence of the Organization in its cooperation with the private entity is guaranteed;

(i) cooperation with the private entity does not interfere with the transmission of international cooperation requests and alerts;

(j) the private entity undertakes, in the agreement, to respect the processing principles and the general obligations incumbent upon all sources, as set out in the present Rules.

(6) Data supplied to private entities must be limited to analytical data and may not be personal in nature. Nevertheless, in exceptional cases, data supplied to private entities may be extended, as part of a specific project, to include personal data (but not nominal data, unless the National Central Bureaus or international entities which have supplied the data give their express authorization to do so) and/or data used in an operational context. In that case, the following additional conditions must be met:

(a) the scope of the project must be clearly defined;

(b) the project must be the subject of a prior agreement with the entities concerned;

(c) access to these data is strictly limited to the entity's need to know such data;

(d) the use made of the data must be proportional to the aims referred to in Article 10(2) of the present Rules.

(7) The conditions relating to the processing of data by private entities shall be set out in the agreement concluded between the private entity and the Organization.

(8) Before providing private entities with data, according to the authorizations and conditions under the agreement, the General Secretariat shall notify the source of that data. The source shall have 45 days with effect from the date of notification to signify its opposition to this data communication.

(9) The ways in which data are communicated to private entities must be defined in the agreement in order to guarantee the security and integrity of the data processed in the INTERPOL Information System.

(10) The General Secretariat shall ensure that the means used by private entities to supply or obtain data processed in the INTERPOL Information System allow those entities to access only the data authorized, in conformity with the agreements concluded to that effect. The General Secretariat shall ensure that private entities are not able to access operational data, to compromise, or to interfere with police communications.

(11) Under no circumstances shall the INTERPOL Information System be used to circumvent restrictions imposed by any national laws governing police cooperation with private entities.

(12) The list of agreements concluded shall be forwarded each year to the Executive Committee, to the Commission for the Control of INTERPOL's Files and to the General Assembly.

TITLE 3: PROCEDURES FOR PROCESSING DATA

CHAPTER I: POLICE DATABASES

SECTION 1: AUTHORIZATION

Article 29: Creation of a database

(1) The General Secretariat shall submit any proposal to create a police database to the Executive Committee for approval.

(2) To justify its request, the General Secretariat shall provide:

(a) the reasons that led it to develop this project, as well as the financial implications of such a project;

(b) the list of the general characteristics of this database drawn up in consultation with the National Central Bureaus or with their representatives on the advisory bodies set up for that purpose;

(c) the outcome of any tests conducted by the General Secretariat;

(d) the opinion of the Commission for the Control of INTERPOL's Files, if the database contains personal data or is linked to such data.

(3) Any creation of a police database shall immediately be notified to the National Central Bureaus. It shall also be notified to the international entities according to the access rights they have been granted to the INTERPOL Information System.

Article 30: Modification of an existing database

(1) The General Secretariat shall be entitled to modify police databases.

(2) The General Secretariat shall request the opinion of the Commission for the Control of INTERPOL's Files on any proposal to modify a database that would result in the modification of its general characteristics if the database contains personal data or is linked to such data.

(3) The General Secretariat shall submit it to the Executive Committee for approval any proposal to modify a database that would result in the modification of its general characteristics.

(4) To this end, the General Secretariat shall provide:

(a) the reasons that led it to propose a modification of this database, as well as the financial implications of such a modification;

(b) the revised list of the characteristics of this database, drawn up in consultation with the National Central Bureaus or with their representatives on the advisory bodies set up for the purpose;

(c) the outcome of any tests conducted by the General Secretariat;

(d) the opinion of the Commission for the Control of INTERPOL's Files, if the database contains personal data or is linked to such data.

(5) Any modifications to the general characteristics of a police database shall immediately be notified to the National Central Bureaus. They shall also be notified to the international entities according to the access rights they have been granted to the INTERPOL Information System.

Article 31: Deletion of an existing database

(1) The General Secretariat shall report to the Commission for the Control of INTERPOL's Files any intention to delete a database and the processing of data contained in that database.

(2) The General Secretariat shall submit to the Executive Committee for approval any intention to delete a database.

(3) To this end, the General Secretariat shall provide:

(a) the reasons that led it to propose the deletion, as well as the financial implications of the deletion;

(b) the report it submitted to the Commission for the Control of INTERPOL's Files and the Commission's opinion.

(4) Any deletion of a police database shall immediately be notified to the National Central Bureaus. It shall also be notified to the international entities according to the access rights they have been granted to the INTERPOL Information System.

Article 32: Authorizations granted by the Executive Committee

(1) Each year, the Executive Committee shall report to the General Assembly the authorizations it has granted for the creation, modification or deletion of police databases belonging to the Organization, indicating in particular their position in the overall INTERPOL Information System, the purpose of each, the nature of the data they store, and the processing rights attaching to each database.

(2) The Executive Committee shall also report to the General Assembly on the maximum retention period it has set for each type of data processed in the INTERPOL Information System, indicating the underlying reasons.

Article 33: Register of existing databases

(1) The General Secretariat shall keep an updated register of the Organization's police databases. The register shall specify the general characteristics of each database.

(2) National Central Bureaus may consult this register at any time. International entities may consult part of this register according to the access rights they have been granted to the INTERPOL Information System.

SECTION 2: FUNCTIONING

Article 34: Compliance with the Organization's Constitution

(1) In conformity with Article 5 of the present Rules, prior to any recording of data in a police database, the National Central Bureau, national entity or international entity shall ensure that the data are in compliance with Article 2 of the Organization's Constitution, and also that it is authorized to record such data pursuant to applicable national laws and international conventions and to the fundamental human rights enshrined in the Universal Declaration of Human Rights to which the said Article refers.

(2) In conformity with Article 5 of the present Rules, prior to any recording of data in a police database, the National Central Bureau, national entity or international entity shall ensure that the data are in compliance with Article 3 of the Organization's Constitution.

(3) To determine whether data comply with Article 3 of the Constitution, all relevant elements shall be examined, such as:

(a) nature of the offence, namely the charges and underlying facts;

(b) status of the persons concerned;

(c) identity of the source of the data;

(d) the position expressed by another National Central Bureau or another international entity;

(e) obligations under international law;

(f) implications for the neutrality of the Organization;

(g) the general context of the case.

(4) In light of the directives issued by the General Assembly and of developments in international law, the General Secretariat may compile repositories of practice on the application of Articles 2 and 3 of the Constitution, and make them available to the National Central Bureaus, national entities and international entities.

Article 35: Interest of the data for the purposes of international police cooperation

(1) In conformity with Article 5(3) of the present Rules, prior to any recording of data in a police database, the National Central Bureau, national entity or international entity shall ensure that the data are of interest for the purposes of international police cooperation.

(2) Compliance with this condition for recording data shall be assessed in relation to:

(a) the purposes specific to international police cooperation which are laid down in Article 10(2) of the present Rules; and

(b) the international nature of the data and, in particular, the extent to which the data may be used by National Central Bureaus, national entities or international entities other than the source.

Article 36: General characteristics of databases

(1) Each police database shall be defined with regard to the following characteristics:

(a) specific purpose of the database;

(b) nature of the data it contains, especially personal or particularly sensitive data;

(c) sources likely to contribute to the database;

(d) applicable confidentiality levels;

(e) applicable types of restrictions;

(f) applicable security measures;

(g) National Central Bureaus, national entities or international entities likely to record data in the database;

(h) minimum conditions for recording data;

(i) procedures for recording data, in particular any specific processing carried out on data during the recording due to their nature;

(j) procedures for updating recorded data;

(k) retention period of the data and the specific methods for extending or deleting this period;

(l) procedures and mechanisms used to check the compliance of the data;

(m) National Central Bureaus, national or international entities likely to consult the database;

(n) procedures for consulting the database, especially any type of direct access or any interconnection and uploading operations;

(o) procedures for using the data;

(p) procedures to follow if a positive query result is generated on the basis of data recorded in the database;

(q) data which may be disclosed to the public in conformity with Article 61 of the present Rules.

(2) All of the general characteristics above determine the legal framework applicable to each of the Organization's databases.

Article 37: Minimum conditions for recording data in the databases

(1) Minimum conditions shall be set for recording data in each database.

(2) Regardless of the database, the recording of data about a person, object or event must include:

(a) the identity of the source of the data;

(b) the date on which the data were recorded;

(c) the specific purpose for the recording;

(d) for any personal data, the status of the person and the data connecting this person to an event;

(e) the level of confidentiality of the data;

(f) the retention period of the data;

(g) access restrictions;

(h) any additional information ensuring that all the data are relevant to the purpose and of interest for the purposes of international police cooperation.

(3) These conditions shall be established by the General Secretariat in consultation with the National Central Bureaus or with their representatives on the advisory bodies set up for the purpose and communicated to all National Central Bureaus. They shall also be communicated to international entities according to the access rights they have been granted.

(4) All National Central Bureaus, national entities and international entities shall ensure that the minimum recording conditions are met when recording data in a police database.

(5) All National Central Bureaus, national entities and international entities shall keep any items on the basis of which the data were recorded or which justify retaining the information in the database.

Article 38: Additional conditions for recording data on persons

(1) Additional conditions for recording data on persons shall be applicable in the following cases:

(a) data on deceased persons;

(b) data on victims or witnesses;

(c) data on minors;

(d) particularly sensitive data.

(2) All National Central Bureaus, national entities and international entities shall observe these additional recording conditions when recording information in a police database.

Article 39: Additional conditions for recording data on deceased persons

(1) Data on deceased persons shall be recorded only in the following cases:

(a) for identification purposes;

(b) if the person has played a part in a criminal case or an event that has been processed in the Organization's police databases and the data concerning this person are necessary to understand the case or the event;

(c) for crime-analysis purposes.

(2) Data shall be recorded for the time strictly required to achieve one of the processing purposes above.

(3) The status of these persons and the purpose for recording the data shall be specified in a manner such that the data cannot be confused, in any way whatsoever, with data on persons who are the subject of cooperation.

Article 40: Additional conditions for recording data on persons who are victims or witnesses

(1) Data on persons who are victims or witnesses shall be recorded exclusively in the context of the events or acts of which they were victims or to which they were witnesses, and may not be used in relation to other events or acts. The status of these persons and the purpose for recording the data shall be specified in a manner such that the data cannot be confused, in any way whatsoever, with data on persons suspected of, accused of or convicted for these same acts.

(2) An additional indication shall be inserted to the effect that no restrictive measures may be taken against them.

Article 41: Additional conditions for recording data on minors

(1) The additional indication "MINOR" must be inserted whenever the person was a minor at the time of the event or act which is being recorded. The age at which a minor attains majority shall be determined in the light of the national laws of the National Central Bureau or the national entity that recorded the data or, in the case of an international entity, in the light of the applicable rules.

(2) In this case, the National Central Bureau, national entity or international entity which records the data shall specify any particular conditions imposed by applicable national laws.

Article 42: Additional conditions for recording particularly sensitive data

(1) Particularly sensitive data may only be recorded in one of the Organization's police databases if:

(a) they are relevant and of particularly important criminalistic value for achieving the aims of the Organization and the purposes of the processing as described in Article 10(2) of the present Rules;

(b) they are described objectively and contain no judgment or discriminatory comments.

(2) The data shall be recorded in a way which enables them to be identified as such when they are consulted, and shall not be processed, in any form whatsoever, for any discriminatory purpose.

Article 43: Additional conditions for recording copied or uploaded data

(1) Data from one of the Organization's police databases may only be copied into another of the Organization's police databases or into part of the INTERPOL Information System if all the following conditions are met:

(a) if the data are copied for the same purpose, the source of the data has not objected within 10 days;

(b) if the data are copied for another purpose, the source has agreed to their processing for this new purpose;

(c) copying the data is unlikely to prejudice the integrity and the confidentiality of the data copied;

(d) the data are copied exactly;

(e) the data are regularly updated.

(2) The General Secretariat shall ensure that these additional recording conditions are complied with when the data of one of the Organization's police databases are copied into another of the Organization's police databases.

(3) Data may only be uploaded into the INTERPOL Information System if all the following conditions are met:

(a) the uploading is carried out by a National Central Bureau, a national entity, an international entity, or the General Secretariat, and is done with due respect for the provisions of the present Rules;

(b) the data are copied exactly;

(c) the National Central Bureau, national entity or international entity uploading the data ensures they are regularly updated.

Article 43A: Additional conditions for temporarily processing large data sets

(1) The General Secretariat may temporarily process large data sets to determine their potential interest for the purposes of international police cooperation and to assess their compliance with the present Rules.

(2) In consultation with the source of the data, such temporary processing may include, inter alia, data structuring, formatting, assessing, categorizing and comparing against data already processed in the INTERPOL Information System.

(3) The temporary processing shall meet the following conditions:

(a) the data shall comply with the applicable general principles as defined in Title 1 of the present Rules;

(b) the data shall be processed in a protected data-processing environment within the INTERPOL Information System. The data shall be separated from other operational or analytical data and shall be distinguished from data provided by other sources;

(c) the retention period of the data in this environment shall be determined by the source, but shall not exceed the maximum retention period determined by the Executive Committee;

(d) access to the data shall be restricted to authorized departments or members of staff of the General Secretariat to whom specific access has been granted;

(e) any other conditions defined by the source of the data.

(4) Following an assessment of the data, the General Secretariat shall communicate the results of the assessment to the source of the data and shall promptly delete any non-compliant data.

(5) The source of the data may process any compliant data for one or more of the processing purposes listed in Article 10 of the present Rules.

(6) The General Secretariat shall then delete the remaining data from the temporary processing environment and shall inform the source of the data accordingly.

Article 44: Status of persons

(1) When recording any data concerning a person who is the subject of international police cooperation, the National Central Bureau, national entity or international entity must specify the status of that person from the following list:

(a) Convicted: a person who, following a court ruling, has been found guilty of committing an ordinary-law crime;

(b) Charged: a person against whom criminal proceedings have been initiated for allegedly committing an ordinary-law crime;

(c) Suspect: a person who, as part of a criminal investigation, is considered to be a possible offender but against whom no charges have been filed;

(d) Criminal history: a person who is known to law-enforcement departments because of a previous conviction, or previous criminal conduct for which he/she has not been exonerated;

(e) Witness: a person who is not a suspect and who might be able to provide information relevant to a criminal investigation or an investigation into a disappearance;

(f) Victim: a person against whom a crime has been committed;

(g) Missing: a person whose whereabouts are unknown and who has been reported as missing;

(h) Unidentified person: a person, alive, whether criminal or not, the identification of whom is sought;

(i) Unidentified body: a dead person, whether criminal or not, the identification of whom is sought;

(j) Deceased: a person on whom data is kept in INTERPOL's police databases following the confirmation of his/her death;

(k) Possible threat: a person who presents or is likely to present a danger to public safety;

(l) Subject to UN sanctions: a person subject to sanctions decided upon by the United Nations Security Council.

(2) Other statuses may be established by the General Secretariat in consultation with the National Central Bureaus and the international entities or with their representatives on the advisory bodies set up for the purpose.

Article 45: Definition of specific conditions of use when recording data

In accordance with Article 12(1) of the present Rules, any National Central Bureau, national entity or international entity which records data shall specify the conditions for use of these data once they have been entered in the INTERPOL Information System and, in particular, any conditions linked to using the data as evidence in criminal proceedings.

Article 46: Updates

(1) The National Central Bureau, national entity or international entity that recorded data shall update them regularly.

(2) When the purpose for which the data were recorded has been achieved, these data may only be updated or retained in the Organization's police database if the National Central Bureau, national entity or international entity that recorded them determines and justifies a new purpose for their recording.

(3) The National Central Bureau, national entity or international entity that updates data shall ensure that the conditions for recording those data are met.

(4) The National Central Bureau, national entity or international entity that recorded data may also modify, at any time:

(a) the retention period of the data;

(b) their level of confidentiality;

(c) restrictions on access to data;

(d) conditions for consultation;

(e) conditions for use.

Article 47: Recording of data at the initiative of the General Secretariat

In conformity with Article 24(1,b) of the present Rules and for purposes such as assisting in criminal investigations, complementing data already recorded in the INTERPOL Information System, or in the context of crime analyses it may be required to conduct, the General Secretariat may record data taken from sources other than those mentioned in Article 1(6) under the following conditions:

(a) It has ensured that the data comply with the general conditions for recording set out in these Rules, in particular with regard to the quality of data referred to in Article 12 of the present Rules;

(b) The General Secretariat shall be considered as the source of the data for the purposes of the present Rules and shall ensure that data are periodically assessed and updated in accordance with Articles 46, 49, 50 and 51 of the present Rules;

(c) The data are recorded in a way which enables them to be distinguished from data processed by a source mentioned in Article 1(6) and the origin of the data is clearly identified;

(d) Any National Central Bureau or international entity which confirms the accuracy of the data shall be considered as the source of those data for the purposes of the present Rules.

Article 48: Supplementary information and corrections

(1) If a National Central Bureau, national entity or international entity other than the one which recorded the data has specific, relevant reasons for considering that data are incorrect, it shall immediately inform the National Central Bureau which recorded the data or on whose behalf a national entity recorded them, or the international entity which recorded the data.

(2) If a National Central Bureau, national entity or international entity other than the one which recorded the data wishes to supplement them, it may send the supplementary information to the Bureau or to the international entity concerned.

(3) The recording National Central Bureau, national entity or international entity shall promptly examine the information and, if necessary, modify, correct or delete the data immediately.

Article 49: Retention period

(1) In conformity with Article 10 of the present Rules, the data may only be retained in the Organization's police databases for the time required to achieve the purpose for which they were recorded.

(2) Data shall initially be recorded for the maximum period determined by the Executive Committee for this type of data, unless a shorter retention period is set by the source or the purpose has been achieved.

(3) The retention period shall begin from the date on which the data are recorded.

(4) The suspension of a cooperation request or alert, as referred to in Articles 81 and 100 of the present Rules, shall have no bearing on the retention period of the data.

Article 50: Periodic assessments

(1) In order to reassess the purpose of processing data and their quality, in conformity with Articles 10 and 12 of the present Rules, the National Central Bureau, national entity or international entity must, on expiry of the retention period, examine the need for retaining that data and, if necessary, check that the conditions for recording them are still being met.

(2) The General Secretariat shall ask the National Central Bureau, national entity or international entity that recorded the data, at the latest six months before the expiry date, to examine the need to retain the data.

(3) The General Secretariat shall specify, in particular:

(a) if the data are connected with other data from the same National Central Bureau or the same entity;

(b) if the data are processed as part of an analysis project;

(c) if the data concern a form of serious crime or a special crime area for which the General Assembly has defined a specific retention policy implemented by the General Secretariat.

(4) If the National Central Bureau, national entity or international entity decides to retain the data, it shall specify the reasons for the retention. Data shall be recorded for a further period not exceeding the maximum retention period, unless a shorter retention period is set by the source or the purpose has been achieved.

(5) If the National Central Bureau, national entity or international entity decides that the purpose for which the data were recorded has been achieved but that retaining data in the Organization's police databases continues to be of interest for the purposes of international police cooperation, particularly if those data belong to one of the three categories mentioned above, it shall determine and justify a new purpose for recording that data. Data shall be recorded for a further period not exceeding the maximum retention period for this new purpose, unless a shorter retention period is set by the source or the purpose has been achieved.

(6) The National Central Bureau, national entity or international entity that decides to retain the data shall ensure that the conditions for recording the data continue to be met.

(7) For a given database of the Organization, the Executive Committee is empowered to waive the above requirements regarding reassessment, provided such a waiver is necessary.

Article 51: Deletion of data

(1) If the National Central Bureau, national entity or international entity decides not to retain data serving one of the purposes set in Article 10, they shall be deleted for that specific purpose.

(2) The data shall also be deleted automatically on expiry of the retention period if the National Central Bureau, national entity or international entity has not indicated the need to retain the data for the purpose they serve.

(3) When the purpose for which the data were recorded has been achieved, the National Central Bureau, national entity or international entity that recorded the data shall delete them from the police databases, unless it has decided to determine and justify a new purpose for recording them.

(4) When the General Secretariat has specific, relevant reasons for considering that the purpose for which data were recorded has been achieved or that the data no longer meet the minimum conditions for recording, it shall promptly request the National Central Bureau, national entity or international entity that recorded the data to examine the need to retain these data.

(5) When the General Secretariat deletes data recorded by a National Central Bureau, a national entity or international entity concerning a person who is the subject of an international cooperation request or an alert, it shall inform the National Central Bureau or international entity that recorded that data, and explain the reasons for its action.

(6) When data have been deleted from one of the Organization's police databases, all copies of those data contained in the INTERPOL Information System shall also be deleted, unless data are retained for a separate purpose as set out in Article 10, and subject to the prior consent of the National Central Bureau, national entity or international entity that initially recorded the data.

(7) When it is impossible to delete data because of the cost and volume of work involved, the General Secretariat shall take all appropriate steps to ensure that the data cannot be used, to prevent access to that data and their use for the purposes of a criminal investigation, or to indicate clearly that the data must be considered to be non-existent. It shall inform the Commission for the Control of INTERPOL's Files of such measures.

Article 52: Temporary retention of criminal history

(1) The National Central Bureau, national entity or international entity that withdraws an international alert or cooperation request concerning a person who has been convicted, charged, is suspected or constitutes a potential threat may choose to temporarily retain the data on this person in order to provide information about his/her criminal history.

(2) The temporary retention of the criminal history of a person who has been convicted, charged, is suspected or constitutes a threat, but who has been cleared of the charges which led to the data about him/her initially being recorded, shall be prohibited.

(3) The National Central Bureau, national entity or international entity which retains data for reference purposes shall ensure that retention is lawful under national law. The international entity shall ensure that the retention is lawful under its applicable rules.

(4) The purpose of this recording as well as the status of the person concerned shall be specified in accordance with, respectively, Articles 10 and 44(1) of the present Rules, in a manner such that the data cannot be confused with data concerning persons who are the subject of alerts or requests for international cooperation. A record shall be kept of the status initially attributed to the person concerned.

(5) These data may be retained for a period not exceeding the maximum retention period determined by the Executive Committee from the moment at which the National Central Bureau, national entity or international entity indicates that the initial purpose has been achieved, unless a shorter retention period is set by the source. On expiry of the retention period, the data shall be automatically destroyed unless the National Central Bureau, national entity or international entity decides to retain the data for the purposes of redirecting enquiries in conformity with Article 53 below.

Article 53: Retention of data for purposes of redirecting enquiries

(1) The National Central Bureau or entity that deletes data it has recorded about a person suspected, accused or convicted of criminal offences shall indicate whether it wishes to retain those data items that would allow another National Central Bureau or entity to address to it any subsequent enquiries it may have about this person.

(2) The General Secretariat may not retain, for purposes of redirecting enquiries, data it has deleted from the police databases without the express authorization from the National Central Bureau or entity that recorded those data.

(3) The only data that may be retained for purposes of redirecting enquiries are: the name of the National Central Bureau or entity that recorded the data; the reference of the recording; the person's name and forenames; the identity document number and the nature of that document; date and place of birth; and fingerprints and DNA profile.

(4) These data may be retained for a maximum retention period determined by the Executive Committee, unless a shorter retention period is set by the source.

SECTION 3: CONSULTATION

Article 54: Direct access

(1) In accordance with Article 6 of the present Rules, National Central Bureaus may directly consult the Organization's police databases, subject to the restrictions and confidentiality rules laid down by the source. National entities and international entities may also directly consult the Organization's police databases subject to the same restrictions and confidentiality rules and according to the access rights they have been granted.

(2) In accordance with Article 36(1,n), the type of data that can be directly consulted is specified in the list of the general characteristics of this database.

Article 55: Interconnection

(1) Interconnection operations must meet all of the following conditions:

(a) The purpose, the nature and the scope of the interconnection are specified, explicit and conform to the aims and activities of the Organization;

(b) The interconnection is of interest for the purposes of international police cooperation;

(c) The information system to be interconnected offers a level of security at least equivalent to that of the INTERPOL Information System;

(d) The interconnection allows for compliance with the processing conditions established by the sources of data contained in the INTERPOL Information System and in the information system to be interconnected;

(e) The interconnection allows the National Central Bureau, national entity or international entity that entered the data into the INTERPOL Information System, and the General Secretariat, to be notified immediately of any element deriving from the interconnected data that is likely to be of interest for the purposes of international police cooperation.

(2) All requests for interconnection from a national entity must be sent through its National Central Bureau.

(3) The General Secretariat shall submit to the Executive Committee for approval all requests for interconnection. It shall provide:

(a) a copy of the request for interconnection it received, specifying the person who will be responsible for overseeing the interconnection at the National Central Bureau, national entity or international entity;

(b) the assessment of the request by the General Secretariat as well as the financial implications of that request for the Organization;

(c) the outcome of any tests conducted by the General Secretariat;

(d) the opinion of the Commission for the Control of INTERPOL's Files if the database contains or is linked to personal data.

(4) If the Executive Committee authorizes the interconnection, the General Secretariat shall give prior notification to the sources of the data recorded in the database to be interconnected. The Secretariat shall specify the conditions of interconnection.

(5) The General Secretariat shall keep an updated register of interconnection operations which specifies the conditions of each operation. National Central Bureaus may consult this register at any time. International entities may also consult this register according to the access rights they have been granted.

(6) The Executive Committee shall report to the General Assembly each year the authorizations it has granted for interconnection operations.

Article 56: Downloading for the purposes of international police cooperation

(1) All downloading operations must meet all the following conditions:

(a) the purpose of the downloading is specified, explicit and conform to the aims and activities of the Organization;

(b) the request is of interest for the purposes of international police cooperation;

(c) an interconnection operation cannot be carried out due to its cost and the functional or technical characteristics of the information system to be interconnected;

(d) the information system of the National Central Bureau, national entity or international entity offers a level of security at least equivalent to that of the INTERPOL Information System;

(e) the conditions established by the sources for the processing and use of the downloaded data are strictly observed;

(f) the downloading operation is for a set period not exceeding six months;

(g) downloaded data are updated at least once a week, including when such updating implies the deletion of data;

(h) the data are not copied within the information system into which they are downloaded;

(i) the downloaded data must systematically be deleted when the purpose for which they were downloaded has been achieved, and at the very latest when the aforementioned period of six months has expired;

(j) the National Central Bureau, national entity or international entity that downloads data immediately notifies the National Central Bureau, national entity or international entity that entered the data into the INTERPOL Information System, and the General Secretariat, of any item derived from the downloaded data that is likely to be of interest for the purposes of international police cooperation.

(2) All downloading requests from a national entity must be sent through its National Central Bureau.

(3) The General Secretariat shall be empowered to authorize a downloading operation, subject to:

(a) compliance with the conditions above; and

(b) written assurances provided by the National Central or international entity that requested to carry out the downloading operation, by which it undertakes to comply with those conditions, the purpose of the downloading, its nature and its scope; and

(c) the designation of a person to be responsible for overseeing the downloading at the National Central Bureau, national entity or international entity.

(4) If, for technical or other reasons, the General Secretariat cannot comply with one or more of the processing conditions linked to the data to be downloaded, it shall not authorize the downloading of the said data.

(5) The General Secretariat shall notify National Central Bureaus and international entities of any downloading operation it has authorized. It shall specify all the conditions of downloading, particularly the characteristics of the information system of the National Central Bureau or international entity it has authorized to proceed with the downloading. With effect from the date of notification by the General Secretariat, a National Central Bureau, a national entity or an international entity has 15 days to signify its opposition to any possibility of processing by the requesting National Central Bureau or entity of the data that it entered into the INTERPOL Information System. At the end of the prescribed period, the General Secretariat shall be empowered to proceed with the downloading, with the exception of data about which an opposition has been signified.

(6) The General Secretariat shall inform the Executive Committee of the downloading authorization it has granted by providing:

(a) its assessment of the request as well as the financial implications for the Organization;

(b) the characteristics of the information system of the National Central Bureau or national entity or international entity into which the data were downloaded;

(c) a copy of the written assurances provided by the National Central Bureau or international entity which requested to carry out a downloading operation;

(d) the opinion of the Commission for the Control of INTERPOL's Files if the downloaded data contained personal data or were linked to such data.

(7) The General Secretariat shall be responsible for checking that the conditions for downloading are being met throughout the period for which the downloading has been authorized. It shall take all necessary and appropriate measures to perform these checks.

(8) The General Secretariat shall keep a register of the data downloaded which specifies the conditions of each downloading operation. National Central Bureaus may consult this register at any time. International entities may also consult this register according to the access rights they have been granted.

Article 57: Indirect access

(1) When a police database cannot be consulted directly or an international entity only has indirect access to a database, the General Secretariat shall determine the procedures for consulting that database and inform the National Central Bureaus of them. It shall also inform international entities according to the access rights they have been granted.

(2) When a police database can be consulted directly, the General Secretariat may authorize a request for indirect access to the data contained in that database in the following cases:

(a) the international entity does not have direct access rights, or

(b) direct access is temporarily inoperative, or

(c) the request is specific or complex and the data cannot be obtained through direct consultation.

(3) All requests for indirect access from a national entity must be submitted through its National Central Bureau.

(4) When examining a request for indirect access, the General Secretariat shall ensure that:

(a) the request has been made by a National Central Bureau, a national entity, an international entity or a private entity;

(b) if made by an international entity or a private entity, the request corresponds to the purpose for which access to the INTERPOL Information System was granted;

(c) the request is clear and reasoned;

(d) the National Central Bureau or international entity that recorded data likely to correspond to the request has not imposed any access restrictions on the requesting National Central Bureau, international entity or private entity.

Article 58: Access restrictions

(1) In accordance with Article 7(1) of the present Rules, any National Central Bureau or international entity may, at any time, place general restrictions on access by other National Central Bureaus, international entities or private entities to the data it has recorded in a police database. General access restrictions placed by a National Central Bureau shall apply to the data recorded by the national entities it has authorized.

(2) Any National Central Bureau or international entity may, at any time, place additional restrictions on access by other National Bureaus, international entities or private entities to recorded data concerning a person, object or event.

(3) National Central Bureaus and international entities may not place access restrictions applicable solely to the national entities of other National Central Bureaus. Any restrictions on access by a National Central Bureau shall apply to all the national entities that it has authorized.

(4) Access restrictions to data shall apply regardless of the method used to consult the police database.

(5) When a National Central Bureau or an international entity consults a database and it cannot access the data that may match its search, the General Secretariat may forward the request to the National Central Bureau or international entity that placed the access restriction.

(6) Messages for which a National Central Bureau or international entity has authorized the recording in one of the Organization's databases shall be considered to be restricted to their initial recipients, unless otherwise specified by the said Bureau or entity.

(7) Access restrictions may not be lifted by the General Secretariat except in urgent situations, according to the applicable procedure, or when the data have become public.

(8) Access restrictions are confidential data that shall be processed in accordance with Article 112 of the present Rules.

Article 59: Disclosure of data subject to restrictions

The disclosure of data subject to restrictions may only be carried out in the urgent situations referred to in Article 26(2) of the present Rules and according to the following procedure:

(a) The General Secretariat shall notify the National Central Bureau, national entity or international entity that recorded the said data, that the conditions set out in Article 26(2) of the present Rules have been met, and shall set a deadline, proportionate to the threat, for the said National Central Bureau or entity to object to the removal of the restrictions;

(b) All requests to a national entity concerning the removal of restrictions must be sent through its National Central Bureau;

(c) The restrictions will be considered to be lifted upon expiry of the deadline set by the General Secretariat and in the absence of an express objection by the National Central Bureau, national entity or international entity that recorded the restricted data relating to the threat;

(d) The General Secretariat shall inform the Executive Committee and the Commission for the Control of INTERPOL's Files as soon as possible that it has applied this emergency procedure.

Article 60: Access by third parties

(1) The General Secretariat may process requests for access submitted by international organizations or legal persons governed by private law with which the Organization is considering establishing relations for cooperation in data processing.

(2) When a third party requests access to data contained in a police database, the General Secretariat may forward the data only with the express prior authorization of the source of the data.

Article 61: Disclosure of data to the public

(1) The General Secretariat shall request the opinion of the Commission for the Control of INTERPOL's Files on any policy that it may, in accordance with the conditions set out in paragraph 2 below, decide to adopt regarding disclosure to the public of data processed in the INTERPOL Information System, whenever the processing of personal data is concerned.

(2) Data processed in the INTERPOL Information System may only be disclosed to the public if all the following conditions are met:

(a) The disclosure is for at least one of the following purposes:

(i) to alert the public;

(ii) to request help from the public;

(iii) for any other purpose intended to promote international police cooperation;

(b) The source of the data has authorized the disclosure beforehand, including details of the type of data to be disclosed, the method of disclosure, and the potential recipients of the disclosure, and the source has indicated any specific conditions concerning the disclosure;

(c) The disclosure complies with the aims and activities of the Organization and respects the basic rights of the persons who are subjects of international police cooperation;

(d) The disclosure is not such that it might prejudice the Organization's image or interests, or those of its Members;

(e) The disclosure does not concern an offender or an alleged offender who, at the time of the offence in question, was considered to be a minor under the law applicable in the country of the National Central Bureau or of the international entity which entered the data in the system, unless that National Central Bureau or international entity and the General Secretariat consider that such disclosure is essential to international police cooperation, and if the disclosure in question complies with the applicable principles of the national laws and of international law.

(3) If a notice or the data it contains is disclosed by a National Central Bureau, a national entity or an international entity other than the source of the data, in addition to the conditions listed in paragraph 2 above, the following conditions shall be met:

(a) The General Secretariat shall have first authorized such disclosure;

(b) The data contained in the notice shall be copied identically and be updated regularly to ensure they remain accurate.

SECTION 4: USE OF DATA

Article 62: Conditions of use

All National Central Bureaus, national entities and international entities about to use data processed in the INTERPOL Information System shall determine the following:

(a) the accuracy and relevancy of the data;

(b) the purpose for which they are about to use the data;

(c) any special conditions of use;

(d) any access restrictions placed on these data applicable to another National Central Bureau or another international entity to which they are to be forwarded.

Article 63: Verification of the accuracy and relevance of data

(1) All National Central Bureaus, national entities and international entities about to use data processed in the INTERPOL Information System for the purposes of applying coercive measures, including but not limited to detention, arrest, or restriction of movement, must ensure that these data are still accurate and relevant. Notwithstanding the above, any such measures permitted under national law and applicable international treaties may be taken prior to or while the data verification process is carried out.

(2) A National Central Bureau shall conduct the necessary checks directly with the National Central Bureau that recorded the data or, if the data were recorded by a national entity, with the National Central Bureau of this national entity. If the data were recorded by an international entity, it shall conduct the necessary checks with the General Secretariat.

(3) A national entity shall conduct these checks through its National Central Bureau.

(4) An international entity shall conduct these checks with the National Central Bureau or international entity solely through the General Secretariat, unless it has been granted access rights.

Article 64: Use of data for a criminal investigation purpose other than the initial purpose or for an administrative purpose

(1) In accordance with Article 10(6) of the present Rules, all National Central Bureaus, national entities or international entities about to use data for a criminal investigation purpose other than the specific purpose of international police cooperation for which the data were initially recorded in the Organization's police databases, or for an administrative purpose as specified by the source of the data pursuant to paragraph (2) below, or in the absence of such specification, under the applicable law of the entity intending to use the data, shall ensure that this purpose and use:

(a) complies with the aims and activities of the Organization;

(b) is not incompatible with the initial purpose;

(c) is lawful under the applicable law.

(2) Each source of data shall have the right to specify which purposes, other than those listed under Article 10(2) of the present Rules, are considered an administrative purpose under its applicable law.

(3) National Central Bureaus or entities intending to use data as described in paragraph (1) above shall inform in advance the source of the data, as follows:

(a) A National Central Bureau shall directly inform the National Central Bureau that recorded the data or, if the data were recorded by a national entity, the National Central Bureau of this national entity. If the data were recorded by an international entity, it shall inform the General Secretariat;

(b) A national entity shall inform the National Central Bureau, national entity or international entity that recorded the data through its National Central Bureau;

(c) An international entity shall inform the National Central Bureau, national entity or international entity that recorded the data through the General Secretariat, unless it is an international entity with powers of investigation and prosecution in criminal matters which, in conformity with Article 27(5,f) of the present Rules, has been authorized to send the data directly as a message.

(4) With effect from the date of notification, the source has 10 days to signify its opposition or to request additional information or time to respond to the request to use the data for the envisaged purpose. This period may be reduced by the General Secretariat in urgent cases.

Article 65: Use of data for administrative purposes *[deleted]*

Article 66: Special conditions for use

(1) In accordance with Article 45 of the present Rules, when any data are consulted, the General Secretariat shall draw attention to the special conditions for use established by a National Central Bureau, a national entity or an international entity when the data were recorded, in particular any conditions relating to the use of data as evidence in criminal proceedings.

(2) Any National Central Bureau, national entity or international entity which is about to use data recorded in a police database shall observe the special conditions for use established by the National Central Bureau, national entity or international entity that recorded them.

(3) The General Secretariat shall ensure that any National Central Bureau, national entity or international entity that consults the data is aware of those special conditions for use, so that it may take any necessary measures to ensure they are observed.

Article 67: Forwarding data

(1) Any National Central Bureau or international entity which is about to forward to another National Central Bureau or another international entity data contained in the Organization's police databases shall ensure with the General Secretariat or the National Central Bureau, national entity or international entity which recorded these data that they are not subject to restrictions:

(a) A National Central Bureau shall conduct the necessary checks directly with the National Central Bureau that recorded the data or, if the data were recorded by a national entity, with the National Central Bureau of this national entity. If the data were recorded by an international entity, it shall conduct the necessary checks with the General Secretariat;

(b) An international entity shall conduct the necessary checks with the National Central Bureau, national entity or international entity solely through the General Secretariat, unless it is an international entity with powers of investigation and prosecution in criminal matters which has been authorized, in application of Article 27(5,f) of the present Rules, to send data directly by means of a message.

(2) Any National Central Bureau or international entity which is about to forward particularly sensitive data contained in the Organization's police databases shall ensure that the forwarding is relevant and has specific crime-investigation value for achieving the aims of the Organization and the purposes of the processing.

(3) When forwarding data, the National Central Bureau or international entity and the General Secretariat shall, in cases of indirect access, indicate:

(a) the source of the data;

(b) the specific conditions for use established by the source;

(c) the level of confidentiality of the data;

(d) the date they were recorded and their retention period in the police databases;

(e) the person's status and the type of action to be taken regarding him/her, in the case of personal data;

(f) any specific methods for processing the data.

(4) It shall send an exact copy of the forwarded data to the source of the data if it deems it necessary or if the source so requires.

(5) In accordance with Article 58(6) of the present Rules, the General Secretariat may not forward a message it has received to a National Central Bureau or an international entity which is not a recipient without the prior consent of the National Central Bureau or the international entity that originally sent it.

SECTION 5: SPECIFIC RULES RELATING TO CRIME ANALYSIS FILES

Article 68: Analysis files

(1) Analysis files are temporary databases created for crime-analysis purposes, in accordance with a list of general characteristics drawn up on the basis of Article 36(1) of the present Rules and in consultation with the National Central Bureaus, national entities and international entities that may be involved in the crime analysis project concerned.

(2) The processing principles and conditions for recording data in the Organization's databases set out in the present Rules shall be applicable to analysis files, subject to the provisions below.

(3) Analysis files shall be created by the General Secretariat for an initial period not exceeding five years.

(4) The General Secretariat shall inform the Executive Committee about any crime-analysis project involving the creation of an analysis file, and shall provide:

- (a) the reasons that led it to develop this project, as well as the financial implications of such a project;
- (b) the list of the National Central Bureaus, national entities and international entities that may be involved in the project;
- (c) the list of the general characteristics of the analysis file constituting its legal framework;
- (d) the opinion of the Commission for the Control of INTERPOL's Files, if the analysis file contains personal data or is linked to such data.

(5) The Executive Committee may refuse or cancel the creation of an analysis file, if it considers that the requirements set by the present Rules are not met.

(6) The creation of an analysis file, as well as its purpose and the applicable legal framework, shall immediately be notified to the National Central Bureaus and international entities that may be involved in the project. Subsequent participation by a National Central Bureau, a national entity or an international entity in the crime analysis project is subject to the agreement of all the National Central Bureaus international entities already participating in the project.

(7) National Central Bureaus shall be responsible for making necessary notifications to their respective national entities.

(8) The General Secretariat shall submit any proposal to extend an analysis file for a period not exceeding five years to the Executive Committee for approval.

Article 69: Use of analysis files

(1) Access to analysis files shall be restricted to authorized departments or members of staff of the General Secretariat involved in the crime analysis and to whom specific access has been granted.

(2) The General Secretariat shall be entitled, when required, to authorize staff of National Central Bureaus, national entities and international entities participating in the project and involved in the crime analysis to access a given analysis file, and to determine the extent of their access and processing rights. Access and processing rights shall be granted to staff of national entities in consultation with the National Central Bureaus concerned.

(3) The analysis files may or may not be connected to the Organization's police databases, depending on the purpose of the files in question and the required security and confidentiality conditions.

(4) Data recorded in an analysis file may be copied into a database of the Organization, or, conversely, data recorded in a database of the Organization may be copied into an analysis file provided that the data meet the minimum conditions for recording information in the said database, and that the copying is subject to the express consent of the National Central Bureau, national entity or international entity that supplied the data.

(5) If the data or other items of information recorded in an analysis file are such that they might allow updates to one or several of the Organization's other databases or conversely if the data recorded in other databases might allow updates to one or several analysis files, the General Secretariat must take all appropriate measures to that end.

Article 70: Additional conditions for recording data on criminal analysis purposes

(1) Data referred to in Article 1(2) of the present Rules, as well as other items of information that may be necessary for the crime analysis, may be recorded in analysis files.

(2) Data and other items of information recorded in analysis files shall be retained for a maximum retention period determined by the Executive Committee, unless a shorter retention period is set by the source or the crime-analysis file which contains them is closed earlier.

(3) If the data are recorded both in an analysis file and in one of the Organization's police databases, the purposes for recording the data shall be specified in a manner such that the data cannot be confused.

(4) When recording in an analysis file any data or other items of information about a person who is the subject of international police cooperation, the status of that person shall be specified with reference to the following list, which shall only be used in the context of criminal analysis:

(a) The statuses listed in Article 44(1) of the present Rules;

(b) Other statuses below created in application of Article 44(2) of the present Rules:

(i) Associate: person who has sporadic or regular contact with a person of interest in a criminal investigation, and/or against whom criminal proceedings have been initiated;

(ii) Person of interest: person who can provide information about an ordinary-law crime.

Article 71: Crime analysis reports

(1) Crime analysis reports prepared for analysis files must:

(a) make a clear distinction between the information obtained by the General Secretariat and the conclusions that the General Secretariat has drawn from that information;

(b) indicate the sources of the information cited, the status of the persons mentioned and the date when the analysis was made;

(c) specify that, prior to making any use of such reports and the data and other items of information they contain, the General Secretariat and the sources of the data should be consulted to ascertain the rights and restrictions attaching to them.

(2) Crime-analysis reports shall be disclosed to the National Central Bureaus, national entities and international entities participating in the crime analysis project concerned. Crime-analysis reports may be disclosed to other National Central Bureaus, national entities and international entities, subject to authorization by the General Secretariat and any access restrictions that may be determined by the sources of the data contained in the reports. Disclosure must comply with the confidentiality level assigned to the analysis file by the General Secretariat, as well as any other applicable security measures.

(3) The crime-analysis reports may be retained for a maximum retention period determined by the Executive Committee after the completion of the analysis project concerned, provided that they are used in a manner that is relevant and in compliance with the processing rules set out in the present Rules.

Article 72: Completion of crime analysis projects

(1) When a crime analysis project is completed:

(a) the analysis files concerned, as well as the data and other items of information recorded in them, must be destroyed;

(b) the crime analysis report may be retained provided that steps are taken to prevent any use which is not relevant or is contrary to the processing rules set out in the present Rules.

(2) Disclosure of a crime analysis report or any of the data it contains must conform to any restrictions that may have been imposed by their sources on the data it contains and any other measures attaching to it concerning security or confidentiality.

CHAPTER II: NOTICES AND DIFFUSIONS

SECTION 1: PROVISIONS COMMON TO NOTICES

Article 73: INTERPOL notices system

(1) The INTERPOL notices system consists of a set of colour-coded notices published for specific purposes, and special notices published within the framework of specific cooperation not covered by the previous categories of notices.

(2) A category of notices or special notices may only be created with the approval of the General Assembly which, if the notice contains or is linked to personal data, shall have obtained the opinion of the Commission for the Control of INTERPOL's Files.

(3) The conditions for publishing notices are defined for each category of notice or special notice. These conditions are at least identical to the general conditions required for recording these data in the Organization's databases.

(4) The conditions for publishing each category of notice are defined below. The conditions for publishing each category of special notice are specified in an agreement.

Article 74: Role of the General Secretariat

(1) The General Secretariat shall be responsible for publishing INTERPOL notices on behalf of the Organization.

(2) In particular, it is responsible for:

(a) checking the compliance of all notice requests with the present Rules and publishing, as soon as possible, any notice requests it deems to be in compliance;

(b) simultaneously recording any published notices in a database of the Organization for direct consultation by National Central Bureaus, national entities and international entities according to the access rights they have been granted;

(c) translating any notices into the Organization's working languages according to the directives decided upon by the General Assembly;

(d) assisting National Central Bureaus and international entities in the event of a positive query result;

(e) ensuring that published notices continue to comply with the conditions for their publication and are regularly assessed by the National Central Bureau or international entity that requested their publication. To that end, the General Secretariat shall review published notices on a regular basis and shall consult the National Central Bureaus and international entities that requested their publication, as well as the other National Central Bureaus.

Article 75: Structure of INTERPOL notices

(1) The General Secretariat, in consultation with the National Central Bureaus, or with their representatives on the advisory bodies set up for the purpose, shall define and modify, when necessary, the structure of each category of notices, in due compliance with the conditions for their publication, as well as any other directives or decisions taken by the General Assembly or by the Executive Committee.

(2) Without prejudice to the principles set out in Title 1 of the present Rules, the international entity and the Organization shall define the structure of special notices in an agreement.

(3) A notice may contain data from different sources if all the following conditions have been met:

(a) the sources have agreed to the processing;

(b) the processing is of specific interest to the requesting National Central Bureau or international entity for this cooperation request or alert;

(c) the data are clearly identified as having been submitted by different sources;

(d) the processing does not incur significant additional costs.

Article 76: Requests for the publication of notices

(1) Notice requests shall be submitted in at least one of the Organization's working languages.

(2) Prior to requesting the publication of a notice, the National Central Bureau or international entity shall ensure:

(a) the quality and lawfulness of the data it provides in support of its request;

(b) that the conditions attached to its request for publication are met;

(c) that the data are of interest for the purposes of international police cooperation;

(d) that its request complies with INTERPOL's rules, specifically with Articles 2(1) and 3 of the Constitution, as well as with the obligations imposed on the requesting entity under international law.

Article 77: Examination of requests by the General Secretariat

(1) All notice requests shall be examined by the General Secretariat for compliance with the present Rules.

(2) The General Secretariat may not publish a notice on behalf of the Organization if:

(a) the data provided do not meet the conditions for publishing a notice;

(b) publication of the notice is not, in the case in point, of interest for the purposes of international police cooperation. This interest is assessed in light of the possibility that the request could be processed by all the Organization's Members;

(c) publication of the notice could prejudice the Organization's or its Members' interests.

(3) While requests for notices are being examined by the General Secretariat, they are temporarily recorded in a database of the Organization. An additional indication must be inserted so that, when consulted, these requests can be identified as such and not be confused with published notices.

Article 78: Incomplete or non-compliant requests for notices

(1) When a request is incomplete, the requesting National Central Bureau or international entity shall provide, at the earliest opportunity and after consultation with the General Secretariat, all additional data required to publish the notice.

(2) The General Secretariat shall propose to the requesting National Central Bureau or international entity, whenever possible, the publication of other notices when the data provided are insufficient to allow publication of the requested notice but correspond to the purposes and conditions for publication of another notice.

(3) The General Secretariat shall propose to the requesting National Central Bureau or international entity, whenever possible, that it circulates a diffusion when the request is not intended for all the Organization's Members, or when the data provided are insufficient for the requested notice to be published but correspond to the purpose and conditions for recording a diffusion.

Article 79: Publication of notices

(1) Notices shall be published by the General Secretariat for the attention of all National Central Bureaus as follows:

(a) National Central Bureaus shall be informed of the publication of a notice on the day of its publication;

(b) National Central Bureaus shall be able to directly consult all published notices on a police database of the Organization, subject to the interim measures referred to in Article 129 of the present Rules.

(2) Notices may also be consulted by:

(a) national entities, according to the access authorizations they have been granted by their respective National Central Bureaus;

(b) international entities, when expressly provided for in the agreement concluded with the Organization.

(3) Notwithstanding Article 58 of the present Rules, any National Central Bureau or international entity which requests a notice shall agree not to place restrictions on access to the data it provides by any National Central Bureau or national entity that the said National Central Bureau has authorized to consult notices. It shall retain the possibility of placing restrictions on access to the data it provides by international entities that do not have powers of investigation and prosecution in criminal matters.

Article 80: Implementation of notices

(1) National Central Bureaus shall forward to:

(a) all relevant national authorities, as soon as possible and in accordance with their national laws, all the data contained in the notices they receive, as well as the updates regarding those notices;

(b) the requesting National Central Bureau or international entity, as well as the General Secretariat, all available data concerning the person or purpose for which the notice was published, in particular, whenever those data could enable the purpose of the notice to be achieved. A national entity must submit those data via its National Central Bureau;

(c) the General Secretariat any information that may give rise to doubts about the conformity of a notice with the present Rules.

(2) The National Central Bureau or international entity which originally requested the notice shall:

(a) continue to ensure that the data it has provided in the notice remains accurate and relevant;

(b) forward to the General Secretariat any data that would modify the content of the published notice, and assess whether the modifications require the said notice to be withdrawn.

Article 81: Suspension, withdrawal or cancellation of a notice

(1) The requesting National Central Bureau or international entity can suspend its cooperation request or its alert for a period not exceeding six months. It shall indicate the reasons for this suspension to the General Secretariat, which will then suspend the notice.

(2) The National Central Bureau or international entity requesting a notice shall withdraw its cooperation request or its alert and ask the General Secretariat to cancel the notice immediately:

(a) once the purpose of this request or alert has been achieved; or

(b) if this request or alert is linked to one or several other requests or alerts whose purpose has been achieved and without which it cannot be maintained; or

(c) if it no longer wishes to maintain the request; or

(d) if the notice no longer meets the conditions for publication of the notice.

(3) The General Secretariat shall cancel a notice if:

(a) the purpose of the cooperation request or the alert on the basis of which the notice was published has been achieved, and this information has been confirmed by the source National Central Bureau or international entity; or

(b) if this request or alert is linked to one or several other requests or alerts whose purpose has been achieved and without which it cannot be maintained; or

(c) the notice no longer meets the conditions for publishing a notice; or

(d) the National Central Bureau or international entity that requested the notice obtains data allowing it to carry out the required action but has not taken any steps to this end and, after being consulted, has not provided reasonable grounds for its lack of action.

SECTION 2: PROVISIONS SPECIFIC TO RED NOTICES

Article 82: Purpose of red notices

Red notices are published at the request of a National Central Bureau or an international entity with powers of investigation and prosecution in criminal matters in order to seek the location of a wanted person and his/her detention, arrest or restriction of movement for the purpose of extradition, surrender, or similar lawful action.

Article 83: Specific conditions for publication of red notices

(1) Minimum criteria

(a) Red notices may be published only if the following cumulative criteria are met:

(i) The offence concerned is a serious ordinary-law crime.

Red notices may not be published for the following categories of offences:

- offences that in various countries raise controversial issues relating to behavioural or cultural norms;
- offences relating to family/private matters;
- offences originating from a violation of laws or regulations of an administrative nature or deriving from private disputes, unless the criminal activity is aimed at facilitating a serious crime or is suspected of being connected to organized crime.

The General Secretariat shall keep, update and share with National Central Bureaus and international entities a non-exhaustive list of specific offences that fall within the above categories.

(ii) Penalty threshold:

- if the person is sought for prosecution, the conduct constituting an offence is punishable by a maximum deprivation of liberty of at least two years or a more serious penalty;
- if the person is sought to serve a sentence, he/she is sentenced to at least six months of imprisonment and/or there is at least six months of the sentence remaining to be served.

(iii) The request is of interest for the purposes of international police cooperation.

(b) The General Secretariat may decide to publish a red notice where the criteria in (i) and/or (ii) above are not met if, following consultation with the requesting National Central Bureau or international entity, it considers that publication of the requested red notice would be of particular importance to international police cooperation.

(c) Several offences: if the request includes several offences, the red notice may be published for all offences that meet INTERPOL's Rules provided that at least one offence meets the above criteria.

(2) Minimum data

(a) Identity particulars:

Red notices may be published only when sufficient identifiers have been provided. Sufficient identifiers will be considered to include at least one of the following two combinations of identifiers:

(i) family name, forename, sex, date of birth (at least the year) and one of the following identifiers:

- physical description; or
- DNA profile; or
- fingerprints; or
- data contained in identity documents (e.g. passport, national identity card).

(ii) photograph of good quality with some additional data (e.g. alias, name of the parent(s), further physical description, DNA profile, fingerprints, etc.).

(b) Judicial data:

Red notices may be published only when sufficient judicial data has been provided. Sufficient judicial data will be considered to include at least:

(i) summary of facts of the case, which shall provide a succinct and clear description of the criminal activities of the wanted person, including the time and location of the alleged criminal activity; and

(ii) charge(s); and

(iii) law(s) covering the offence (whenever possible, and subject to national law or the rules governing the operation of the international entity, the requesting National Central Bureau or international entity shall provide the wording of the relevant penal provision(s)); and

(iv) maximum penalty possible, sentence imposed, or sentence remaining to be served; and

(v) reference to a valid arrest warrant or judicial decision having the same effect (whenever possible, and subject to national law or the rules governing the operation of the international entity, the requesting National Central Bureau or international entity shall provide a copy of the arrest warrant or judicial decision).

Article 84: Assurances provided by the requesting National Central Bureau or international entity

The requesting National Central Bureau or international entity shall ensure that:

(a) the authority which issued the arrest warrant or handed down the judicial decision has the necessary power;

(b) the red notice request has been coordinated with the relevant authorities responsible for extradition, and assurances have been given that extradition will be sought upon arrest of the person, in conformity with national laws and/or the applicable bilateral and multilateral treaties;

(c) if the arrest warrant has not been issued by a judicial authority, the laws of the requesting country or the rules governing the operation of the international entity provide for a mechanism of appeal before a judicial authority.

Article 85: Provision of documents that could support extradition or surrender proceedings

When it considers it useful and appropriate, the requesting National Central Bureau or international entity shall provide the General Secretariat with additional documents that could support extradition or surrender proceedings. The General Secretariat could serve as a repository for such documents and provide them upon request to the relevant countries.

Article 86: Legal review by the General Secretariat

The General Secretariat shall conduct a legal review of all red notices prior to their publication to ensure compliance with INTERPOL's Constitution and Rules, in particular with Articles 2 and 3 of INTERPOL's Constitution.

Article 87: Steps to be taken following the location of the person

If a person who is the subject of a red notice is located, the following steps shall be taken:

(a) The country where the person has been located shall:

(i) immediately inform the requesting National Central Bureau or international entity and the General Secretariat of the fact that the person has been located, subject to limitations deriving from national law and applicable international treaties;

(ii) take all other measures permitted under national law and applicable international treaties, such as provisionally arresting the wanted person or monitoring or restricting his/her movement.

(b) The requesting National Central Bureau or international entity shall act immediately once it has been informed that the person has been located in another country and, in particular, shall ensure the swift transmission – within the time limits defined for the case in question – of data and supporting documents requested by the country where the person was located or by the General Secretariat.

(c) The General Secretariat shall provide assistance to the relevant National Central Bureaus or international entities by, *inter alia*, facilitating the transfer of documents related to the provisional arrest or the extradition procedures in accordance with the relevant national laws and international treaties.

SECTION 3: PROVISIONS SPECIFIC TO OTHER NOTICES

Article 88: Blue notices

(1) Blue notices are published in order to:

(a) obtain information on a person of interest in a criminal investigation, and/or

(b) locate a person of interest in a criminal investigation, and/or

(c) identify a person of interest in a criminal investigation.

(2) Blue notices may only be published under the following conditions:

(a) The subject of the notice has been convicted or charged, or is a suspect, a witness or a victim;

(b) Additional information on the possible criminal history, location or identity of the person or any other information relevant to the criminal investigation is sought;

(c) Sufficient data relating to the criminal investigation or the person are provided to allow the cooperation requested to be effective.

(3) A blue notice may only be published if it contains sufficient identifiers. Sufficient identifiers mean at least:

(a) If the person is identified:

(i) either the family name, forename, sex, date of birth (at least the year), along with the physical description, DNA profile, fingerprints or data contained in identity documents (passport or national identity card, for example); or

(ii) a photograph of good quality, along with at least one identifier such as an alias, the name of one of the parents, or a specific physical characteristic not visible in the photograph.

(b) If the person is unidentified:

(i) a photograph of good quality, and/or

(ii) fingerprints, and/or

(iii) DNA profile.

Article 89: Green notices

(1) Green notices are published to warn about a person's criminal activities.

(2) Green notices may only be published under the following conditions:

(a) The person is considered to be a possible threat to public safety;

(b) This conclusion has been drawn from an assessment by a national law-enforcement authority or an international entity;

(c) This assessment is based on the person's previous criminal conviction(s) or other reasonable grounds;

(d) Sufficient data concerning the threat are provided for the warning to be relevant.

(3) A green notice may only be published if it provides sufficient identifiers. Sufficient identifiers mean at least:

(a) either the family name, forename, sex, date of birth (at least the year), along with the physical description, DNA profile, fingerprints or data contained in identity documents (passport or national identity card, for example); or

(b) a photograph of good quality, along with at least one identifier such as an alias, the name of one of the parents, or a specific physical characteristic not visible in the photograph.

(4) The National Central Bureaus and national entities that receive green notices shall take the appropriate measures, in conformity with their national laws.

Article 90: Yellow notices

(1) Yellow notices are published to locate a missing person or to identify a person unable to identify himself/herself.

(2) Yellow notices may only be published under the following conditions:

(a) The person's disappearance or discovery has been reported to and recorded by the police;

(b) The whereabouts of the missing person or the identity of the discovered person are unknown to the police;

(c) If the person is an adult, applicable national privacy laws do not prevent a request being made;

(d) Sufficient data on a person or the circumstances surrounding the disappearance or discovery of the person are provided for his/her identification.

(3) A yellow notice may only be published if it provides sufficient identifiers. Sufficient identifiers mean at least:

(a) If it concerns a missing person:

(i) the family name, forename, sex, date of birth (at least the year); and

(ii) physical description, a photograph of good quality, DNA profile or fingerprints;

(b) If it concerns a person who is unable to identify him/herself:

(i) physical description, sex of the person; and

(ii) photograph of good quality, fingerprints or DNA profile.

Article 91: Black notices

(1) Black notices are published to identify dead bodies.

(2) Black notices may only be published under the following conditions:

(a) the discovery of a dead body has been recorded by the police;

(b) this dead body has not been identified;

(c) enough data on this dead body or the circumstances surrounding its discovery are provided for its identification.

(3) A black notice may only be published if it provides sufficient identifiers. Sufficient identifiers mean at least:

(a) a photograph of good quality, and/or

(b) fingerprints, and/or

(c) DNA profile.

Article 92: Purple notices

(1) Purple notices are published in order to:

(a) warn about modi operandi, objects, devices or concealment methods used by offenders, and/or

(b) request information on offences to resolve them or assist in their investigation.

(2) A purple notice may only be published under the following conditions:

(a) If the facts are no longer under investigation:

(i) the modus operandi is known in detail, is complex or different from other identified modi operandi for similar offences;

(ii) the publication of the notice is intended to prevent these offences from being repeated;

(iii) the request includes enough data on the modus operandi, objects, equipment or hiding places used by perpetrators of these crimes to allow effective prevention;

(iv) the request provides sufficient identifiers for matches to be made with similar offences in order to resolve them.

(b) If the facts are still under investigation:

(i) they are serious offences;

(ii) the offences draw the attention of the Organization's Members to a specific modus operandi, object, device or concealment method;

(iii) the request includes enough data on this modus operandi and these objects, equipment or hiding places for matches to be made.

Article 93: Orange notices

(1) Orange notices are published to notify about an event, a person, an object, a process or a modus operandi representing an imminent threat to public safety and likely to cause serious damage to property or injury to persons.

(2) Orange notices may only be published under the following conditions:

(a) In the case of a person:

(i) he/she is considered to represent an imminent threat to public safety, or is preparing to commit, or is imminently about to commit a particularly serious ordinary-law crime;

(ii) this conclusion is based on an assessment by a national law-enforcement authority or an international entity;

(iii) this assessment is based on the person's previous criminal conviction(s) and/or other reasonable grounds;

(b) In the case of an object, event or modus operandi:

(i) it is considered an imminent threat to public safety;

(ii) this conclusion is based on an assessment by a national law-enforcement authority.

(3) An orange notice may only be published if sufficient data relating to the imminent threat are provided for the alert to be relevant.

(4) The National Central Bureaus and national entities that receive orange notices shall take the appropriate measures, in conformity with their national laws

(5) When the threat which led to the publication of an orange notice is no longer imminent, the General Secretariat, in consultation with the National Central Bureau or international entity which requested its publication, may replace it with any other appropriate notice.

Article 94: Stolen work of art notices

(1) Stolen work of art notices are published to locate works of art or items of cultural value which have been stolen, or to identify such objects discovered in suspicious circumstances.

(2) Stolen work of art notices may only be published under the following conditions:

(a) the work of art or item of cultural value is of interest in a criminal investigation;

(b) it has some unique characteristic and/or is of considerable commercial value.

(3) A notice on a stolen work of art may only be published if enough data is provided for its identification.

Article 95: INTERPOL-United Nations Security Council Special Notices

(1) INTERPOL-United Nations Security Council Special Notices are published in order to inform INTERPOL's Members that an individual or an entity is subject to UN Security Council Sanctions.

(2) INTERPOL-United Nations Security Council Special Notices are published consistent with the Arrangement on Cooperation between the International Criminal Police Organization-INTERPOL and the United Nations in relation to the United Nations Security Council Sanctions Committees.

(3) The conditions for publication of these special notices shall be established in accordance with procedures agreed upon by the United Nations Secretariat and INTERPOL in consultation with the relevant Committees.

Article 96: Other special notices

(1) The purpose, conditions for publication and the structure of any other category of special notices shall be established under the agreement referred to in Article 28 of the present Rules, in conformity with the Organization's aims and activities set out in Title 1 of the present Rules.

(2) A special notice may only be published if the data satisfy the conditions for publishing this category of special notices, as laid down in the said agreement.

SECTION 4: DIFFUSIONS

Article 97: Diffusions system

(1) The diffusions system consists of standardized requests for cooperation and alerts each corresponding to a specific purpose:

(a) to arrest, detain or restrict the movements of a convicted or accused person;

(b) to locate and trace;

(c) to obtain additional information;

(d) for identification purposes;

(e) to warn about a person's criminal activities;

(f) for information purposes.

(2) The conditions for sending a diffusion are the same as the general conditions for recording data in the Organization's police databases.

(3) The General Secretariat shall submit any proposal to create a new category of diffusion to the Executive Committee for approval. To justify its request, the General Secretariat shall provide:

(a) the reasons that led it to propose this creation, as well as the financial implications of such a creation;

(b) the specific purpose of this new category of diffusion, the conditions for its circulation as well as the type of data it will contain;

(c) the outcome of any tests conducted by the General Secretariat;

(d) the opinion of the Commission for the Control of INTERPOL's Files, if the new category of diffusion contains personal data or is linked to such data.

Article 98: Diffusion forms

(1) The General Secretariat shall make tools and mechanisms available to the National Central Bureaus and international entities to enable them to carry out the automated and standard processing of diffusions in the INTERPOL Information System and to consult them directly.

(2) The General Secretariat shall provide National Central Bureaus and international entities with the necessary forms to enable them to send cooperation requests and alerts by means of a diffusion.

(3) The General Secretariat, in consultation with the National Central Bureaus or with their representatives on advisory bodies set up for the purpose, shall define and modify, when necessary, the structure of each form.

Article 99: Circulation of diffusions

(1) Diffusions shall be circulated in at least one of the Organization's working languages.

(2) Before circulating a diffusion, the National Central Bureau or international entity shall ensure:

(a) the quality and lawfulness of the data it provides in support of its diffusion;

(b) that its diffusion complies with the general conditions for recording data;

(c) that the data are of interest for the purposes of international police cooperation;

(d) that its request complies with INTERPOL's rules, specifically with Articles 2(1) and 3 of the Constitution, as well as with the obligations imposed on the requesting entity under international law.

(3) A National Central Bureau or international entity must use a diffusion rather than a notice if:

(a) it wishes to limit the circulation of its cooperation request or alert to selected National Central Bureaus or international entities;

(b) it wishes to limit the access to the data contained in its cooperation request or alert to a restricted number of National Central Bureaus or international entities;

(c) its request does not justify or does not qualify for the publication of a notice.

Article 100: Suspension or withdrawal of a diffusion

(1) The National Central Bureau or international entity that has sent an alert or a cooperation request by diffusion may suspend its diffusion for a period not exceeding six months. It shall indicate to the General Secretariat the reasons for the suspension.

(2) The National Central Bureau or international entity that has sent an alert or a cooperation request by diffusion must assess the need to maintain its diffusion whenever any changes are made to data contained in the diffusion.

(3) The National Central Bureau or international entity that has sent an alert or a cooperation request by diffusion must notify the National Central Bureaus, international entities, and the General Secretariat of its withdrawal once the purpose of the diffusion has been achieved or if it no longer wishes to maintain the request.

Article 101: Recording of cooperation requests or alerts circulated in messages

(1) In conformity with Article 9(4) of the present Rules, a National Central Bureau or an international entity may ask the General Secretariat to record in one of the Organization's police databases a request for cooperation or an international alert that it initially circulated in a message of which the General Secretariat was not initially a recipient.

(2) The General Secretariat shall record the cooperation request or alert in accordance with the present Rules and any rules on restricted access and conditions for use of data which may have been established by the National Central Bureau or international entity.

SECTION 5: NOTICES AND DIFFUSIONS PUBLISHED AT THE INITIATIVE OF THE GENERAL SECRETARIAT

Article 102: Requests for information

(1) The General Secretariat may request information from sources for cooperation purposes in the following cases:

(a) The request is made in the context of either a specific project or an event with specific interest for the purposes of international police cooperation;

(b) It has reasons to believe that this is necessary to achieve the objectives of the Organization and is in keeping with the aims pursued.

(2) The General Secretariat must obtain the prior authorization of the National Central Bureau concerned if it wishes to request information from a national entity. This authorization shall be deemed to have been granted if the National Central Bureau has not replied to the General Secretariat within 30 days of the request for authorization. It is understood that the National Central Bureau retains the right to oppose this request for information from one of its national entities at any moment.

Article 103: Publication of notices

(1) In conformity with Article 25(4) of the present Rules, the General Secretariat may publish notices at its own initiative:

(a) for the purposes of issuing an alert;

(b) to request information.

(2) Before publishing a notice at its own initiative, the General Secretariat shall ensure that:

(a) the publication of the notice complies with the conditions for its publication;

(b) the source(s) of the data have consented to this publication and, in particular, that any access restrictions have been lifted and the confidentiality level set for these data permits their publication;

(c) the publication of the notice is not likely to interfere with a pending cooperation request and that no similar notice request has been submitted by a National Central Bureau or an international entity.

SECTION 6: POSITIVE QUERY RESULTS

Article 104: Generation of positive query results

(1) A positive query result is generated in the INTERPOL Information System whenever sufficient correlation is established between the query and data recorded in one of the Organization's permanent operational police databases. The establishment of a sufficient correlation will depend on the characteristics of each database.

(2) When a positive query result is generated, subject to the characteristics of each database, a notification shall be sent to the National Central Bureau or international entity that consulted the database, and to the General Secretariat. A notification shall also be sent to the National Central Bureau or the international entity that recorded the initial data, depending on its indicated preference for receiving positive query result notifications.

(3) The notification of the positive query result shall include, at the very least, the reference of the National Central Bureau or international entity that consulted the database and that of the National Central Bureau or the international entity which recorded the initial data, as well as the main data relating to the recorded person, object or event.

(4) When data are processed by private entities in the context of specific projects, all the conditions and modalities relating to the positive query results shall be laid down in the agreements concluded between the Organization and the private entities pursuant to Article 28 of the present Rules.

Article 105: Procedure for managing positive query results

(1) The National Central Bureau or the international entity that generated the positive query result shall contact the National Central Bureau or the international entity that recorded the initial data in accordance with Article 63(1).

(2) The National Central Bureau or international entity that recorded the initial data shall examine the relevance of the positive query result as soon as possible.

(3) Procedures shall be determined by the General Secretariat, in consultation with National Central Bureaus or with their representatives on the advisory bodies set up for that purpose, to define the measures to be taken and response deadlines, according to the nature of the cooperation request.

(4) The National Central Bureaus shall determine the procedures for notifying positive query results to their national entities, with due regard to the applicable national laws.

Article 106: Record of positive query results

(1) The General Secretariat shall keep a record of the positive query results generated for a given cooperation request. This record shall be retained for such time as the data are recorded in the police databases.

(2) The National Central Bureau or international entity that recorded the initial data may consult this record.

CHAPTER III: DATA SECURITY

SECTION 1: MANAGEMENT OF RIGHTS OF ACCESS TO THE INTERPOL INFORMATION SYSTEM

Article 107: Designation of a new National Central Bureau

(1) The General Secretariat shall inform the National Central Bureaus and the international entities of any new membership to the Organization and designation of a National Central Bureau.

(2) With effect from the date of notification by the General Secretariat, a National Central Bureau or an international entity shall have 45 days to signify its opposition to granting this new National Central Bureau the right to process the data it has recorded in the police databases.

Article 108: Granting a right of access to a new national entity

(1) Prior to granting a new national entity a right of access to the INTERPOL Information System, the National Central Bureau shall take all the necessary measures to ensure that the said national entity observes the obligations arising from the present Rules.

(2) Each National Central Bureau shall notify the General Secretariat of any rights it has granted to a new national entity to access the INTERPOL Information System.

(3) It shall specify the scope of the authorizations granted.

Article 109: Granting a right of access to a new international entity

(1) The General Secretariat shall notify National Central Bureaus and international entities of any new right of access granted by the Organization to a new international entity.

(2) It shall specify the scope of authorizations granted under the agreement concluded with the Organization.

(3) With effect from the date of notification by the General Secretariat, a National Central Bureau or an international entity shall have 45 days to signify its opposition to granting this international entity the right to access the data it has recorded in the police databases.

Article 110: Register of rights of access to the INTERPOL Information System

The General Secretariat shall keep an up-to-date register of all the National Central Bureaus, and all national entities, international entities and private entities authorized to process data, directly or indirectly, in the INTERPOL Information System and ensure it is permanently available for consultation. This register shall specify the purpose, the nature and the scope of processing rights, and shall record any recent changes to these rights.

Article 111: Individual rights to access the INTERPOL Information System

(1) In conformity with Article 15(4) and (5) of the present Rules, the rights to access the INTERPOL Information System shall be granted to expressly authorized persons, solely on a need-to-know basis, taking into account the confidentiality levels.

(2) These rights shall be defined by:

(a) the National Central Bureaus for their staff and staff of their national entities;

(b) the General Secretariat for its staff and the staff of international entities.

(3) The National Central Bureaus and international entities shall be required to take all appropriate measures to ensure that their authorized users of the INTERPOL Information System observe the provisions of the present Rules.

(4) The National Central Bureaus and the international entities shall:

(a) use all appropriate means to ensure that the authorized users are aware of and are able to observe the provisions of the present Rules and that they receive necessary training for that purpose;

(b) forward the information communicated by the General Secretariat to the authorized users.

(5) The National Central Bureaus, international entities and the General Secretariat shall keep a register of the names of persons and the access rights they have been granted. They shall indicate the databases and the data to which they are authorizing user access.

(6) A National Central Bureau may choose to delegate to a national entity the management of access rights for the national entity's users. It shall ensure that the said national entity observes the obligations set out above. The delegation arrangements shall be defined in the agreement concluded between the National Central Bureau and the national entity in conformity with Article 21(3) of the present Rules. The National Central Bureau shall regularly check that these obligations and the defined arrangements are being observed by the entity.

SECTION 2: CONFIDENTIALITY

<u>Article 112: Confidentiality levels</u>

(1) There are three confidentiality levels reflecting the increasing risks that may arise from unauthorized disclosure of data:

(a) "INTERPOL FOR OFFICIAL USE ONLY"

(b) "INTERPOL RESTRICTED"

(c) "INTERPOL CONFIDENTIAL".

(2) The data shall be classified:

(a) "INTERPOL FOR OFFICIAL USE ONLY" if their unauthorized disclosure is likely to adversely affect law-enforcement action or to disadvantage or discredit the Organization, its staff, its Members, National Central Bureaus, national entities, and international entities or persons concerned by the data;

(b) "INTERPOL RESTRICTED" if their unauthorized disclosure could compromise law-enforcement action or cause harm to the Organization or its staff, its Members, National Central Bureaus, national entities, and international entities or persons concerned by the data;

(c) "INTERPOL CONFIDENTIAL" if their unauthorized disclosure might seriously compromise law-enforcement action or cause serious harm to the Organization or its staff, its Members, National Central Bureaus, national entities, international entities or persons concerned by the data.

(3) If no confidentiality level is attributed to the data by their source, the data shall be classified "INTERPOL FOR OFFICIAL USE ONLY".

(4) If a National Central Bureau, national entity or international entity needs, in a specific case, to classify certain data at a higher level of confidentiality than above, the General Secretariat shall assess with the National Central Bureau or entity concerned whether it is possible. If it is possible, they shall conclude a special arrangement defining the conditions attached to the processing of these data.

(5) A National Central Bureau, national entity or international entity may, at any time, modify the level of confidentiality that it has attributed to data, in particular by attributing a lower confidentiality level than the one previously indicated, if it considers that the data requires less protection.

<u>Article 113: Additional measures taken by the General Secretariat</u>

(1) The General Secretariat may, with the consent of the National Central Bureau, national entity or international entity that recorded the data, attribute a confidentiality level to the data which is higher than that attributed by the source, in the light of the risks to international police cooperation or to the Organization, its staff, and its Members that the processing and, more particularly, disclosure of the data might entail.

(2) The General Secretariat shall determine, in the same way, the confidentiality level of the value it adds to data, in particular when it carries out analysis work or publishes a notice. In such cases, it shall inform the source or sources of the data of this additional measure.

(3) The General Secretariat may also classify a database in the same conditions as those mentioned above.

(4) When the General Secretariat attributes a confidentiality level to data which is higher than that attributed by the National Central Bureau, national entity or international entity which recorded them, it may modify that higher confidentiality level at any time.

Article 114: Respecting confidentiality in the INTERPOL Information System

(1) The General Secretariat shall be responsible for determining authorization procedures or a system of security clearance at each data-confidentiality level. Access to a given confidentiality level shall be understood to be subject to any restrictions determined by the National Central Bureaus, international entities or the General Secretariat.

(2) The communication facilities and infrastructure used for processing data shall, depending on the confidentiality level attributed to the data, be equipped with the appropriate security controls to prevent the risk of unauthorized disclosure or to detect such a disclosure.

(3) The General Secretariat shall develop the administrative and technical processing procedures which must be observed by its staff for each confidentiality level.

(4) The National Central Bureaus, national entities and international entities shall put in place internal administrative and technical processing procedures, at least equivalent to those established by the General Secretariat, in order to ensure that the confidentiality level requested by the National Central Bureau, national entity or international entity which recorded the data is duly observed.

(5) The General Secretariat shall, in coordination with the National Central Bureaus and the entities concerned, draw up equivalence tables for its levels of classification and those used by the National Central Bureaus, national entities and international entities, whenever necessary.

SECTION 3: MANAGEMENT OF THE SECURITY SYSTEM

Article 115: Security rules

(1) In conformity with Article 15 of the present Rules, the General Secretariat shall lay down security rules defining procedural, technical and administrative security controls that ensure appropriate levels of confidentiality, integrity and availability for the INTERPOL Information System.

(2) The General Secretariat shall perform the necessary risk assessment.

(3) The General Secretariat shall develop appropriate control mechanisms to ensure that the security of data is maintained.

(4) The General Secretariat may, if necessary, establish specific security rules for a part of the communication infrastructure, a database or a specific department.

Article 116: Implementation by the National Central Bureaus and entities

The National Central Bureaus, national entities and international entities shall be responsible for adopting an appropriate level of security at least equivalent to the minimum level of security laid down in the security rules established by the General Secretariat.

Article 117: Appointment of a security officer

(1) Each National Central Bureau, national entity or international entity shall appoint one or more security officers to carry out security operations for their country or international organization in the INTERPOL Information System.

(2) The security officer shall, in particular:

(a) ensure compliance with the security procedures established by his/her National Central Bureau, national entity or international entity;

(b) update these procedures, notably in the light of the rules adopted by the General Secretariat;

(c) conduct further training on data security for the staff in his/her National Central Bureau, national entity or international entity.

(3) Whenever necessary, the security officer shall coordinate with the data protection officer.

(4) The security officer shall ensure the necessary coordination with the General Secretariat with regard to security matter.

SECTION 4: SECURITY INCIDENTS

Article 118: Information on security incidents

(1) In the event of intrusion or serious attempted intrusion affecting the network or one of the Organization's databases, or of violation or attempted violation of the integrity or confidentiality of data, the General Secretariat shall inform the source of that data, the National Central Bureau if the source is an entity that it has authorized, the Executive Committee, and the Commission for the Control of INTERPOL's Files.

(2) In the event of violation or attempted violation of the integrity or confidentiality of data initially processed in the INTERPOL Information System and processed in the information system of a National Central Bureau or an international entity, the latter shall inform the source of that data and the General Secretariat, and the Commission for the Control of INTERPOL's Files if the security incident concerns personal data. When any violation or attempted violation occurs in the information system of a national entity, the National Central Bureau that authorized it to access the INTERPOL Information System shall inform the source of the data and the General Secretariat.

Article 119: Partial or complete restoration of the INTERPOL Information System

The General Secretariat shall take all necessary and appropriate steps to be able to restore, as quickly as possible, in the event of damage, the proper functioning of the INTERPOL Information System, in particular its databases and its communications infrastructure.

TITLE 4: SUPERVISION AND MONITORING

CHAPTER I: TYPES OF SUPERVISION

Article 120: Supervision of users

(1) All National Central Bureaus, national entities and international entities shall regularly ensure that their users observe the present Rules, particularly with regard to the quality of the data they enter in the system and their use of the data consulted therein. Supervision shall be carried out in the context of spot checks and processing incidents.

(2) They shall take, within the limits set by the present Rules, all necessary measures to correct or to ensure the correction of possible processing errors.

Article 121: Designation of a data protection officer within National Central Bureaus and national and international entities

(1) All National Central Bureaus, national entities and international entities shall designate a data protection officer who shall be responsible for organizing and carrying out this monitoring. The duties of the data protection officer shall generally be carried out separately from the duties of the security officer.

(2) The data protection officer shall, in particular:

(a) establish processing procedures at his/her National Central Bureau, national entity or international entity which are in compliance with the present Rules;

(b) carry out supervision in the context of spot checks or processing incidents with the aim of guaranteeing compliance with the said Rules and procedures;

(c) update the said procedures and mechanisms;

(d) implement suitable ongoing training programmes in data processing for the staff of his/her National Central Bureau, national entity or international entity.

(3) Whenever necessary, the data protection officer shall cooperate with the security officer and with the INTERPOL data protection officer.

Article 121A: Designation of a data protection officer within the General Secretariat

(1) In accordance with Article 29 of the Constitution, and Articles 17(5,6) and 22(1,5) of the present Rules, after consulting the Executive Committee and the Commission for the Control of INTERPOL's Files, the Secretary General shall designate a data protection officer, hereinafter called the INTERPOL Data Protection Officer (IDPO).

(2) The IDPO shall be appointed for a period of five years, renewable once.

(3) In the performance of his/her duties, the IDPO shall be independent and shall report directly to the Secretary General.

(4) The IDPO shall, in particular:

(a) monitor the lawfulness and compliance of the processing of data in the INTERPOL Information System in accordance with the Organization's Constitution and rules;

(b) provide on his/her own initiative, or at the request of the General Secretariat, National Central Bureaus or other entities using the INTERPOL Information System with advice on processing operations which are likely to result in a high risk for the rights and freedoms of individuals, including data protection impact assessments, and monitor the actions taken in the light of that advice;

(c) liaise, collaborate and ensure coordination with all data protection officers designated pursuant to Article 121 of the present Rules, including through the provision of training and raising awareness on data protection issues;

(d) examine the yearly reports of data protection officers submitted in accordance with Article 17(4,5,6) and Article 123(3) of the present Rules;

(e) provide training on and raise awareness of data processing issues among the General Secretariat's staff;

(f) liaise with the Commission for the Control of INTERPOL's Files on data processing issues;

(g) liaise with data protection officers of other institutions and bodies, in particular by exchanging experience and best practices.

(5) For the purpose of carrying out his/her functions effectively, the IDPO shall have free and unlimited access to all data processed in the INTERPOL Information System and to any system within the INTERPOL Information System for processing such data, irrespective of the place, form or medium involved.

(6) In performing his/her duties, the IDPO may submit to the General Secretariat:

(a) Recommendations regarding measures to be taken in relation to data processing issues within the General Secretariat, including the correction of processing errors;

(b) Recommendations regarding the need to apply corrective measures in accordance with Article 131 of the present Rules;

(c) Reports relating to the non-implementation of the IDPO's recommendations within the General Secretariat.

(7) The IDPO may, on his/her own initiative or at the request of the CCF, share with the CCF the recommendations made and reports issued for information, and for any action deemed appropriate by the Commission.

(8) The IDPO may seek expert advice on general matters related to his/her duties.

(9) The IDPO shall submit an annual report to the Executive Committee, which will be made available to the Commission for the Control of INTERPOL's Files.

(10) The Secretary General shall adopt implementing rules concerning the work of the IDPO, including with regard to specific tasks within the IDPO's mandate, internal procedures, and safeguards for the independence of the IDPO.

Article 122: Monitoring the use of data

(1) Any National Central Bureau may request information about how another National Central Bureau, a national entity or an international entity is using data which it or its national entities have processed in the INTERPOL Information System. If the data have been consulted or used by a national entity, it shall carry out checks through that national entity's National Central Bureau.

(2) The General Secretariat shall assist the international entities in exercising the same monitoring rights.

(3) Any National Central Bureau, national entity or international entity which is subject to such monitoring must provide the requested data.

Article 123: Evaluation of national entities

(1) In accordance with Article 17(4) of the present Rules, the National Central Bureaus shall evaluate the operations, in the light of the present Rules, of the national entities they have authorized to directly access the INTERPOL Information System.

(2) Due observance by a national entity of the obligations set out in the present Rules is an essential condition for the national entity to retain direct access to the INTERPOL Information System.

(3) Every year, each National Central Bureau shall report to the General Secretariat on the spot checks it has carried out, the processing incidents it has handled, the training resources it has provided to its staff and the new measures it has adopted to meet the obligations of these Rules.

(4) The General Secretariat shall be empowered either to ask the National Central Bureau to apply corrective measures to a national entity, or to terminate access to the INTERPOL Information System if the said entity has repeatedly processed data in a non-compliant manner, if no evaluations have been carried out by the National Central Bureau concerned, or if any such evaluations have been inadequate.

Article 124: Evaluation of National Central Bureaus

(1) In accordance with Article 17(5) of the present Rules, the General Secretariat shall evaluate the operation of the National Central Bureaus in the light of the present Rules.

(2) The evaluation of National Central Bureaus in the light of the present Rules shall be performed by the General Secretariat in accordance with the directives decided upon by the General Assembly.

CHAPTER II: SUPERVISORY TOOLS

Article 125: Compliance management database

(1) In accordance with Article 10(4) of the present Rules, the General Secretariat may set up any databases to ensure that data recorded in the Organization's police databases comply with the present Rules and to avoid unauthorized or erroneous processing of data in the databases.

(2) A compliance management database shall be set up under the following conditions:

(a) It shall contain only those data which are necessary to avoid unauthorized or erroneous processing of data;

(b) The retention of data in this database shall be limited to a maximum retention period determined by the Executive Committee. This may be extended, after the Commission for the Control of INTERPOL's Files has been notified, if the examination of compliance management has not been completed by the end of this period;

(c) Access to these databases shall be restricted to authorized departments and/or staff of the General Secretariat involved in the processing of data and to whom specific access has been granted.

(3) When the General Secretariat deletes data from a police database or a compliance management database, it may nevertheless retain, for a maximum retention period determined by the Executive Committee, those data making it possible to avoid unauthorized or erroneous processing of the said data.

Article 126: Register of processing operations

(1) In accordance with Article 13 of the present Rules, the General Secretariat shall keep an up-to-date register of processing operations in the INTERPOL Information System to record:

(a) accesses to the INTERPOL Information System by users;

(b) the data recorded by users;

(c) updates made by users;

(d) decisions made by users to retain data;

(e) decisions made by users to delete data;

(f) consultations by users with direct access;

(g) requests for information received and replies sent.

(2) The register shall contain only those data necessary for verifying the conformity of processing with the present Rules. To this end, it shall include: the user identifier, the name of the user's National Central Bureau, national entity or international entity, the type of the processing operation, the date, the database concerned, and any additional items of data intended for monitoring purposes.

(3) These records shall be retained for no longer than a maximum retention period determined by the Executive Committee.

(4) These records may be accessed:

(a) solely for monitoring and checking purposes;

(b) by General Secretariat staff authorized to carry out checking operations;

(c) by the source, for monitoring purposes, on request to the General Secretariat.

(5) These records may not be used for the purposes of a criminal investigation unless this investigation is linked to checking the compliance of data processing with the present Rules.

Article 127: Comparison of data for verification purposes

(1) Any National Central Bureau, national entity or international entity which has processed in its information system data that were initially processed in the INTERPOL Information System may send a request to the General Secretariat to compare them with the data currently contained in the INTERPOL Information System in order to verify their quality. All requests from a national entity must be sent through its National Central Bureau.

(2) Any data comparison for verification purposes may be carried out by either uploading or downloading the data:

(a) any data comparison made by uploading data must meet all the following conditions:

(i) the uploading is performed solely to allow the General Secretariat to verify, on behalf of the National Central Bureau or the international entity which sent the request, the quality of the data that it has entered in its information system;

(ii) the uploaded data are not further copied within the INTERPOL Information System into which they are uploaded;

(iii) the uploaded data are systematically deleted after the data-comparison operation.

(b) any data comparison made by downloading data must meet all the following conditions:

(i) the downloading is performed solely to allow the National Central Bureau, national entity or international entity to verify the quality of the data that it has entered in its information system;

(ii) the information system of the National Central Bureau, national entity or international entity offers a level of security at least equivalent to that of the INTERPOL Information System;

(iii) the downloaded data are not further copied within the information system into which they are downloaded;

(iv) the downloaded data are systematically deleted after the data-comparison operation.

(3) The General Secretariat shall be empowered to authorize comparisons of data for verification purposes, subject to:

(a) compliance with the conditions above; and

(b) written assurances provided by the National Central or international entity that requested to carry out an operation to compare data, by which it undertakes to respect those conditions, the purpose of the operation, its nature and its scope; and

(c) the designation of a person to be responsible for overseeing the comparison of data at the National Central Bureau, national entity or international entity.

(4) The General Secretariat shall keep an updated register of the data-comparison operations carried out by downloading or uploading.

CHAPTER III: SUPERVISION MEASURES

Article 128: Examination procedure

(1) Data are, a priori, considered to be accurate and relevant when entered by a National Central Bureau, a national entity or an international entity into the INTERPOL Information System and recorded in a police database of the Organization.

(2) If a doubt arises regarding compliance with the conditions for data processing, including cases where data have been processed by a national entity, the General Secretariat shall consult the National Central Bureau concerned in order to obtain clarifications or supplementary data which may remove the doubt. The General Secretariat shall also consult any international entity if there is any doubt over compliance with the conditions for processing data.

(3) The General Secretariat shall take any other appropriate steps to ensure that these conditions have actually been met.

(4) The examination procedure shall be deemed closed if the General Secretariat concludes that the processing of data:

(a) complies with the present Rules and validates the recording of data;

(b) does not comply with the present Rules and decides to correct the data processing or to delete the data.

(5) The General Secretariat shall inform the National Central Bureau or the international entity that the examination procedure has ended. If it decides to correct or delete the data, it shall indicate reasons for its action and the corrections made to the said National Central Bureau or international entity.

Article 129: Interim measures

(1) If a doubt arises regarding compliance with the conditions for data processing, the General Secretariat shall take all appropriate steps to prevent any direct or indirect prejudice the data may cause to the Organization, its staff, its Members, the National Central Bureaus, the national entities, the international entities or the individuals that the data concern.

(2) The General Secretariat shall inform the National Central Bureau or the international entity of any interim measures taken and shall specify reasons for them.

Article 130: Measures applicable to users

If users infringe the rules applicable to the processing of data in the INTERPOL Information System, the General Secretariat may:

(a) request the National Central Bureau or international entity to suspend or withdraw the access rights it granted them;

(b) suspend or withdraw the rights itself. It shall inform the Bureau or international entity concerned of the suspension or withdrawal.

Article 131: Corrective measures applicable to National Central Bureaus and international entities

(1) If a National Central Bureau or an international entity encounters difficulties when processing data in the INTERPOL Information System or does not fulfil its obligations under the present Rules, the General Secretariat shall be entitled to take the following corrective action:

(a) correction of processing errors;

(b) supervision, for a period no longer than three months, of the processing operations carried out by the National Central Bureau or international entity;

(c) suspension of the access rights granted to users of the National Central Bureau or the international entity;

(d) dispatching an assessment team to the National Central Bureau or the international entity.

(2) The General Secretariat may send the National Central Bureaus and international entities recommendations relating to the implementation of the present Rules with a view to helping them – for instance, through staff training or by enhancing working procedures – to resolve difficulties or bring processing incidents to an end.

(3) The General Secretariat shall submit to the Executive Committee for decision all proposals to take corrective measures which may result in the long-term suspension of the following processing rights of a National Central Bureau or international entity:

(a) the right to record data in one or several police databases of the Organization;

(b) the right to consult one or several databases;

(c) interconnection or downloading authorizations.

(4) Whenever necessary, and at least once a year, the General Secretariat shall remind the National Central Bureaus and international entities of their role and responsibilities connected with the data they process in the INTERPOL Information System.

TITLE 5: FINAL PROVISIONS

CHAPTER I: PROCESSING FOR ANY OTHER LEGITIMATE PURPOSE

Article 132: Definition of processing for any other legitimate purpose

(1) In accordance with Article 10(7) of the present Rules, when data have been deleted from a police database of the Organization or a compliance management database, the General Secretariat may nevertheless retain the data necessary for the pursuit of any other legitimate purpose.

(2) Any other legitimate purpose means:
- (a) the defence of the Organization's interests, particularly in litigation and pre-litigation procedures and transactions;
- (b) scientific, historical or journalistic research and publication;
- (c) the compilation of statistics.

(3) When data initially processed for the purposes of police cooperation undergo further processing for any other legitimate purpose, they may no longer be used, in any way whatever, for the purposes of police cooperation and must not appear in the Organization's police databases.

(4) Only the processing of personal data carried out in application of paragraph 2(b) shall be subject to prior authorization by the source of the data. However, when personal data have been processed in application of paragraph 2(a) above, the source of the data shall be informed by the General Secretariat of their use or transmission.

(5) The General Secretariat shall take the necessary technical and organizational measures, particularly with regard to security, to guarantee that this further processing is not incompatible with the initial processing.

Article 133: Processing conditions

(1) When processing is carried out for any other legitimate purpose, the reasons must be specified. The specific purpose of this processing must be clearly indicated and the processing must be limited to those items of data which are strictly necessary for the purpose intended.

(2) Processing shall be carried out, if possible, using data which have been made anonymous or, failing that, encoded, whenever the intended purpose can be achieved by such means.

(3) The access to data processed for any other legitimate purpose shall be restricted to authorized departments or staff of the General Secretariat to whom specific access has been granted.

Article 134: Retention of data

(1) Data processed for any other legitimate purpose shall be retained for a period strictly necessary to achieve the purpose for which they were processed, and not exceeding a maximum retention period determined by the Executive Committee.

(2) This period may be extended solely when data have been retained for historical purposes or if the data have been made anonymous or encoded for processing, on condition that the extension itself remains necessary to accomplish the aims for which the processing is being carried out.

CHAPTER II: SETTLEMENT OF DISPUTES

Article 135: Settlement of disputes

(1) Disputes that arise in connection with the application of the present Rules should be solved by concerted consultation. If this fails, the matter may be submitted to the Executive Committee and, if necessary, to the General Assembly.

(2) All national entities shall be represented in the settlement of disputes by their National Central Bureaus.

****

**APPENDIX:
CHARTER RELATING TO ACCESS TO THE INTERPOL INFORMATION SYSTEM BY NATIONAL ENTITIES**

The purpose of the present Charter is to clearly set out the conditions under which national entities may be authorized by the National Central Bureaus of their respective countries, pursuant to Article 21 of INTERPOL's Rules on data processing, to directly consult data processed in the INTERPOL Information System or to directly supply data for processing purposes in this System.

(1) Direct access to the INTERPOL Information System shall be subject to the following conditions:

(a) Direct access to and use of the INTERPOL Information System shall be subject to INTERPOL's Rules on the Processing of Data;

(b) The national entity shall accept and agree to comply with the provisions of these Rules and with any procedures established in application of the said Rules to allow access to and use of INTERPOL's Information System;

(c) The national entity shall designate and assign a security officer and a data protection officer, and put in place procedures with the aim of ensuring on a permanent basis that its users are respecting the present Rules;

(d) The national entity shall agree, in particular, to allow the National Central Bureau that authorized it:

(i) to carry out regular checks, remotely or on site, on its processing of data entered or consulted in the INTERPOL Information System to ensure compliance with the Rules;

(ii) to take the necessary preventive or corrective measures against it in the event of a processing incident;

(iii) to withdraw the national entity's access to the INTERPOL Information System in the event of failure to comply with its obligations under these Rules or the repeated non-compliant processing of data.

(e) The national entity shall also agree that the INTERPOL General Secretariat:

(i) shall be responsible for the general administration of the INTERPOL Information System and ensure that the conditions for processing data in the Organization's databases are met;

(ii) may take any appropriate measures within the scope of these Rules to terminate any non-compliant processing of data, including withdrawing access to the INTERPOL Information System.

(2) The extent of the national entity's access rights to the INTERPOL Information System shall be determined by its National Central Bureau in accordance with INTERPOL's Rules on the Processing of Data.

****

Appendix 3 Statute of the Commission for the Control of Interpol's Files

REFERENCES

73rd General Assembly session, Resolution AG-2004-RES-08, approving the Rules relating to the Control of Information and Access to INTERPOL's Files, which replace the second part (Articles 15 to 27) of the "Rules on International Police Cooperation and on the Internal Control of INTERPOL's Archives" which is abrogated.

78th General Assembly session, Resolution AG-2009-RES-13, amending Article 2(a) and 2(b) of the Rules.

85th General Assembly session, Resolution AG-2016-RES-06, adopting the Statute of the Commission for the Control of INTERPOL's Files and abrogating the Rules on the Control of Information and Access to INTERPOL's Files.

CONTENTS

Article 1:Aim 4
CHAPTER 1: GENERAL PROVISIONS 4
Article 2: Definitions 4
Article 3: Competence and powers of the Commission 4
Article 4: Independence of the Commission 4
Article 5: Cooperation of the Members of the Organization 4
CHAPTER 2: Organization of the Commission 4
SUB-CHAPTER 1: STRUCTURE AND COMPOSITION OF THE COMMISSION 4
Article 6: Structure 4
Article 7: Chairperson 5
Article 8: Composition 5
SUB-CHAPTER 2: MEMBERS OF THE COMMISSION 5
Article 9: Election 5
Article 10: Terms of office 5
Article 11:Independence 6
Article 12: Impartiality 6
Article 13:Remuneration 6
Article 14: Dismissal and temporary suspension from office 6
SUB-CHAPTER 3: SECRETARIAT OF THE COMMISSION 6
Article 15: Secretariat 6
SUB-CHAPTER 4: FUNCTIONING OF THE COMMISSION 7
Article 16: Sessions 7
Article 17: Delegation of powers 7
Article 18: Languages 7
Article 19: Access to the INTERPOL Information System 7
Article 20: Confidentiality and professional secrecy 7
Article 21: Consultation 8
Article 22: Experts 8
Article 23: INTERPOL General Secretariat 8
Article 24: Budget 8
Article 25: Operating Rules 8

CHAPTER 3: THE SUPERVISORY AND ADVISORY CHAMBER 8

Article 26: Powers of the Supervisory and Advisory Chamber 8

Article 27: Decisions, opinions and recommendations 9

CHAPTER 4: THE REQUESTS CHAMBER 9

Article 28: Powers of the Requests Chamber 9

SUB-CHAPTER 1: INSTITUTION OF THE PROCEEDINGS 9

Article 29:Right to access, correct and delete data 9

Article 30: Submission of requests 9

Article 31: Communication after the submission of a request 10

Article 32: Admissibility of requests 10

SUB-CHAPTER 2: PROCEDURE AFTER A REQUEST HAS BEEN DECLARED ADMISSIBLE 10

Article 33 Examination of requests 10

Article 34: Consultations 10

Article 35: Communication of information 10

Article 36: Written submissions and hearings 11

Article 37: Provisional measures 11

SUB-CHAPTER 3: DECISIONS AND REMEDIES 11

Article 38: Nature and content of decisions 11

Article 39: Remedies 11

Article 40: Timeframe for decisions 11

Article 41: Notification and implementation of decisions 12

Article 42: Revision 12

CHAPTER 5: PUBLICATIONS AND RETENTION OF FILES 12

Article 43: Annual report 12

Article 44: Publication of decisions, recommendations and opinions 12

Article 45: Retention of the Commission's files 12

CHAPTER 6: FINAL PROVISIONS 13

Article 46: Non-interference with the Organization's functioning 13

Article 47: Status 13

Article 48: Abrogation 13

Article 49: Amendment 13

Article 50: Entry into force 13

Article 1:Aim

(1) The aim of the present Statute is to define the work of the Commission for the Control of INTERPOL's Files.

(2) The Commission for the Control of INTERPOL's Files shall be constituted and shall function in accordance with the present Statute.

CHAPTER 1: GENERAL PROVISIONS

Article 2: Definitions

(1) The definitions given in Article 1 of INTERPOL's Rules on the Processing of Data shall apply to the present Statute.

(2) "The Commission" refers to the Commission for the Control of INTERPOL's Files, as provided for in Articles 5 and 36 of INTERPOL's Constitution.

(3) "INTERPOL's rules" refers to INTERPOL's Constitution and its Rules on the Processing of Data, unless otherwise specified in the present Statute.

Article 3: Competence and powers of the Commission

(1) The Commission shall be competent to perform the functions conferred on it by Article 36 of the Constitution, namely:

(a) Ensure that the processing of personal data by the Organization is in compliance with INTERPOL's rules;

(b) Provide the Organization with advice about any project, operation, set of rules or other matter involving the processing of personal data in the INTERPOL Information System;

(c) Examine and decide on requests for access to data, and/or for the correction or deletion of data, processed in the INTERPOL Information System.

(2) To perform its functions, the Commission shall have:

(a) full access to the INTERPOL Information System in accordance with Article 19 of the present Statute;

(b) the power, as provided for in Article 26 of the present Statute, to carry out the necessary checks and to take decisions binding on the Organization and give opinions concerning the processing of personal data in the INTERPOL Information System;

(c) the exclusive power, as provided for in Article 28 of the present Statute, to examine and take decisions that are final and binding with regard to requests for access to, or correction and/or deletion of, data processed in the INTERPOL Information System.

Article 4: Independence of the Commission

The Commission shall be independent in the performance of its functions.

Article 5: Cooperation of the Members of the Organization

The Members of the Organization shall:

(1) respect the competence and independence of the Commission;

(2) respond diligently to requests from the Commission in accordance with their national laws;

(3) to the extent permitted by their national laws, ensure that no national authority within their territories interferes in the Commission's work or attempts to take decisions directed at the Organization in matters falling within the Commission's competence.

CHAPTER 2: ORGANIZATION OF THE COMMISSION

SUB-CHAPTER 1: STRUCTURE AND COMPOSITION OF THE COMMISSION

Article 6: Structure

(1) The Commission shall consist of two chambers:

(a) A Supervisory and Advisory Chamber, which shall have the power to perform the functions described in Article 3(1)(a) and (b) of the present Statute;

(b) A Requests Chamber, which shall have the power to perform the function described in Article 3(1)(c) of the present Statute.

(2) The members of each Chamber of the Commission may consult and/or participate as non-voting members in the work and deliberations of the other Chamber.

Article 7: Chairperson

(1) The Chairperson shall preside over both Chambers of the Commission, direct their work, and supervise the administration of the Commission and the work of its Secretariat.

(2) The Chairperson shall be elected by all the members of the Commission from among the members of the Requests Chamber.

Article 8: Composition

(1) The Commission shall be composed of seven members, elected from among persons of high moral character, impartiality and integrity who possess the qualifications required for appointment to senior positions in their field of expertise.

(2) The members of the Commission shall be nationals of the Organization's Members, be of different nationalities, and be fluent at least in one of the working languages of the Organization. As far as possible, the members of the Requests Chamber should represent the principal legal systems of the world.

(3) The Supervisory and Advisory Chamber shall consist of the Chairperson, a member with expertise in data protection, and a member with expertise in electronic data processing.

(4) The Requests Chamber shall consist of five members:

(a) A lawyer with data-protection expertise;

(b) A lawyer with recognized international experience in police matters, in particular international police cooperation;

(c) A lawyer with international criminal law expertise;

(d) A lawyer with human rights expertise;

(e) A lawyer who holds or has held a senior judicial or prosecutorial position, preferably with experience in international judicial cooperation.

SUB-CHAPTER 2: MEMBERS OF THE COMMISSION

Article 9: Election

(1) The members of the Commission shall be elected by the General Assembly.

(2) Whenever necessary, the Secretary General shall address a written request to the Organization's Members inviting them to nominate, within a given time, persons with the required qualifications and expertise to perform the duties of a member of the Commission. Each Member may propose one candidate per post.

(3) Every nomination shall be accompanied by a statement specifying the candidate's qualifications for the position.

(4) The Executive Committee shall prepare a list of all eligible candidates who possess the required qualifications, with the accompanying documents, and submit that list to the General Assembly.

(5) The General Assembly shall elect the members of the Commission by secret ballot in accordance with the Rules of Procedure of the General Assembly. Those candidates who obtain a simple majority of votes shall be considered as elected. Depending on his or her experience, a person may be candidate for several vacant posts.

Article 10: Terms of office

(1) The terms of office of the members of the Commission shall be five years, renewable once for an additional term of three years.

(2) For the purposes of the first election under the present Statute:

(a) one of the members of the Supervisory and Advisory Chamber shall be selected by lot to serve for a term of four years;

(b) two of the members of the Requests Chamber shall be selected by lot to serve for a term of four years;

(c) the other members shall serve for a term of five years;

(d) the current members of the Commission may be elected for one non-renewable term.

(3) If a member of the Commission is no longer able to perform his/her functions, or has resigned, a new member shall be elected for the remainder of his/her predecessor's term of office. The new member may subsequently be re-elected for one non-renewable term of three years. A temporary replacement may be appointed by the Executive Committee to serve until the next General Assembly session.

Article 11:Independence

(1) The members of the Commission shall serve in their personal capacity.

(2) In the exercise of their functions, the members of the Commission shall be independent, remain free from external influence, whether direct or indirect, and neither solicit nor accept instructions from any person, body or government.

(3) Members of the Commission shall abstain from any action or activity likely to interfere with the exercise of their functions or to affect confidence in their independence.

(4) The Organization and its Members shall abstain from any action which might influence the members of the Commission or its Secretariat, or be prejudicial to the discharge of their functions.

(5) The Chairperson of the Commission shall ensure that the rules on the independence of the Commission and its members are respected.

Article 12: Impartiality

(1) A member of the Commission shall not participate in any case in which his/her impartiality might reasonably be doubted.

(2) The Commission's Operating Rules shall set out the criteria and procedures regarding the application of this Article.

Article 13:Remuneration

The General Assembly shall decide on the remuneration of the members of the Commission. Such remuneration shall not be reduced during their terms of office.

Article 14: Dismissal and temporary suspension from office

(1) A member of the Commission may be dismissed only by the General Assembly in the following instances:

(a) on the proposal of the Commission in the event of the member's misconduct or incapacity;

(b) on the proposal of the Executive Committee and after consulting the Commission in the event of the member's repeated or serious misconduct.

(2) In urgent cases, the Executive Committee may, after consulting the Commission, temporarily suspend a member until the next session of the General Assembly, in the event of his/her misconduct or incapacity.

SUB-CHAPTER 3: SECRETARIAT OF THE COMMISSION

Article 15: Secretariat

(1) The Secretariat shall be a permanent body headed by a Secretary who shall act under the authority of the Commission. The Secretary shall be a legal professional with wide experience, notably in the fields of international criminal law, human rights and/or data protection.

(2) The staff of the Secretariat shall be selected by the Commission. In the selection of the Secretariat's staff, account shall be taken of the need for:

(a) the representation of all working languages of the Organization;

(b) the representation of the principal legal systems of the world;

(c) the appropriate presence of staff members with judicial or court registry experience and/or familiarity with international criminal law, human rights law and/or data protection, and demonstrated skills in legal analysis and writing.

(3) The Secretariat shall assist the Commission in effectively carrying out its functions under the present Statute. In particular, it shall take all appropriate steps to:

(a) perform administrative operations for the Commission, or arrange for them to be performed;

(b) prepare files for consideration by the Commission;

(c) act as an interface and coordinator between the Commission and the Organization or any other body;

(d) carry out studies and other tasks as instructed by the Commission or its Chairperson.

(4) The staff of the Secretariat shall exercise their duties in complete independence and shall receive and accept instructions exclusively from the Commission.

(5) For administrative purposes exclusively, the staff of the Secretariat shall have the rights and obligations of a member of the General Secretariat's staff.

SUB-CHAPTER 4: FUNCTIONING OF THE COMMISSION

Article 16: Sessions

(1) The Commission shall determine the venue, number and duration of its sessions to carry out its functions effectively, but shall meet at least three times a year. Sessions shall be convened by the Chairperson of the Commission.

(2) The Commission's sessions shall be held *in camera* and, in principle, only members of the Commission and its Secretariat may attend them. Nonetheless, the Commission may invite other persons whose presence it considers is necessary.

(3) The Commission shall make publicly available the general timeframe of its planned sessions for each calendar year.

(4) To facilitate the preparation for its sessions, the Commission shall provide the General Secretariat in due time, and preferably one month before each session, with the list of issues to be discussed by both Chambers.

Article 17: Delegation of powers

Each of the Commission's Chambers may delegate some of its powers to one or several of its members in order to perform its functions effectively. Such delegation may include the power to take decisions in between sessions.

Article 18: Languages

(1) The working languages of the Commission shall be those of the Organization as specified in Article 54 of the General Regulations, namely Arabic, English, French and Spanish.

(2) The Commission may decide which of the working languages it will use for its internal files and deliberations.

Article 19: Access to the INTERPOL Information System

For the purpose of carrying out its functions effectively, the Commission shall have free and unlimited access to all data processed in the INTERPOL Information System, irrespective of the place, form or medium involved.

Article 20: Confidentiality and professional secrecy

(1) The files of the Commission shall be confidential.

(2) The requests submitted to the Commission under Chapter 4 of the present Statute shall be treated by the Requests Chamber as confidential and shall not be recorded in the INTERPOL Information System. However, the Requests Chamber may decide:

(a) in order to examine the requests, to disclose information, when deemed necessary in the exercise of its functions, having regard to the facts of the case and the rights and freedoms of the applicant;

(b) to record a request or parts of it in the INTERPOL Information System in order to update or correct data already contained in the INTERPOL Information System.

(3) The members of the Commission, its Secretariat, and any expert appointed by the Commission under the present Statute shall consider as confidential all information that comes to their knowledge in the exercise of their functions, unless the proper discharge of their functions requires otherwise. The obligation of confidentiality shall continue to apply after they cease to be active in any of those capacities.

Article 21: Consultation

(1) The Commission may directly consult the General Secretariat, sources of data or other entities which have access to the INTERPOL Information System as provided for in INTERPOL's Rules on the Processing of Data. Consultation of national entities shall take place through the National Central Bureau of the Member concerned.

(2) The Commission may consult other international or national bodies, including data protection bodies, on matters related to its functions, whereas consultation of national authorities shall take place through the National Central Bureau of the Member concerned.

(3) In consulting other entities or bodies, the Commission shall take into consideration confidentiality requirements and any restrictions.

Article 22: Experts

The Commission may entrust any individual or body with recognized expertise with the task of providing expert advice, subject to confidentiality requirements and restrictions.

Article 23: INTERPOL General Secretariat

The INTERPOL General Secretariat shall provide in due time the necessary support to the Commission to enable it to carry out its functions effectively, in particular by:

(a) providing premises and the necessary infrastructure;

(b) forwarding to the Commission any request made under Chapter 4 of the present Statute as soon as the General Secretariat receives it;

(c) communicating to the Commission any information requested by the Commission and available to the General Secretariat or as provided for in INTERPOL's Rules on the Processing of Data;

(d) communicating to the Commission any other relevant information to enable it to perform its functions;

(e) facilitating its sessions;

(f) respecting and protecting the Commission's competence and independence.

Article 24: Budget

Following a proposal from the Commission, the General Assembly shall allocate to the Commission the annual budget necessary to perform its functions.

Article 25: Operating Rules

(1) Subject to the provisions of this Statute, the Commission shall enact its own operating rules to carry out its functions.

(2) The operating rules of the Commission shall include, *inter alia*, provisions on the following points:

(a) Organization of work;

(b) Procedures for maintaining and protecting the confidentiality of the Commission's work;

(c) Election procedure and term of office of the Chairperson;

(d) Venue, number and duration of the Commission's sessions;

(e) Procedures concerning the adoption of decisions by the Commission's Chambers;

(f) Criteria and procedure for the withdrawal of its members;

(g) Procedure to determine the admissibility of requests;

(h) Other matters relating to the effective functioning of the Commission.

(3) The operating rules adopted by the Commission shall be made public in all working languages of the Organization.

CHAPTER 3: THE SUPERVISORY AND ADVISORY CHAMBER

Article 26: Powers of the Supervisory and Advisory Chamber

In accordance with Article 3 of the present Statute, the Supervisory and Advisory Chamber of the Commission shall have the power to:

(1) in its supervisory capacity, carry out the necessary checks to ensure that the processing of personal data by the Organization is in compliance with INTERPOL's rules, and take decisions binding on the Organization on the measures

required to remedy any non-compliance with INTERPOL's rules as well as recommendations on how to improve the processing of personal data by the Organization;

(2) in its advisory capacity, give opinions on all matters referred to in the INTERPOL Rules on the Processing of Data and on any other matter involving the processing of personal data, either on its own initiative or at the request of the General Secretariat.

Article 27: Decisions, opinions and recommendations

(1) The decisions, opinions and recommendations shall be made in writing and shall be reasoned.

(2) The Supervisory and Advisory Chamber shall communicate its decisions, opinions and recommendations to the General Secretariat.

(3) The General Secretariat shall implement the decisions of the Supervisory and Advisory Chamber as soon as possible, and shall report to the Commission on such implementation.

(4) The General Secretariat shall strive to follow up on opinions and recommendations made by the Supervisory and Advisory Chamber as soon as possible, and shall report to the Commission on their implementation.

(5) If the General Secretariat disagrees with the opinions or recommendations made by the Supervisory and Advisory Chamber, it shall so inform the Commission as soon as possible and indicate the reasons for its disagreement. In such a case, the Commission may inform the Executive Committee of that disagreement, so that the latter may take any appropriate measure.

CHAPTER 4: THE REQUESTS CHAMBER

Article 28: Powers of the Requests Chamber

(1) In accordance with Article 3 of the present Statute, the Requests Chamber shall have exclusive power to:

(a) decide on its competence to process requests submitted under the present Statute;

(b) examine and decide on requests for access to, or correction and/or deletion of, data processed in the INTERPOL Information System.

(2) Nothing in the present Statute shall prevent:

(a) any person or entity from submitting a request to the competent authorities of the source of the data asking those authorities to take action regarding the data processed by that source in the INTERPOL Information System;

(b) the source of data from correcting or deleting the data it processes in the INTERPOL Information System;

(c) the General Secretariat from blocking, correcting or deleting, in accordance with INTERPOL's rules, data processed in the INTERPOL Information System.

SUB-CHAPTER 1: INSTITUTION OF THE PROCEEDINGS

Article 29: Right to access, correct and delete data

(1) Any person or entity shall have the right to submit directly to the Commission a request for access to, or correction and/or deletion of, data processed in the INTERPOL Information System and concerning that person or entity.

(2) The Organization and its Members undertake to respect this right.

Article 30: Submission of requests

(1) For the purposes of the present Chapter, any individual or entity submitting a request to the Commission shall be referred to as an applicant.

(2) A request shall be submitted to the Commission in writing, in one of INTERPOL's working languages, by the applicant or a duly authorized representative. A request for correction or deletion of data shall set out the reasons therefor.

(3) There shall be no charge for the submission of a request.

Article 31: Communication after the submission of a request

(1) The Requests Chamber shall acknowledge the receipt of a request at the earliest opportunity, and shall inform the applicant of the applicable procedure and timeframe.

(2) The Requests Chamber shall be the only point of contact for the applicant during the entire proceedings.

(3) On request or at its own initiative, the Requests Chamber shall inform both the applicant and the source of data of the status of the request and any relevant developments. In addition, the Requests Chamber shall inform them of the date on which the request will be examined and the deadline for any additional submissions.

(4) The Requests Chamber shall communicate with the applicant and the source of the data in the working languages of the Organization used by them, and shall use different forms of communication as appropriate, including electronic forms of communication.

Article 32: Admissibility of requests

(1) The Requests Chamber shall examine the admissibility of each request and inform the applicant, at the earliest opportunity and no later than one month from its receipt by the Commission, whether the request is admissible.

(2) The Commission shall declare inadmissible any request considered to be incompatible with the provisions of the present Statute and the admissibility criteria defined by the Commission in its Operating Rules.

(3) If the request is declared inadmissible in whole or in part, the Requests Chamber shall explain the reasons to the applicant.

SUB-CHAPTER 2: PROCEDURE AFTER A REQUEST HAS BEEN DECLARED ADMISSIBLE

Article 33 Examination of requests

(1) When a request is considered admissible, the Requests Chamber shall determine whether data concerning the applicant are being processed in the INTERPOL Information System.

(2) If no data concerning the applicant are being processed at the time the request is examined, the Requests Chamber may decide on appropriate measures, taking into consideration confidentiality requirements.

(3) If data concerning the applicant are being processed in the INTERPOL Information System, and if the request is for correction or deletion, the Requests Chamber shall examine the compliance of the processing of the data with INTERPOL's rules. If the request only concerns access to the data, the Requests Chamber may nonetheless decide to examine the compliance of the processing of those data with INTERPOL's rules. The scope of review of a request shall be limited to examining the compliance of the processing of data with INTERPOL's rules.

Article 34: Consultations

(1) If additional information is required to examine the request, the Requests Chamber shall seek information or clarification from the source of the data and/or the General Secretariat.

(2) The Requests Chamber may also seek information or clarification from any other entity in accordance with Article 21 of the present Statute.

Article 35: Communication of information

(1) Information connected with a request shall be accessible to the applicant and the source of the data, subject to the restrictions, conditions and procedures set out in this article.

(2) Prior to disclosing information, the Requests Chamber shall consult the owner of that information, namely the applicant or source of the data.

(3) The communication of information may be restricted at the decision of the Requests Chamber, on its own initiative or at the request of the source of data, the General Secretariat or the applicant, for one or more of the following reasons:

- (a) To protect public or national security or to prevent crime;
- (b) To protect the confidentiality of an investigation or prosecution;
- (c) To protect the rights and freedoms of the applicant or third parties;

(d) To enable the Commission or the Organization to properly discharge their duties.

(4) Any restriction on the disclosure of information must be justified and must specify whether some information, such as summaries, may be provided. The absence of justification alone will not lead to the disclosure of the content of the information but may be taken into consideration by the Requests Chamber in assessing and deciding on a request.

(5) Where deemed appropriate, and provided that this does not compromise the confidentiality of the case, the Requests Chamber may direct the applicant to contact the competent authorities of the source(s) of data.

Article 36: Written submissions and hearings

The Requests Chamber shall examine a request on the basis of written submissions. Hearings may be held only if deemed necessary by the Requests Chamber for the examination of requests.

Article 37: Provisional measures

(1) At any time during the proceedings, the Requests Chamber may decide on provisional measures to be taken by the Organization in relation to the processing of the data concerned.

(2) Provisional measures shall be implemented in accordance with the procedure specified in Article 41 of the present Statute.

SUB-CHAPTER 3: DECISIONS AND REMEDIES

Article 38: Nature and content of decisions

(1) The decisions of the Requests Chamber shall be final and binding on the Organization and the applicant.

(2) Decisions shall be given in writing in one of the Organization's working languages. They shall be reasoned and shall contain, *inter alia*, a summary of the proceedings, the submissions of the parties, a statement of the facts, the application of INTERPOL's rules, an analysis of legal arguments, and operative parts.

(3) Decisions shall be provided to the applicant and the source of data, subject to confidentiality requirements and restrictions and in accordance with Article 41 of the present Statute.

Article 39: Remedies

(1) The Requests Chamber may decide on any appropriate corrective actions to ensure that data are processed in the INTERPOL Information System in accordance with INTERPOL's rules.

(2) If the Requests Chamber finds that data have not been processed in accordance with those rules, in addition to any decision on the corrective actions to be taken with regard to such data, it may decide on other appropriate remedies to be granted by the Organization to the applicant.

(3) Any remedy to be granted by the Organization may only relate to the Organization's responsibilities in the particular case and to the processing of data in the INTERPOL Information System.

(4) To determine such remedies, the Requests Chamber shall take into consideration, *inter alia*, the following factors:

(a) The information available to the Organization when the data were processed;

(b) The role and responsibilities of the relevant entities involved in the processing of data;

(c) The steps that have been taken or should reasonably have been taken by the applicant before the competent authorities of the source of the data;

(d) Any remedy already provided to the applicant by the competent authorities of the source of data, or available to him/her from those authorities;

(e) The position expressed by the Organization;

(f) The obligation of non-interference with the Organization's functions, as provided for in Article 46 of the present Statute.

Article 40: Timeframe for decisions

(1) The Requests Chamber shall decide on a request for access to data within four months from the date on which the request was declared admissible.

(2) The Requests Chamber shall decide on a request for correction and/or deletion of data within nine months from the date on which the request was declared admissible.

(3) The Requests Chamber may decide that the circumstances of a particular request warrant an extension of the time limit. Any such extension shall be reasonable, promptly communicated to the General Secretariat, the source of data and the applicant, and shall also be explained in the decision.

(4) The Requests Chamber may take decisions between sessions and devise any appropriate procedures in order to discharge its function effectively within the time limits set by the present Article.

Article 41: Notification and implementation of decisions

(1) The written decision of the Requests Chamber shall be provided to the General Secretariat within one month from the date on which the decision was made.

(2) The General Secretariat shall implement a decision within one month from the date on which it was received, unless it seeks further clarifications needed for the implementation of the decision. In the latter case, the General Secretariat shall proceed with the implementation within one month from the date on which the clarifications were received. The General Secretariat shall promptly notify the Commission of the implementation of its decision.

(3) The Requests Chamber shall provide its written decision to the applicant and to the source of data and notify them of the implementation of its decision by the Organization taking into consideration confidentiality requirements and restrictions. Decisions on requests for access shall be provided within one month from the date on which they were adopted by the Requests Chamber. Decisions on requests for correction and/or deletion of data shall be provided promptly and no later than one month from the date on which the Requests Chamber received notification of their implementation.

(4) If data have been corrected or deleted as a result of a decision by the Commission, the General Secretariat shall promptly notify the Organization's Members which had received the data concerned, other than the source of the data, of any corrections or deletions. At the request of a Member other than the source of data, and subject to confidentiality requirements and restrictions, the Commission may supply its decision and any clarification.

Article 42: Revision

(1) Applications for the revision of decisions of the Requests Chamber may be made only when they are based on the discovery of facts which could have led the Requests Chamber to a different conclusion if that fact had been known at the time at which the request was being processed.

(2) Applications for revision must be made within six months after the discovery of the fact.

(3) The timeframe for a decision on a request for revision shall be that provided for in Article 40 of the present Statute.

CHAPTER 5: PUBLICATIONS AND RETENTION OF FILES

Article 43: Annual report

(1) The Commission shall produce an annual report on all its activities and submit it to the General Assembly.

(2) The Commission's annual report shall be made public in all working languages of the Organization.

Article 44: Publication of decisions, recommendations and opinions

Subject to the confidentiality requirements, restrictions and other conditions set forth in the present Statute, the Commission shall endeavour to make its decisions, opinions, recommendations and reports public in all working languages of the Organization.

Article 45: Retention of the Commission's files

(1) The Commission shall keep its files, its decisions, opinions and recommendations for a period of 30 years.

(2) The Commission may nevertheless retain the files, decisions, opinions and recommendations necessary for the pursuit of any other legitimate purpose set out in Article 132 and in accordance with the timeframe specified in Article 134 of INTERPOL's Rules on the Processing of Data.

CHAPTER 6: FINAL PROVISIONS

Article 46: Non-interference with the Organization's functioning

Nothing in the present Statute shall be interpreted as allowing any fundamental interference with the assets and activities necessary for the functioning of the Organization.

Article 47: Status

The present Statute constitutes an appendix to the Organization's Constitution.

Article 48: Abrogation

The present Statute abrogates and replaces the Rules on the Control of Information and Access to INTERPOL's Files which were adopted by the General Assembly at its 73rd session by Resolution AG-2004-RES-08.

Article 49: Amendment

The present Statute may be amended by a decision of the General Assembly in accordance with Article 44 of the Constitution and the General Assembly's Rules of Procedure.

Article 50: Entry into force

The present Statute shall enter into force on 11 March 2017.

****

Appendix 4 Rules on the Control of Information and Access to Interpol's Files

REFERENCES

73rd General Assembly session, Resolution AG-2004-RES-08, approving the Rules relating to the Control of Information and Access to INTERPOL's Files, which replace the second part (Articles 15 to 27) of the "Rules on International Police Cooperation and on the Internal Control of INTERPOL's Archives" which is abrogated.

78th General Assembly session, Resolution AG-2009-RES-13, amending Article 2(a) and 2(b) of the Rules.

CONTENTS

PREAMBLE 3

CHAPTER 1: COMMISSION FOR THE CONTROL OF INTERPOL'S FILES 3

Article 1: Role of the Commission 3

Article 2: Composition of the Commission 3

Article 3: Commission members' terms of office 3

Article 4: Matters submitted to the Commission 4

Article 5: Functioning of the Commission 4

Article 6: Findings of the Commission 5

Article 7: Secretariat of the Commission 5

Article 8: Budget of the Commission 5

CHAPTER 2: ACCESS BY REQUESTING PARTIES TO PERSONAL INFORMATION PROCESSED BY INTERPOL 5

Article 9: Access conditions and procedures 5

Article 10: Control carried out by the Commission 6

Article 11: Results of the Commission's processing of a request 6

Article 12: Final provisions and interim measures 6

PREAMBLE

The aim of the present Rules is to organize the independent control of INTERPOL's files. It establishes a Commission for the Control of INTERPOL's Files and governs the composition, role and functions of that Commission. The present Rules also set out the general conditions under which a person may gain access to the Organization's files.

CHAPTER 1: COMMISSION FOR THE CONTROL OF INTERPOL'S FILES

Article 1: Role of the Commission

(a) The Commission shall ensure that the rules and operations relating to the processing of personal information by the Organization, and particularly its projects to create new files or new methods of circulating personal information, conform to all the relevant rules adopted by the Organization, and that they do not infringe the basic rights of the people concerned, as referred to in Article 2 of the Organization's Constitution, which refers in turn to the Universal Declaration of Human Rights, or the general principles of data protection.

(b) The Commission shall provide the Organization with advice about any project, operation, set of rules or other matter involving the processing of personal information.

(c) The Commission shall process requests for access to INTERPOL's files and shall reply to requesting parties. On request, the Commission shall make the list of INTERPOL's files available to any national or permanent resident of a Member State of the Organization.

Article 2: Composition of the Commission

(a) The Commission shall comprise five members, appointed because of their expertise and in such a way as to allow the Commission to carry out its mission completely independently:

- a Chairperson, appointed because he holds or has held senior judicial or data protection posts;
- two data protection experts, who hold or have held senior positions in this field;
- an electronic data processing expert, who holds or has held a senior position in this field;
- an expert with recognized international experience in police matters, in particular international police cooperation.

(b) The members shall be appointed as follows:

- The experts referred to in Article 2(a) above shall be appointed by the General Assembly from amongst the candidates put forward by Member States and selected by the Executive Committee.
- The Chairperson shall be appointed by the other four members.

(c) The members of the Commission must be nationals of INTERPOL Member States, and speak at least one of the working languages of the Organization's General Secretariat. The applications sent in by the Member States must therefore give sufficient detail to make it possible to assess the candidates' qualifications.

(d) As far as possible, the members shall be of different nationalities and represent at least two regions.

Article 3: Commission members' terms of office

(a) The terms of office of the members of the Commission shall be three years, commencing on the date on which the Chairperson of the Commission is appointed, it being understood that the Commission shall be considered to have been composed on the date on which the Chairperson was appointed.

(b) The term of office of a Commission member, may be renewed once, in the same position. However, the term of office may be renewed twice if, in the light of circumstances, the Executive Committee considers it advisable.

(c) Except in cases of force majeure, the terms of office of the Commission members shall not all be renewed at the same time.

(d) If a member of the Commission is no longer in a position to perform his duties, or has resigned, a new member shall be appointed for the remainder of his term of office. If the member concerned is one of those appointed by the General Assembly, a temporary replacement may be appointed by the Executive Committee pending the next General Assembly session.

Article 4: Matters submitted to the Commission

(a) The Commission may receive requests from any person wishing to access personal information concerning him or the person he represents, as long as the requests meet the conditions on admissibility laid down by the Commission.

(b) The General Secretariat must consult the Commission in all the cases referred to in the Rules on the Processing of Information for the purposes of International Police Cooperation.

(c) The General Secretariat may in addition consult the Commission on any issue or operation concerning the processing of personal information, particularly with regard to the interpretation of an existing rule, the adoption of a new rule or of implementing rules, or the setting up of databases or the conclusion of agreements with third parties involving the processing of personal information.

(d) The Commission may also decide to carry out controls in the context of its spot checks.

Article 5: Functioning of the Commission

(a) The Commission shall be completely independent in the exercise of its duties.

(b) The Commission shall determine the venue and number of its annual meetings, on the understanding that it shall meet at least three times a year in order to perform its duties. Meetings shall be convened by the Chairperson of the Commission.

(c) The sessions of the Commission shall be held in camera. Only members of the Commission and the Commission's Secretariat shall be considered as permanent participants in those meetings. However, any other persons whose presence the Commission considers necessary for discussion of an item on the agenda for the session, may also take part in the meetings.

(d) The Commission shall determine its own operating rules, insofar as they are not laid down in the present Rules.

(e) The Commission shall take all appropriate steps to exercise its duties and ensure its independence. To that effect, it is agreed that:

(1) In the exercise of their duties, the members of the Commission shall neither solicit nor accept instructions from any persons or bodies, and shall be bound by professional secrecy;

(2) The Commission shall have free and unlimited access to all personal information processed by INTERPOL, and to any system for processing such information, irrespective of the place, form or medium involved; as far as possible, the Commission shall exercise its right of access in such a way as not to interfere unnecessarily with the day-to-day work of the General Secretariat;

(3) The Commission may consult the General Secretariat and ask to hear its representatives;

(4) The Commission may also consult the NCBs concerned or the other information sources concerned, or even the Executive Committee;

(5) The Commission may ask the Executive Committee to permit it address the General Assembly, in accordance with the provisions of Article 6 (d) below.

(f) To enable the Commission to perform its duties, the General Secretariat shall:

(1) Forward to the Commission any request it receives, as soon as it receives it, it being understood that requests forwarded by the Organization to the Commission and the correspondence between the Organization and the Commission shall not be recorded in the Organization's files, unless the Commission so recommends, in order to update an item of information already contained in INTERPOL's files;

(2) Communicate to the Commission any information which the Commission requires or requests, and in particular the list of the computerized and other files containing personal information, as well as their structure and the access rights attached to them;

(3) Provide the Commission with the necessary assistance, particularly in order to facilitate its meetings and to guarantee its independence;

(4) Inform the Commission of any new measures taken concerning the processing of personal information;

(5) May also ask to be heard by the Commission to present or defend its position, particularly in the event of a recognized disagreement with a recommendation made by the Commission.

Article 6: Findings of the Commission

(a) The Commission, through its Secretariat if appropriate, shall:

(1) Inform the General Secretariat of its investigations and recommendations so that its decisions and opinions may be notified to the entities and persons concerned, and indeed implemented;

(2) If it considers it appropriate, communicate to the General Secretariat certain items of information taken from requests or certain documents prepared at its request by the Commission's own Secretariat, either before or after a session, in order to understand and review the processing of personal information by the Organization.

(b) If the General Secretariat considers that it is unable to follow one of the Commission's recommendations:

(1) It shall take any appropriate steps to ensure that INTERPOL's processing of the personal information concerned complies with the provisions of INTERPOL's information-processing rules;

(2) It shall submit a report explaining its decision at the Commission's next meeting.

(c) If the Commission disagrees with the General Secretariat about an operation or project to process personal information, it may inform the Executive Committee, so that the Committee may, if necessary, take any appropriate measures.

(d) The Commission shall produce an annual report on its activities for the information of the Executive Committee and for submission to the General Assembly along with any comments made by the Executive Committee. With the authorization of the Executive Committee, the Commission itself may present the report to the General Assembly.

(e) The Commission shall decide how to reply to requesting parties, and shall send those replies.

(f) The Commission shall be empowered to make public statements, and in particular to disclose its annual report.

Article 7: Secretariat of the Commission

(a) The General Secretariat shall act as the Commission's Secretariat. It shall appoint a Secretary, who shall be completely independent of the General Secretariat in the exercise of the assigned duties. If the Secretary is unable to perform his duties, the General Secretariat shall appoint a replacement.

(b) The Secretariat of the Commission shall take all appropriate steps to:

(1) Carry out any administrative operations for the Commission, or arrange for them to be carried out;

(2) Act as interface and coordinator between the Commission and INTERPOL's permanent departments;

(3) Examine requests, carry out studies and other work as requested by the Commission;

(4) Carry out any other task as instructed by the Commission or its Chairperson.

(c) The Commission's Secretariat shall assist the General Secretariat in order to ensure that the Commission is composed in conformity with the present Rules.

Article 8: Budget of the Commission

The General Secretariat shall make available to the Commission the necessary budget to enable it to perform its duties.

CHAPTER 2: ACCESS BY REQUESTING PARTIES TO PERSONAL INFORMATION PROCESSED BY INTERPOL

Article 9: Access conditions and procedures

(a) Any person who so wishes may, freely and free of charge, exercise the right of access to personal information concerning him which has been recorded in INTERPOL's files.

(b) The Commission shall acknowledge receipt of any request and process the request at the earliest opportunity.

(c) Requests for access to personal information shall only be admissible if they emanate from persons who may actually be the subject of such information or from the duly authorized or legal representatives of such persons.

(d) When the requests submitted to the Commission are clearly unreasonable, for instance because of their number or because of their repetitive or systematic nature, the Commission may refrain from carrying out the verifications and shall not be obliged to reply to the person requesting them.

Article 10: Control carried out by the Commission

(a) When the Commission receives a request, it shall check that any personal information about a requesting party, or about the person he represents, that may be stored by the Organization complies with the information processing conditions which must be respected by the Organization.

(b) In accordance with the provisions of Article 6 above, the Commission shall also send any recommendations it may have to the General Secretariat if it feels that action is required of the General Secretariat.

Article 11: Results of the Commission's processing of a request

(a) Subject to the agreement of the source, if any, of the information requested, the Commission may communicate to the requesting party the information which INTERPOL may have about him and which has been supplied by the said source.

(b) Irrespective of its decisions, but **subject to the provisions of Article 9(d)** above, the Commission shall notify requesting parties that it has carried out the checks requested.

Article 12: Final provisions and interim measures

(a) The present Rules, which constitute an appendix to the Organization's General Regulations, shall enter into force on 1 January 2005.

(b) The definitions given in Article 1 of the Rules on the Processing of Information for the purposes of International Police Cooperation shall apply to the present Rules.

****

Appendix 5 Commission for the Control of Interpol's Files: Operating rules

OPERATING RULES
OF THE COMMISSION FOR THE CONTROL OF INTERPOL'S FILES

TABLE OF CONTENTS

PREAMBLE 4

TITLE 1 ORGANIZATION AND WORK OF THE COMMISSION 4

CHAPTER 1 INDEPENDENCE AND IMPARTIALITY OF THE COMMISSION 4

Rule 1: Incompatible activities 4

Rule 2: Withdrawal of members 4

Rule 3: Solemn declaration 5

Rule 3A: Status of the members 5

CHAPTER 2 RESIGNATION AND DISMISSAL OF MEMBERS 5

Rule 4: Resignation 5

Rule 5: Dismissal from office 5

CHAPTER 3 CHAIRPERSON AND VICE-CHAIRPERSON 6

Rule 6: Election 6

Rule 7: Term of office 6

Rule 8: Functions 6

Rule 9: Replacement of the Chairperson 6

CHAPTER 4 RAPPORTEURS 6

Rule 10: Appointment and functions of the Rapporteurs 6

Rule 11: Term of office 6

CHAPTER 5 SECRETARIAT OF THE COMMISSION 7

Rule 12: Functions of the Secretariat 7

CHAPTER 6 GENERAL FRAMEWORK FOR THE WORK OF THE COMMISSION 7

Rule 13: Confidentiality and professional secrecy 7

Rule 14: Working languages 7

Rule 15: Timeframes set by the Commission 7

Rule 16: Organization of sessions 7

Rule 17: Attendance at sessions 7

Rule 18: Relations between Chambers 8

CHAPTER 7 CONCLUSIONS OF THE COMMISSION 8

Rule 19: Conclusions 8

Rule 20: Quorum 8

Rule 21: Votes 8

TITLE 2 SUPERVISORY AND ADVISORY CAPACITY 8

Rule 22: General provisions 8

Rule 23: Supervision and advice 9

Rule 24: Notification of conclusions ... 9

TITLE 3 REQUESTS ... 9

CHAPTER 1 GENERAL PROVISIONS ... 9

Rule 25: Registration ... 9

Rule 26: Joint examination ... 9

Rule 27: Additional information ... 9

Rule 28: Hearings ... 9

Rule 29: Confidentiality ... 9

CHAPTER 2 ADMISSIBILITY OF REQUESTS ... 10

Rule 30: Criteria of admissibility of requests ... 10

Rule 31: Decision on admissibility of requests ... 10

CHAPTER 3 CONCLUSIONS OF THE REQUESTS CHAMBER ... 11

Rule 32: Notification of conclusions ... 11

TITLE 4 FINAL PROVISIONS ... 11

Rule 33: Non-derogation ... 11

Rule 34: Temporary measures ... 11

Rule 35: Entry into force of the Rules and amendments ... 11

PREAMBLE

The Commission for the Control of INTERPOL's Files ("the Commission");

Having regard to the Statute of the Commission (hereinafter referred to as "the Statute"), which entered into force on 11 March 2017, and in particular Articles 3 and 25 (1) of the Statute;

Adopts the following Operating Rules on 1 February 2019 which replace the Commission's Operating Rules that entered into force on 28 March 2017.

TITLE 1
ORGANIZATION AND WORK OF THE COMMISSION

CHAPTER 1
INDEPENDENCE AND IMPARTIALITY OF THE COMMISSION

Rule 1: Incompatible activities

(1) In accordance with Article 11 (1) and (2) of the Statute, the members of the Commission shall serve in their personal capacity and represent neither their administration, nor the NCB of their country, nor their country, nor any other entity.

(2) In accordance with Article 4, Article 11 (3) and (4), and Article 12 of the Statute, the members of the Commission shall not, during their term of office, engage in any action or activity which may appear to be incompatible with their independence or impartiality, in accordance with the present Rules. They shall take all appropriate measures to ensure respect of the independence and impartiality of their function and of the Commission. In particular, they shall take all necessary measures to ensure that they do not have, or are not seen by a reasonable observer as having, a conflict of interest.

(3) The members of the Commission shall not participate in INTERPOL's official meetings and/or INTERPOL's conference as delegates appointed by their countries. However, subject to the prior approval of the Chairperson and/or a decision of the Commission taken by a majority of the members present and voting, they may participate in such meetings as Commission members representing the Commission.

(4) In accordance with Article 11 (5) of the Statute, each member shall communicate to the Chairperson any concern regarding his/her independence and/or impartiality.

(5) In the event of a disagreement between the Chairperson and the member concerned, the Commission shall decide on any question arising.

Rule 2: Withdrawal of members

(1) A member of the Commission may not take part in any way in the consideration of a case, if he/she may be seen to have a real or perceived, direct or indirect conflict of interest with respect to the case concerned, that would challenge his/her independence or impartiality, that is if:

(a) he/she has a personal interest in the case (including a spousal, parental or other close family relationship), personal or professional relationship, or a subordinate relationship with any of the parties;

(b) he/she has previously acted in the case, either as a consultant, advocate or adviser of a party or of a person having an interest in the case, or as a member of another international or national body, or in any other capacity;

(c) he/she engages in any political, administrative, professional or any other activity which is incompatible with his/her independence or impartiality;

(d) he/she is a national of the country source of the data challenged by an applicant;

(e) for any other reason, when his/her independence or impartiality may legitimately be called into doubt.

(2) When a member withdraws for one of the reasons referred to above, he/she:

(a) shall notify the Chairperson, who shall exempt the member from sitting,

(b) shall not be present during discussions and deliberations of the case and shall not have access to documents concerning the case.

(3) In the event of any doubt or disagreement on the part of the member concerned or the Chairperson as to the existence of one of the grounds referred to in Rule 2(1), that issue shall be decided by all members of the Commission. After hearing the views of the member concerned, the Commission shall deliberate and vote, without that member being present. The decision shall be taken by a majority of the members present and voting.

(4) In case of withdrawal of the Chairperson, Rule 9 below shall apply.

(5) The withdrawal of a member shall be recorded in the minutes of the session and in the text of the Decision of the case concerned.

Rule 3: Solemn declaration

(1) Before taking up office, each member shall, at the first meeting of the Commission at which the member is present or, in case of need, before the President of the Commission, make the following solemn declaration: "I solemnly declare that I will exercise my functions as a member of the Commission honorably, independently and impartially and that I will keep secret all materials, information and deliberations".

(2) The declaration shall be signed by the member and kept in the records of the Commission.

(3) This act shall be recorded in the minutes.

Rule 3A: Status of the members

In accordance with Articles 8(1), 8(2) and 9(1) of the Statute, the members of the Commission are elected by the General Assembly from among qualified nationals of member countries of the Organization. Consequently, they do not have the status of officials of the Organization and the term "remuneration", as used in Article 13 of the Statute, is defined as a lump-sum payment which does not qualify as a salary.

CHAPTER 2
RESIGNATION AND DISMISSAL OF MEMBERS

Rule 4: Resignation

(1) The resignation of a member of the Commission is a personal prerogative, which must be freely given without any direct or indirect influence, pressure, intimidation or coercion from anyone.

(2) The resignation of a member of the Commission shall be notified to the Chairperson who shall inform the other members of the Commission. The resignation of a member of the Commission must be reasoned. At the request of the Commission or its Chairperson, the resigning member may be invited to provide additional information as to the reasons for his/her decision.

(3) The Chairperson shall forward the resignation to the General Secretariat. Article 10(3) of the Statute shall apply for the election of a new member.

Rule 5: Dismissal from office

(1) In accordance with Article 14(1)(a) of the Statute, the Commission may propose the dismissal from office of a member who has ceased to fulfil the required conditions for office, due to misconduct or incapacity. Such decision shall be taken in session by at least five votes of the other members, cast in a secret ballot.

(2) Any member of the Commission may set in motion the procedure for dismissal from office.

CHAPTER 3
CHAIRPERSON AND VICE-CHAIRPERSON

Rule 6: Election

(1) The Chairperson shall be elected by all the members of the Commission from among the members of the Requests Chamber in accordance with Article 7(2) of the Statute. Only the members who are present shall take part in the election. To be elected, the Chairperson shall receive at least five votes cast in a secret ballot.

(2) If no candidate achieves the required majority in the first round of voting, a second round shall take place between the two candidates having received the most votes. In the event of a tie between two candidates in the final round, preference shall be given to the member having precedence according to the date of his/her taking up office as member of the Commission. If the length of time they have served as members is the same, they shall take precedence according to age.

(3) The Commission shall also elect a Vice Chairperson, pursuant to the same procedure.

Rule 7: Term of office

(1) The Chairperson and the Vice-Chairperson shall be elected for a term of office of 3 years.

(2) They may be re-elected for a second term, for the remainder of their mandate.

Rule 8: Functions

(1) The functions of the Chairperson are established in Article 7(1) and Article 16(1) of the Statute.

(2) The Chairperson of the Commission shall convene and preside over sessions of the Commission, and direct the discussions over both Chambers.

(3) The Chairperson shall represent the Commission and, in particular, be responsible for its relations with the authorities of INTERPOL.

(4) For the purposes of the first election under the present Rules, the session shall be convened and chaired by the member of the Commission having precedence according to the date of his/her taking up office as member of the Commission. If the length of time they have served as members is the same for all, the member having precedence according to age shall act as Chairperson.

(5) The Vice-Chairperson shall assume the functions of the Chairperson in the circumstances outlined in Rule 9 below.

Rule 9: Replacement of the Chairperson

The Vice-Chairperson shall assume the functions of the Chairperson in case of resignation, dismissal, withdrawal or absence of the Chairperson, or if he/she is unable to carry out his/her duties, as long as the office is vacant.

CHAPTER 4
RAPPORTEURS

Rule 10: Appointment and functions of the Rapporteurs

(1) In application of Article 17 of the Statute, which provides for the possibility for the Commission to delegate some powers to one or several members, the members of each Chamber may appoint from among themselves one or more Rapporteurs with the function of facilitating the Commission's work and taking decisions in between sessions of the Commission.

(2) The Rapporteurs may be assisted by any other member of the Commission. They shall report back to the Commission.

(3) The Rapporteurs shall participate in discussions and deliberations of the cases for which they serve as Rapporteurs.

Rule 11: Term of office

(1) The Rapporteurs shall be appointed for three years.

(2) They may be reappointed for the remainder of their mandate.

CHAPTER 5
SECRETARIAT OF THE COMMISSION

Rule 12: Functions of the Secretariat

(1) In accordance with Article 15 of the Statute, the Secretariat of the Commission shall take all necessary and appropriate measures, within the limits of its remit, to ensure the smooth operation of the Commission's work. The Secretariat shall assist the members of the Commission in performing their duties.

(2) The Commission shall supervise the work of the Secretariat, relating in particular to its relation with the Chairperson, the Vice Chairperson or the Rapporteurs, the selection of its staff, and/or the preparation of the decisions of the Commission.

CHAPTER 6
GENERAL FRAMEWORK FOR THE WORK OF THE COMMISSION

Rule 13: Confidentiality and professional secrecy

(1) The work and the files of the Commission are confidential.

(2) The Commission's files and reports are reserved for internal use only, unless it expressly decides otherwise in conformity with Article 20 of the Statute.

(3) In the exercise of their duties, members of the Commission and its Secretariat shall consider as confidential all documents and information that come to their knowledge as a consequence of, or in connection with, their membership of the Commission.

(4) Members of the Commission and its Secretariat shall take all appropriate measures to ensure respect of the confidentiality requirements of the Commission's work, as described in Rule 29: below.

Rule 14: Working languages

(1) The working languages of the Commission shall be those of the Organization, namely Arabic, English, French and Spanish.

(2) In accordance with Article 18(2) of the Statute, the working language selected by the Commission for the processing of its internal files is English.

(3) Interpretation in Arabic, English, French and Spanish may be provided during the sessions of the Commission.

Rule 15: Timeframes set by the Commission

(1) In addition to the timeframes established in Article 40 of the Statute, the Commission may set deadlines within which it wants to receive any information requested.

(2) Such deadlines may be extended by the Commission upon receipt of a reasoned demand.

Rule 16: Organization of sessions

(1) In accordance with Article 16(1) of the Statute, the Commission shall meet at least three times a year. The sessions of the Commission shall be held at the Organization's headquarters, unless otherwise decided by the Commission. Where necessary, the Commission may decide to allow remote participation by telephone and video.

(2) The dates of the Commission's sessions shall be set by its Chairperson after consultation with the members of the Commission.

Rule 17: Attendance at sessions

(1) In accordance with Article 16 of the Statute, the Commission's sessions shall be held *in camera*. Its deliberations shall remain secret. In principle, only members and the Commission's Secretariat shall attend the Commission's sessions.

(2) In case of unavailability, the member concerned shall inform the Chairperson as soon as possible.

(3) The Commission may nonetheless invite other persons whose presence it may consider useful.

(4) If the person is not already bound by rules of confidentiality of the Organization, Rule 3 above shall apply *mutatis mutandis*.

Rule 18: Relations between Chambers

The meetings of the Supervisory and Advisory Chamber and of the Requests Chamber shall be scheduled in a manner that allows members of each Chamber of the Commission to consult and/or participate as non-voting members in the work and deliberations of the other Chamber, as provided in Article 6(2) of the Statute.

CHAPTER 7
CONCLUSIONS OF THE COMMISSION

Rule 19: Conclusions

(1) For the purposes of the present Rules, conclusions of the Commission include any decisions, opinions and recommendations made by the Commission.

(2) In accordance with Articles 26(1) and 38(1) of the Statute, decisions of the Chambers of the Commission which require any action by the General Secretariat to ensure compliance with INTERPOL's rules are binding decisions.

(3) Conclusions of the Commission are in principle reached during its sessions, except in the case of delegation of powers in accordance with Article 17 of the Statute. Conclusions may be reached by the Commission also in between the sessions, if necessary and deemed possible.

(4) In accordance with Article 27(1) of the Statute, when the Commission considers that it has received sufficient information to reach a conclusion on a question or case under examination, it shall draw reasoned conclusions.

Rule 20: Quorum

(1) The quorum of the Commission as a whole shall be four members present and voting.

(2) The quorum of the Supervisory and Advisory Chamber shall be two members of that Chamber present and voting.

(3) The quorum of the Requests Chamber shall be three members of that Chamber present and voting.

(4) If there is no quorum, the Chairperson shall adjourn the session of the Chamber concerned.

Rule 21: Votes

(1) Each member shall vote in the Chamber he/she has been elected to. The Chairperson shall vote in both Chambers.

(2) Each member of the Commission shall have one vote. Votes shall be taken by a show of hands, unless decided otherwise.

(3) The conclusions of the Commission as a whole shall be reached by a majority of the members of the Commission, subject to Rule 34 below. The conclusions of each Chamber shall be reached by a majority of the members present and voting of the Chamber concerned. Members shall not abstain from deciding on the admissibility of a request and from adopting conclusions.

(4) In the event of an equality of votes, a fresh vote shall be taken. If there is still equality, the Chairperson shall have a casting vote.

TITLE 2
SUPERVISORY AND ADVISORY CAPACITY

Rule 22: General provisions

(1) For the performance of its functions, as stated in Article 26 of the Statute, the Supervisory and Advisory Chamber may seek information or clarification from the General Secretariat, in particular its Data Protection Officer, and the sources of data processed through INTERPOL's channels, or may invite them to provide any information.

(2) In this respect the Supervisory and Advisory Chamber may set timeframes within which the General Secretariat or the source of data consulted shall provide the information requested or any comments concerning its decisions, opinions or recommendations.

Rule 23: Supervision and advice

(1) The Supervisory and Advisory Chamber may examine and assess in light of INTERPOL's rules, any matter involving the processing of personal data in the INTERPOL Information System, to identify any potential sources of risks and to provide guidance on the processing of data, including to ensure effective implementation of applicable rules.

(2) For that purpose, the Supervisory and Advisory Chamber may undertake various checks. These checks may be decided in light of issues identified or questions raised by the Requests Chamber.

(3) The Supervisory and Advisory Chamber may determine the scope and subject of these checks and the way in which they shall be carried out.

(4) The Supervisory and Advisory Chamber shall inform the General Secretariat of the checks undertaken in the context of its supervisory capacity.

Rule 24: Notification of conclusions

(1) The Supervisory and Advisory Chamber shall provide its findings to the General Secretariat. It may decide to address provisional findings to the General Secretariat, for comments or information.

(2) The Supervisory and Advisory Chamber may also provide its findings to the Requests Chamber. It shall do so when the Requests Chamber asked it to address an issue identified in the context of the examination of requests.

TITLE 3
REQUESTS

CHAPTER 1
GENERAL PROVISIONS

Rule 25: Registration

The Requests Chamber shall register all the requests it receives.

Rule 26: Joint examination

At the request of the applicants or at its own initiative, the Requests Chamber may decide to process together requests that relate to the same case or which raise the same or similar issues.

Rule 27: Additional information

(1) In addition to consultations foreseen in Articles 21 and 34 of the Statute, the Commission may invite the applicant to provide further information or clarifications relating to his/her request, as well as to supply any additional items which may be needed in support of the request, within a set deadline.

(2) The Commission may also invite the General Secretariat to provide its views on a case or on the implementation of INTERPOL's rules, within a set deadline.

Rule 28: Hearings

In accordance with Article 36 of the Statute, the Commission shall meet applicants, or their duly authorized representatives or hold hearings, if it considers this necessary for the examination of a request.

Rule 29: Confidentiality

(1) In accordance with Article 20(2) of the Statute and with Rule 13: above, the information, work and files of the Commission are confidential. In the exercise of their duties, the members of the Commission and its Secretariat shall consider as confidential all information, work and files that come to their knowledge as a consequence of, or in connection with their membership of the Commission. They shall take all appropriate measures to respect the confidentiality of a request, and of the items making up the request submitted to the Commission.

(2) When necessary, special handling procedures may be adopted by the Requests Chamber to ensure specific confidentiality requirements.

CHAPTER 2
ADMISSIBILITY OF REQUESTS

Rule 30: Criteria of admissibility of requests

(1) A request shall be considered admissible if the following conditions are met:

(a) the request includes a letter signed by the applicant, explaining the purpose of the request;

(b) it is written in one of the Organization's working languages (Arabic, English, French and Spanish);

(c) the request comes from the person whom it concerns, or from that person's duly authorized representative(s);

(d) where the applicant is represented by a duly authorized representative, the request shall be accompanied by a power of attorney signed by the applicant authorizing his/her representative to access any information about him/her recorded in INTERPOL's files;

(e) where the applicant is represented by a legal representative, the request shall be accompanied by the corresponding written declaration or certificate;

(f) where the applicant is an entity, the request shall be accompanied by documents showing that the individual who lodged the application on behalf of the entity has standing or authority to represent the entity, for example an extract from the Chamber of Commerce register or minutes of the governing body;

(g) the request shall be accompanied by a copy of a readable and non-redacted identity document belonging to the applicant in order to prove his/her identity. Where the applicant is an entity, the full name, date of incorporation or registration, the official registration number (if any), and the official address shall be provided;

(h) where the applicant submits a request for correction and/or deletion of information processed in the INTERPOL Information System, the request shall set out the reasons, and be accompanied by a summary of arguments in support of the request, making specific reference to any relevant attached document in the form provided for by the Secretariat. The Requests Chamber shall only take into consideration the attached documents which are or have been translated into one of INTERPOL's working languages, as described in paragraph 1 (b) of the present Rule.

(2) If, upon receipt of such request, further information is needed from the applicant to determine the admissibility of the request, the Requests Chamber shall invite the applicant to submit any missing or additional information within a given time limit. At the same time, the Commission shall inform the applicant that as a consequence of the failure to provide the information requested within the deadline that it specified, no admissibility decision nor further action will be taken in respect to the request concerned.

(3) The examination of such request may continue if the requested information is submitted at a later date.

(4) The Requests Chamber shall not deal with requests when it considers them as:

(a) clearly unreasonable, for instance, because of their repetitive or systematic nature;

(b) not within the Requests Chamber's competence, as set out in the Statute.

In such cases, the Commission may refrain from carrying out the action or actions requested and shall not be obliged to reply to the person or persons introducing the request.

Rule 31: Decision on admissibility of requests

(1) Once the criteria of admissibility established in Rule 30 above have been

fulfilled, the request shall be declared admissible.

(2) If the criteria of admissibility established in Rule 30 above have not been fulfilled, the Requests Chamber shall declare the request inadmissible.

(3) In both situations, the Requests Chamber shall inform the applicant of its decision at the earliest opportunity in accordance with Article 32(1) of the Statute.

(4) A decision not to deal with a request in whole or in part shall be explained to the applicant.

CHAPTER 3
CONCLUSIONS OF THE REQUESTS CHAMBER

Rule 32: Notification of conclusions

(1) In compliance with Articles 40 and 41 of the Statute and with Rule 19:(4) above, when its conclusions have become final, the Requests Chamber shall provide the reasoned conclusions to the General Secretariat and to the applicant, within the time frames set by the Statute and by the Commission.

(2) The Requests Chamber may also decide to address interim conclusions or interim replies to the General Secretariat and to the applicant.

TITLE 4
FINAL PROVISIONS

Rule 33: Non-derogation

The present Rules shall not be construed as derogating from any of the provisions of the Statute of the Commission.

Rule 34: Temporary measures

(1) In case of unforeseeable circumstances seriously disrupting the proper functioning of the Commission (or its Secretariat) or the discharge of its mandate, the Commission may adopt such interim emergency measures it considers adequate to allow for the conduct of its activities.

(2) These measures, adopted upon proposal of the Chairperson and by a simple majority of members of the Commission, may derogate from current provisions of the Operating Rules but must in any case comply with the Statute of the Commission. They must be strictly necessary to allow for the Commission's proper functioning, and must be proportionate to the impact of events or circumstances on the Commission's activities.

(3) Due to their temporary nature, they can only be applied for a maximum non-renewable period of six months, before they are either rescinded or integrated into permanent provisions of the Operating Rules, further to the procedure described in Rule 35.

Rule 35: Entry into force of the Rules and amendments

(1) The present Rules shall enter into force upon adoption by at least five members of the Commission.

(2) Any proposal for amendment to the present Rules shall be communicated to the Secretariat to the Commission at least one month before the session at which it is to be discussed. On receipt of such a proposal, the Secretariat shall inform all members of the Commission at the earliest possible moment.

(3) Any Rule may be amended by a majority of five members of the Commission. The amendments shall enter into force upon adoption.

Appendix 6 Commission for the Control of Interpol's Files: Application Form for Access and/or Correction/Deletion

Please complete all relevant fields and submit the required documents so that your request can be considered admissible and properly examined.

A. NATURE OF YOUR REQUEST

☐ Request for access ☐ Correction/deletion

B. APPLICANT

Please ensure that a clear, readable copy of the applicant's identity document is sent in attachment to this form. If the applicant is a minor, please include a document which attests to your relationship to him/her.

1. IF THE APPLICANT IS A PERSON:

- FAMILY NAME ______________________________
- FORENAME(S) ______________________________
- DATE OF BIRTH ______________________________
- PLACE AND COUNTRY OF BIRTH ______________________________
- NATIONALITY ______________________________
- ADDRESS *(Please note it is required to indicate a valid postal address, so the Commission can send you notifications related to your application. Should you have a representative, you may indicate only their address, in Part C of this form.)*

- E-MAIL *(optional)* ______________________________
- Do you authorize the Commission to send all future correspondence relating to your request via e-mail? No ☐ Yes ☐

- Is the applicant currently detained?
  No ☐ Yes ☐ (if yes, please specify in which country: ______________________________)
- Does the applicant currently hold a protective status in a third country?
  No ☐ Yes ☐ (if yes, please provide a document certifying the status and mention it in the list of appendices)

2. IF THE APPLICANT IS AN ENTITY:

- FULL NAME OF THE ENTITY ______________________________
- DATE OF INCORPORATION OR REGISTRATION ______________________________
- PLACE OF INCORPORATION OR REGISTRATION ______________________________
- OFFICIAL REGISTRATION NUMBER (if any) ______________________________
- OFFICIAL ADDRESS:

Page 1/4

- PERSON WITH STANDING/AUTHORITY:
  FAMILY NAME ____________________
  FORENAME(S) ____________________
  DATE AND PLACE OF BIRTH ____________________
  CAPACITY ____________________
- E-MAIL *(optional)* ____________________
- Do you authorize the Commission to send all future correspondence relating to your request via e-mail? No ☐ Yes ☐

C. REPRESENTATIVE OF THE APPLICANT (IF APPLICABLE)

An applicant may have several representatives, but only one may act as the point of contact with the Commission. Please attach a separate document with the names of all representatives (if more than one) and provide the point of contact's information below.

- FAMILY NAME ____________________
- FORENAME(S) ____________________
- CAPACITY *(lawyer, family member, etc.)* ____________________
- NAME OF THE REPRESENTATIVE BODY *(law firm, NGO, etc., if applicable)* ____________________
  ____
- ADDRESS:
- E-MAIL ADDRESS *(optional)* ____________________
- Do you authorize the Commission to send all future correspondence relating to your request via e-mail? No ☐ Yes ☐

D. POWER OF ATTORNEY

If the applicant is represented, he/she must give express authorization to the representative to act on his/her behalf.

I, ____________________ (family name and forename of the applicant), hereby authorize the person indicated above (Part C) to represent me before the Commission for the Control of INTERPOL's Files.

Date: ____________________ Signature: ____________________

*If the power of attorney is provided on a separate sheet of paper, **please check this box** ☐ and indicate this document in the list of appendices (Part F). Please note that the Power of Attorney must specifically authorize the representative to represent the applicant before the Commission for the Control of INTERPOL's Files and must be signed by the applicant. No additional formality, such as the authentication by a notary, is needed.*

E. THE FACTS

This field is not compulsory for requests for access. For correction/deletion requests, please provide a precise but brief statement of facts concerning your complaint. This section should be completed in one of the Commission's working languages: Arabic, English, French, Spanish.

Should you wish to give further explanations, please do so in a separate document not exceeding 10 pages. You may include any information concerning the applicant that might be relevant for the examination of the request, such as previous and current functions, pending legal actions, etc.

F. RULES ALLEGEDLY VIOLATED

This field is not compulsory for requests for access. Please indicate the main legal instruments that you consider have been violated. Please explain how each article/rule to which you refer was allegedly violated by the member country. We remind you that the role of the Commission is to control whether the processing of data in INTERPOL's files meets INTERPOL's applicable legal requirements and that it is not empowered to conduct an investigation, to weigh evidence, or to make a determination on the merits of a case. That is the role of the competent national/regional authorities.

G. JUDICIAL DECISIONS ISSUED IN THE CASE

Please list and, if possible, attach a simple copy of any relevant judicial decisions that may have been issued concerning the applicant's case specifically. Please indicate clearly and concisely how each decision is relevant to your request, and please include the title, date, case reference number, issuing authority, as well as the website link to the decision and/or related appendix, if they are available.

H. LIST OF ATTACHED APPENDICES

Please list below the documents enclosed for the admissibility of your request.
Then list, in chronological order, any documents provided to support your request. For each, indicate references to the pages you would like to bring to the particular attention of the Commission.

Remark: *The Commission will only take into consideration legible documents, provided in one of the Commission's working languages: Arabic, English, French or Spanish (Rule 14 of the Operating Rules of the Commission for the Control of INTERPOL's Files).*

1. Identity document(s): ☐ *passport* ☐ *national identity card* ☐ *other (specify):* ______________
2. ______________________________ Page(s) ______________
3. ______________________________ Page(s) ______________
4. ______________________________ Page(s) ______________
5. ______________________________ Page(s) ______________
6. ______________________________ Page(s) ______________
7. ______________________________ Page(s) ______________
8. ______________________________ Page(s) ______________
9. ______________________________ Page(s) ______________
10. ______________________________ Page(s) ______________
11. ______________________________ Page(s) ______________
12. ______________________________ Page(s) ______________
13. ______________________________ Page(s) ______________
14. ______________________________ Page(s) ______________
15. ______________________________ Page(s) ______________

DATE ______________________________

FAMILY NAME AND FORENAME ______________________________

SIGNATURE ______________________________

The duly completed request and the appendices listed above should be sent to the Commission

Either by postal mail at the following address:

Commission for the Control of INTERPOL's Files
200 quai Charles de Gaulle
69006 Lyon
France

Or by e-mail: CCF@interpol.int

Page 4/4

Index

[All references are to paragraph number]

Adeishvili case
asylum status, and, 4.27–4.29
Admissibility
challenging Red Notices, 6.14–6.16
Article 2 of the Constitution
assessment by Requests Chamber, 6.51–6.53
generally, 6.32–6.34
human rights violations, 6.35–6.50
Article 3 of the Constitution
background development, 6.56–6.61
charges, 6.65–6.67
context of the case, 6.79–6.80
generally, 6.54–6.55
identity of source of data, 6.71–6.72
nature of offence, 6.65–6.67
neutrality of organisation, 6.77–6.78
obligations under international law, 6.74–6.76
position expressed by NCB or international entity, 6.73
predominance test, 6.62–6.80
status of persons concerned, 6.68–6.70
underlying facts, 6.65–6.67
Ascertaining existence of Red Notices
Commission for Control of Files, from, 5.7–5.19
French NCB, from, 5.31–5.40
German NCB, from, 5.41–5.50
Hong Kong NCB, from, 5.51–5.60
informal police co-operation, from, 5.97
Interpol, from, 5.3–5.19
introduction, 5.1–5.2
Italian NCB, from, 5.61–5.63
Netherlands NCB, from, 5.64–5.73
non-requesting NCB, from, 5.85–5.87
other issues
informal police co-operation, 5.97
introduction, 5.88
preventative requests, 5.89–5.96
police co-operation, from, 5.97
practical guidance, 7.4–7.10
Preventative Requests to CCF
generally, 5.89–5.96
practical guidance, 7.11–7.14
private Red Notices, 5.6–5.5
Ascertaining existence of Red Notices – *contd*
public Red Notices, 5.4–5.5
requesting NCB, from
France, 5.31–5.40
Germany, 5.41–5.50
Hong Kong, 5.51–5.60
introduction, 5.30
Italy, 5.61–5.63
Netherlands, 5.64–5.73
Spain, 5.74
UK, 5.24–5.29
US, 5.75–5.84
Spanish NCB, from, 5.74
UK NCB, from, 5.24–5.29
US NCB, from, 5.75–5.84
Assange case
asylum status, 4.24–4.25
Asylum status of subject
Adeishvili case, 4.27–4.29
Assange case, 4.24–4.25
conclusion, 4.55–4.58
introduction, 4.22–4.23
new policy, 4.26–4.34
refoulement risk, 4.22
Refugee Policy (2014), 4.26–4.34

Cancellation requests
challenging Red Notices, 6.29–6.31
Challenges
admissibility, 6.14–6.16
approach of Interpol
deletion of data, to, 6.26–6.28
retention of data, to, 6.19–6.25
Article 2 of the Constitution, under
assessment by Requests Chamber, 6.51–6.53
generally, 6.32–6.34
human rights violations, 6.35–6.50
Article 3 of the Constitution, under
background development, 6.56–6.61
charges, 6.65–6.67
context of the case, 6.79–6.80
generally, 6.54–6.55
identity of source of data, 6.71–6.72
nature of offence, 6.65–6.67

Challenges – *contd*
Article 3 of the Constitution, under – *contd*
neutrality of organisation, 6.77–6.78
obligations under international law, 6.74–6.76
position expressed by NCB or international entity, 6.73
predominance test, 6.62–6.80
status of persons concerned, 6.68–6.70
underlying facts, 6.65–6.67
breaches of RPD, based on, 6.81–6.95
cancellation request to Secretariat, by, 6.29–6.31
conclusion, 6.124–6.125
deletion of data
approach of Interpol, 6.19–6.25
discretion of Secretariat, 6.26–6.28
domestic jurisdictions, in
France, 6.97–6.99
Germany, 6.100–6.106
Hong Kong, 6.107
Italy, 6.108–6.109
Netherlands, 6.110–6.113
Spain, 6.114–6.118
USA, 6.119–6.123
France, 6.97–6.99
Germany, 6.100–6.106
Hong Kong, 6.107
Interpol Refugee Resolution 2017, under, 6.96
introduction, 6.1–6.3
Netherlands, 6.110–6.113
practical guidance, 7.15–7.20
procedure
admissibility, 6.14–6.16
deletion of data, 6.26–6.28
pre-emptive requests, 6.11–6.13
requests, 6.4–6.10
retention of data, 6.19–6.25
revisiting a decision, 6.17–6.18
requests
general, 6.4–6.10
pre-emptive, 6.11–6.13
retention of data, 6.19–6.25
revisiting a decision, 6.17–6.18
RPD, via
deletion of data, 6.26–6.28
general approach, 6.29–6.31
retention of data, 6.19–6.25
Secretariat's discretion, 6.26–6.28
Spain, 6.114–6.118
USA, 6.119–6.123
Commission for the Control of Files (CCF)7
ascertaining existence of Red Notices, 5.7–5.19
generally, 2.19–2.20
Preventative Requests, 5.89–5.96
Committee on Legal Affairs and Human Rights reports
2017, 4.36–4.42
2019, 4.43–4.47
Criticisms
asylum status of subject
Adeishvili case, 4.27–4.29
Assange case, 4.24–4.25
introduction, 4.22–4.23
new policy, 4.26–4.34
refoulement risk, 4.22
Refugee Policy (2014), 4.26–4.34
Committee on Legal Affairs and Human Rights reports
2017, 4.36–4.42
2019, 4.43–4.47
conclusion, 4.55–4.58
current analysis of policy approach
Committee on Legal Affairs and Human Rights, 4.36–4.47
introduction, 4.35
LIBE Committee, 4.48–4.52
summary, 4.53–4.54
expressions of concern
OSCE, 4.3
UNHCR, 4.4
Fair Trials International report
generally, 4.9–4.10
inadequate opportunity to challenge, 4.11–4.12
insufficient procedural protections, 4.9–4.10
introduction, 4.6
generally, 4.8
inadequate opportunity to challenge, 4.11–4.12
insufficient procedural protections against abuse, 4.9–4.10
introduction, 4.1–4.7
LIBE Committee study (2022), 4.48–4.52
Notices and Diffusions Task Force, 4.21
OSCE expression of concern, 4.3
reform efforts, 4.13–4.21
UNHCR expression of concern, 4.4
Working Group on Processing of Information
generally, 4.15–4.20
introduction, 4.13

Data criteria
generally, 3.15
introduction, 3.6
Deletion of data
approach of Interpol, 6.19–6.25
discretion of Secretariat, 6.26–6.28
Diffusions
See **Wanted Person Diffusions**
Discretion of Secretariat
generally, 3.13–3.14
introduction, 3.6

Fair Trials International report (2013)
generally, 4.9–4.10
inadequate opportunity to challenge, 4.11–4.12
insufficient procedural protections, 4.9–4.10
introduction, 4.6
France
challenging Red Notices, 6.97–6.99
existence of Red Notices, 5.31–5.40

Germany
challenging Red Notices, 6.100–6.106
existence of Red Notices, 5.41–5.50

Hong Kong
challenging Red Notices, 6.107
existence of Red Notices, 5.51–5.60

Identifiers
generally, 3.15
introduction, 3.6
Identifying existence of Red Notices
Commission for Control of Files, from, 5.7–5.19
French NCB, from, 5.31–5.40
German NCB, from, 5.41–5.50
Hong Kong NCB, from, 5.51–5.60
informal police co-operation, from, 5.97
Interpol, from, 5.3–5.19
introduction, 5.1–5.2
Italian NCB, from, 5.61–5.63
Netherlands NCB, from, 5.64–5.73
non-requesting NCB, from, 5.85–5.87
other issues
informal police co-operation, 5.97
introduction, 5.88
preventative requests, 5.89–5.96
police co-operation, from, 5.97
practical guidance, 7.4–7.10
Preventative Requests to CCF
generally, 5.89–5.96
practical guidance, 7.11–7.14

Identifying existence of Red Notices – *contd*
private Red Notices, 5.6–5.5
public Red Notices, 5.4–5.5
requesting NCB, from
France, 5.31–5.40
Germany, 5.41–5.50
Hong Kong, 5.51–5.60
introduction, 5.30
Italy, 5.61–5.63
Netherlands, 5.64–5.73
Spain, 5.74
UK, 5.24–5.29
US, 5.75–5.84
Spanish NCB, from, 5.74
UK NCB, from, 5.24–5.29
US NCB, from, 5.75–5.84
Informal police co-operation
ascertaining existence of Red Notices, 5.97
International Criminal Police Commission (ICPC)
establishment, 1.10
International Criminal Police Congress
First IPC (Monaco, 1914), 1.4–1.7
General Assembly of 1934, 1.16–1.17
General Assembly of 1938, 1.18
post-WWII renewal, 1.21–1.30
Second IPC (Vienna, 1923), 1.8–1.15
World War II, during, 1.16–1.20
International Criminal Records Office (ICRO)
establishment, 1.12
International Wanted Notices
establishment, 1.14
Interpol
advisers on scientific matters, 2.18
aims, 2.4
annual financial statements, 2.24
asylum status of subject
Adeishvili case, 4.27–4.29
Assange case, 4.24–4.25
introduction, 4.22–4.23
new policy, 4.26–4.34
refoulement risk, 4.22
Refugee Policy (2014), 4.26–4.34
Commission for the Control of Files, 2.19–2.20
constitution, 2.4–2.7
criticisms
asylum status, and, 4.22–4.34
conclusions, 4.55–4.58
future issues, 4.53–4.54
generally, 4.8
inadequate opportunity to challenge, 4.11–4.12

Interpol – *contd*
criticisms – *contd*
insufficient procedural protections against abuse, 4.9–4.10
introduction, 4.1–4.7
Notices and Diffusions Task Force, 4.21
post-2017, 4.35–4.52
reform efforts, 4.13–4.21
Working Group on Processing of Information, 4.15–4.20
culture, 2.21–2.22
Executive Committee, 2.11–2.12
field operations, 2.29
functions, 2.4–2.6
investigation of crime, 2.28–2.29
funding
budget, 2.25
contributions, 2.25–2.26
external donors, 2.26
financial statements, 2.24
introduction, 2.23
regular budget, 2.25
special account, 2.26
trust fund, 2.26
future of, 4.53–4.54
General Assembly, 2.9–2.10
General Secretariat, 2.13–2.15
headquarters, 2.1
historical development, 1.4–1.31
independent advisers, 2.18
international partners, 2.27
membership, 2.1–2.2
National Central Bureaus, 2.16–2.17
Notices and Diffusions Task Force
generally, 3.25–3.33
reforms, 4.21
origins, 1.4–1.31
priorities, 2.21–2.22
prohibited activities, 2.5
Red Notices
See also **Red Notices**
criticisms, 4.1–4.58
generally, 3.4–3.25
introduction, 3.1–3.3
reform efforts
generally, 4.13–4.14
Notices and Diffusions Task Force, 4.21
Working Group on Processing of Information, 4.15–4.20
Refugee Policy (2014), 4.26–4.34
role, 3.1–3.2
Secretariat, 2.13–2.15
strategic priorities, 2.22
structure 2.8–2.22
Task Force, 4.21

Interpol – *contd*
Working Group on Processing of Information, 4.15–4.20
Interpol Refugee Resolution 2017
challenging Red Notices, 6.96
Italy
existence of Red Notices, 5.61–5.63

Judicial data
generally, 3.15
introduction, 3.6

Legal review
issue of Red Notice, 3.18–3.19
LIBE Committee study (2022)
asylum status of subject, 4.48–4.52

Media campaigns
practical guidance, 7.27

National central bureaus (NCB)
action pursuant to Red Notice, 3.20–3.21
ascertaining existence of Red Notice from non-requesting NCB, 5.85–5.87
ascertaining existence of Red Notice from requesting NCB
France, 5.31–5.40
Germany, 5.41–5.50
Hong Kong, 5.51–5.60
introduction, 5.30
Italy, 5.61–5.63
Netherlands, 5.64–5.73
Spain, 5.74
UK, 5.24–5.29
US, 5.75–5.84
establishment, 1.13
generally, 2.16–2.17
Netherlands
challenging Red Notices, 6.110–6.113
existence of Red Notices, 5.64–5.73
Notices and Diffusions Task Force (NDTF)
generally, 3.25–3.33
reforms, 4.21

'Of importance to international co-operation'
generally, 3.13
introduction, 3.6
'Of interest for purposes of international co-operation'
generally, 3.12
introduction, 3.6

Penalty threshold
generally, 3.11
introduction, 3.6

PR campaigns
practical guidance, 7.27
Preventative Requests
generally, 5.89–5.96
practical guidance, 7.11–7.14

Red Notices
action by NCB pursuant to, 3.20–3.21
ascertaining existence
Commission for Control of Files, from, 5.7–5.19
French NCB, from, 5.31–5.40
German NCB, from, 5.41–5.50
Hong Kong NCB, from, 5.51–5.60
informal police co-operation, from, 5.97
Interpol, from, 5.3–5.19
introduction, 5.1–5.2
Italian NCB, from, 5.61–5.63
Netherlands NCB, from, 5.64–5.73
non-requesting NCB, from, 5.85–5.87
other issues, 5.88–5.96
police co-operation, from, 5.97
practical guidance, 7.4–7.10
Preventative Requests to CCF, 5.89–5.96
private Red Notices, 5.6–5.5
public Red Notices, 5.4–5.5
requesting NCB, from, 5.30–5.84
Spanish NCB, from, 5.74
UK NCB, from, 5.24–5.29
US NCB, from, 5.75–5.84
asylum status of subject
Adeishvili case, 4.27–4.29
Assange case, 4.24–4.25
conclusion, 4.55–4.58
current analysis of policy approach, 4.35–4.54
introduction, 4.22–4.23
new policy, 4.26–4.34
refoulement risk, 4.22
Refugee Policy (2014), 4.26–4.34
challenging
admissibility, 6.14–6.16
Article 2 of the Constitution, under, 6.32–6.53
Article 3 of the Constitution, under, 6.54–6.80
breaches of RPD, based on, 6.81–6.95
cancellation request to Secretariat, by, 6.29–6.31
conclusion, 6.124–6.125
deletion of data, 6.26–6.28
domestic jurisdictions, in, 6.97–6.123
Interpol Refugee Resolution 2017, under, 6.96
introduction, 6.1–6.3
practical guidance, 7.15–7.20

Red Notices – *contd*
challenging – *contd*
procedure, 6.4–6.28
requests, 6.4–6.13
retention of data, 6.19–6.25
revisiting a decision, 6.17–6.18
RPD, via, 6.19–6.25
Committee on Legal Affairs and Human Rights reports
2017, 4.36–4.42
2019, 4.43–4.47
contents of representation, 7.21–7.26
criteria
discretion, 3.13–3.14
introduction, 3.5
minimum, 3.6–3.7
request, 3.6–3.7
specific, 3.8–3.12
criticisms
asylum status, and, 4.22–4.34
conclusions, 4.55–4.58
future issues, 4.53–4.54
generally, 4.8
inadequate opportunity to challenge, 4.11–4.12
insufficient procedural protections against abuse, 4.9–4.10
introduction, 4.1–4.7
Notices and Diffusions Task Force, 4.21
post-2017, 4.35–4.52
reform efforts, 4.13–4.21
Working Group on Processing of Information, 4.15–4.20
data criteria, 3.6
discretion of Secretariat, 3.13–3.14
first steps, 7.2–7.3
general operation, 3.4–3.5
identifiers, 3.6
introduction, 3.1–3.3
judicial data, 3.6
legal review by Secretariat, 3.18–3.19
LIBE Committee study (2022), 4.48–4.52
minimum criteria, 3.6–3.7
minimum data
generally, 3.15
introduction, 3.6
nature, 3.4
non-exhaustive list of offences, 3.10
Notices and Diffusions Task Force, 4.21
of importance to international co-operation
generally, 3.13
introduction, 3.6
of interest for purposes of international co-operation
generally, 3.12

Red Notices – *contd*
of interest for purposes of international co-operation – *contd*
introduction, 3.6
origins, 1.14
penalty threshold
generally, 3.11
introduction, 3.6
PR and media, 7.27
practical guidance
ascertaining existence, 7.4–7.10
challenges, 7.15–7.20
conclusion, 7.28–7.29
contents of representation, 7.21–7.26
first steps, 7.2–7.3
introduction, 7.1
PR and media, 7.27
Preventative Requests, 7.11–7.14
publication, 3.6
purpose, 3.4
reforms
introduction, 4.13–4.14
Notices and Diffusions Task Force, 4.21
Working Group on Processing of Information, 4.15–4.20
request
further obligations, 3.16–3.17
generally, 3.6–3.7
minimum data, 3.15
review by Secretariat, 3.18–3.19
Rules on the Processing of Data (RPD)
deletion of data, 6.26–6.28
general approach, 6.29–6.31
introduction, 3.6
retention of data, 6.19–6.25
steps to be taken by NCB pursuant to, 3.20–3.21
Working Group on Processing of Information, 4.15–4.20
Refoulement
asylum status of subject, 4.22
Refugee Policy (2014)
asylum status of subject, 4.26–4.34
Representations
contents, 7.21–7.26
Request for Red Notice
further obligations, 3.16–3.17
generally, 3.6–3.7
minimum data, 3.15
Retention of data
challenging Red Notices, 6.19–6.25
Review
issue of Red Notice, 3.18–3.19
Revisiting a decision
challenging Red Notices, 6.17–6.18
Rules on the Processing of Data (RPD)
challenging Red Notices
deletion of data, 6.26–6.28
general approach, 6.29–6.31
retention of data, 6.19–6.25
generally, 3.6
Russia
Wanted Persons Diffusions, 3.34–3.36

Serious ordinary law crime
generally, 3.8–3.10
introduction, 3.6
Several offences
generally, 3.14
introduction, 3.6
Spain
challenging Red Notices, 6.114–6.118
existence of Red Notices, 5.74

USA
challenging Red Notices, 6.119–6.123
existence of Red Notices, 5.75–5.84

Wanted Person Diffusions
ascertaining existence, 5.1
challenging, 6.1
colour-coded system, 3.23
criticisms
asylum status, and, 4.22–4.34
conclusions, 4.55–4.58
future issues, 4.53–4.54
generally, 4.8
inadequate opportunity to challenge, 4.11–4.12
insufficient procedural protections against abuse, 4.9–4.10
introduction, 4.1–4.7
Notices and Diffusions Task Force, 4.21
post-2017, 4.35–4.52
reform efforts, 4.13–4.21
Working Group on Processing of Information, 4.15–4.20
generally, 3.22–3.24
nature, 3.24
Notices and Diffusions Task Force
generally, 3.25–3.33
reforms, 4.21
Refugee Policy (2014), 4.26–4.34
Russian, 3.34–3.36
Task Force, 4.21
Working Group on Processing of Information, 4.15–4.20
Working Group on Processing of Information
generally, 4.15–4.20
introduction, 4.13